Degrees of Democracy
Politics, Public Opinion, and Policy

This book develops and tests a "thermostatic" model of public opinion and policy. The representation of opinion in policy is central to democratic theory and everyday politics; so too is the extent to which public preferences are informed and responsive to changes in policy. The ongoing coexistence of both "public responsiveness" and "policy representation" is thus a defining characteristic of successful democratic governance, and the subject of this book.

The authors examine both public responsiveness and policy representation across a range of policy domains in the United States, the United Kingdom, and Canada. The story that emerges is one in which representative democratic government functions surprisingly well, although there are important differences in the details. Responsiveness and representation are found to reflect both the public salience of different domains and the design of governing institutions – specifically, federalism (versus unitary government) and presidentialism (versus parliamentarism). The findings alter our understanding of both opinion-policy relationships and the functioning of representative democratic institutions.

Stuart N. Soroka is associate professor and William Dawson Scholar in the Department of Political Science at McGill University, Montreal, Quebec. He is also adjunct professor and director of the Canadian Opinion Research Archive at the School of Policy Studies at Queen's University, Kingston, Ontario, and co-director of the Media Observatory at the McGill Institute for the Study of Canada. He is the author of *Agenda-Setting Dynamics in Canada* (2002) and articles in journals including the *Journal of Politics*, the *British Journal of Political Science*, the *Canadian Journal of Political Science*, and *Comparative Political Studies*.

Christopher Wlezien is professor of political science and faculty affiliate in the Institute for Public Affairs at Temple University. He previously was on the faculty at Oxford University and Nuffield College, where he co-founded the ESRC-funded Oxford Spring School in Quantitative Methods for Social Research. He co-edited *The Future of Election Studies* and *Britain Votes*, and his articles have appeared in numerous journals, including the *American Journal of Political Science*, the *Journal of Politics*, *Public Opinion Quarterly*, *Political Analysis*, and *Comparative Political Studies*. He is co-editor of the international *Journal of Elections, Public Opinion and Parties*.

T0371459

Degrees of Democracy

Politics, Public Opinion, and Policy

STUART N. SOROKA
McGill University

CHRISTOPHER WLEZIEN
Temple University

CAMBRIDGE
UNIVERSITY PRESS

CAMBRIDGE
UNIVERSITY PRESS

32 Avenue of the Americas, New York NY 10013-2473, USA

Cambridge University Press is part of the University of Cambridge.

It furthers the University's mission by disseminating knowledge in the pursuit of education, learning and research at the highest international levels of excellence.

www.cambridge.org
Information on this title: www.cambridge.org/9780521687898

© Stuart N. Soroka and Christopher Wlezien 2010

First published 2010

A catalogue record for this publication is available from the British Library

Library of Congress Cataloguing in Publication data

Soroka, Stuart Neil, 1970–
    Degrees of democracy : Politics, public opinion, and policy / Stuart Soroka, Christopher Wlezien.
      p.   cm.
    Includes bibliographical references and index.
    ISBN 978-0-521-86833-4 (hardback) – ISBN 978-0-521-68789-8 (pbk.)
    1. Political planning.   2. Policy sciences.   3. Public opinion.   4. Representative government and representation.   I. Wlezien, Christopher.   II. Title.
    JF1525.P6S66 2010
    320.6–dc22   2009013068

ISBN 978-0-521-86833-4 Hardback
ISBN 978-0-521-68789-8 Paperback

Contents

Preface

This is a book about representative democracy. We are interested in seeing how well it works – specifically, how consistently governments make policy that reflects public preferences. There is a good deal of academic work demonstrating quite a strong connection between opinion and policy. Even as there seems to be representation, however, there seems to be little basis for it in the public itself. That is, even while showing that governments tend to follow preferences, the body of evidence suggests that the public is largely inattentive to politics, and uninterested and uninformed about the goings-on of governments.

The problem is that the representation of opinion presupposes that the public actually notices and responds to what policymakers do. Without such responsiveness, policymakers have little incentive to represent what the public wants in policy – there is no real benefit for doing so and no real cost for not doing so. Moreover, without public responsiveness to policy, expressed public preferences contain little meaningful information – they are unanchored to the policy status quo. As a result, there is not only a limited basis for holding politicians accountable, but expressed preferences also are of little use even to those politicians motivated to represent the public for other reasons. We need a responsive public; effective democracy depends on it.

A responsive public behaves much like a thermostat. It adjusts its preferences for "more" or "less" policy in response to what policymakers do. Imagine a situation in which the public prefers more defense policy. If policymakers respond, and provide more (but not too much) for defense, then the new policy position will more closely correspond to the public's preferred level of policy. And, if the public is indeed responsive to what policymakers do, then they will not favor as much more activity on defense. They might still favor more, on balance, but not as substantially as in the prior period. (And if policymakers actually overshoot the public's preferred level of spending, they will favor less.) In effect, following the thermostatic metaphor, a departure from the favored policy temperature produces a signal to adjust policy accordingly; once policy has been sufficiently adjusted, the signal stops.

Whether this is the case in reality is the subject of the work that follows. We are interested in capturing the reciprocal, "thermostatic" relationship between public opinion and policy – (a) the degree to which public preferences adjust thermostatically to policy change, and (b) the degree to which government policies reflect these public preferences. We are interested in this relationship not just in one country, or one domain, but across policy domains and countries. Indeed, we are interested not just in whether "public responsiveness" and "policy representation" exist in multiple circumstances, but also in the ways in which they vary across policy and institutional environments. That is, we would like to learn where the opinion-policy relationship is strong (or weak) and the conditions that help make it so.

Before starting in, we have a lot of appreciation to share. This book has been long in progress; it began in 2001 when we both were at Nuffield College, Oxford. We owe a great deal to the institution itself for providing the infrastructure – administrative, intellectual, and social – that was so valuable in the early phases of this work. We are particularly thankful to three Nuffield colleagues, Iain McLean, Tony Atkinson, and Byron Shafer, each of whom provided support and comments as we started the project.

Financial support has come from various sources. We received support from the Nuffield Foundation for a conference on the subject of budgetary policy in the United Kingdom, which was essential to our research there. Subsequent data-gathering and research assistance were funded in part by Nuffield College, by an Internal Research Development Fund Grant from McGill University, and by a Standard Research Grant from the Social Sciences and Humanities Research Council of Canada. We benefited from the expertise of Russell Hubbard, Stuart Mitchell, Allan

Ritchie, Eleanor Ball, and Philippa Todd at Her Majesty's Treasury, and of Terry Moore and Claude Vaillancourt at Statistics Canada. We were also lucky to have had very good research assistants – Robert Bowles, Michelle Meyer, Erin Penner, and Lori Young.

This work also has benefited from comments by scholars at numerous universities and conferences. We are thankful to participants in seminars at the University of British Columbia, Concordia University, Dartmouth College, Harvard University, Indiana University, Juan March Institute, University of Manchester, University of Mannheim, McGill University, Nuffield College, University of Pennsylvania, Queen's University, Sciences-Po, and the University of Washington. We also are thankful to participants in panels at professional meetings in Aarhus, Albuquerque, Chicago, Corpus Christi, Edinburgh, Fukuoka, Halifax, Manchester, Nottingham, Philadelphia, Pisa, Toronto, Washington, D.C., Uppsala, and Vancouver.

Countless scholars have contributed in significant ways, and we note only some of them here. Patrick Fournier gave invaluable advice on a first full draft of this manuscript; Jamie Druckman did the same for the first three chapters. The resulting manuscript has benefited greatly from the contributions of these two reviewers. Additional commentary on previous papers and nascent ideas came from Arash Abizadeh, Kevin Arceneaux, Joseph Bafumi, Keith Banting, Frank Baumgartner, Marc Andre Bodet, Deborah Jordan Brooks, John Carey, Chris Carman, David Cox, Fred Cutler, Dave Cutts, Richard Deeg, Sophie Duchesne, Diana Evans, Ed Fieldhouse, Orfeo Fioretos, Mark Franklin, Emiliano Grossman, Jane Green, Thomas Gschwend, Florence Haegel, Michael Hagen, Armen Hakhverdian, Peter Hall, David Heald, Michael Herron, Sunshine Hillygus, Sara Hobolt, Brian Hogwood, Will Jennings, Peter John, Martin Johnson, Richard Johnston, Bryan Jones, Mark Kayser, Dean Lacy, Patrick Legales, Julia Lynch, Pat Lynch, Jose Maria Maravall, Nonna Mayer, Amy Mazur, Iain McLean, Jose Ramon Montero, Wolfgang Muller, Jack Nagel, Pippa Norris, Josh Pasek, Mark Pollack, Robert Rohrschneider, Andrew Russell, Laura Scalia, Hermann Schmitt, Joseph Schwartz, Robert Shapiro, Robert Stein, James Stimson, Christina Tarnopolsky, Guy Whitten, and Dick Winters. We also thank our many other colleagues over the years at the University of Houston, McGill University, Oxford University, and Temple University.

The book itself would not have happened without many people at Cambridge University Press, from the editor on down. We thank the inimitable Lew Bateman for showing interest in our work and patience as we worked past several deadlines. We also thank Emily Spangler and, especially, Mary Cadette.

Finally, we thank our families for putting up with us over the course of the project.

Degrees of Democracy

Politics, Public Opinion, and Policy

I

Public Opinion and Policy in Representative Democracy

Edmund Burke was a much better political philosopher than he was a politician. Burke was a Member of Parliament for Bristol for six years, from 1774 to 1780. He visited the constituency infrequently during that time, and managed to alienate his electorate through a combination of his rather unpatriotic support for America during the war and a general lack of attention to the principal concerns of Bristol's merchants. It was clear by 1780 – when he withdrew – that Burke stood no chance at reelection.[1]

Burke's political writings remain fundamental to this day, however, including his *Speech to the Electors of Bristol*. In his mind, an elected representative should seek and consider the advice of his constituents, but that advice should not be authoritative instruction. It should not serve as a mandate, dictating what a representative does; it should be but one input into his decision making. Burke's philosophizing did not free him from the burden of representing the interests of his electors, however, and his ideas evidently had only limited appeal for Bristolians at the time. That is, Burke paid the electoral price.

The situation is little changed more than two hundred years later. Active representation of the public's policy preferences remains a – if not *the* – central concern in electoral and inter-electoral politics. Indeed, some argue that the tendency to represent public preferences

---

[1] See Ernest Barker, "Burke and his Bristol Constituency," in *Essays on Government* (Oxford: The Clarendon Press 1951).

has increased as politics has become a career path during the twentieth century, and that politicians have become (out of desire for reelection) more reliably interested in keeping voters happy (e.g., Maestas 2000, 2003).[2] Moreover, Geer argues that the onset and development of public opinion polling has made it easier for politicians to know what public preferences are.[3] Politicians have both a keen interest in representing the public and the seeming means to do so.

Representation is also at the heart of everyday political debate. Citizens care about what they get from government, whether it's tax cuts or prescription drug benefits or education subsidies. They also care about the degree to which what government does matches their preferences for various other things, whether it's the amount of healthcare, the availability of abortion, environmental protection, or going to war.

Not all politics is explicitly about policy, of course. Citizens also care about outcomes, and many argue that this is true now more than ever before (see, e.g., Clarke et al. 2004). People want a growing economy, safe streets, and high-quality healthcare. Not surprisingly, U.S. presidential candidates routinely ask: "Are you better off today than you were four years ago?" This is not a question about policy *per se* – it is a question about outcomes. Policy nevertheless is implicated, of course. Politicians do not have magic wands – they influence outcomes using policy. Politicians offer plans to solve important problems, such as a struggling economy. There are policies to reduce crime, improve education, fix healthcare, and so on, and when conditions improve, politicians don't claim to have been lucky. They explicitly credit policy, for instance, when they declare that "Our tax cut policy got the economy moving again," or that "We put more police on the streets and crime came down." Policy clearly matters for both outcomes and politics. We want things, and, through policy, politicians try to deliver.[4]

This opinion-policy relationship is central not just in everyday politics, but in the theoretical literature on democracy and representation as well, from Jean-Jacques Rousseau, to John Stuart Mill, to Robert A.

---

[2] There is some disagreement on this point, however. See, e.g., Fiorina 1997, Weber 1999.

[3] There is also disagreement on this point. Karol (2007), for instance, argues that polls have not improved representation.

[4] Actually delivering outcomes can be quite complex – see Kelly's (2009) interesting analysis of economic inequality in the United States.

Dahl. Indeed, for each of these theorists the connection between public preferences and public policy is one of the most critical components of representative democracy. Importantly, for each the opinion-policy link is necessarily reciprocal: on the one hand, policymakers need to react to the public's policy preferences; on the other hand, the public needs to have informed preferences, based in part on what policymakers are doing. To put it differently: If we want politicians to make the policy we want, our preferences must be informed by policy itself. This is the theme that guides our investigation, where "degrees of democracy" are conceived as deriving from the extent to which both "policy representation" and "public responsiveness" are evident.

We develop and empirically test a model of democracy in which opinion-policy relationships are paramount. Following Wlezien (1995, 1996a), we posit a very simple but powerful framework that connects opinion and policy, what we call the "thermostatic" model. The model has as its referent the temperature control systems in our homes, where the public is the thermostat and policymakers the furnace or air conditioning unit. If the model works, we will observe three things. First, the difference between the actual policy temperature and the preferred temperature will cause the public to send a signal to change the policy temperature, for example, to turn up the heat. Second, in response to such a signal, policymakers will increase policy. Third, as the policy temperature approaches the preferred temperature, the signal for change will be reduced. This, we argue, is how a functioning democracy should work. Is it what we actually observe out in the world? That is, do policymakers respond to public preference signals? Does the public adjust its signals in response to what policymakers do?

That these are important questions should be clear. They speak to the capacity of citizens, the quality of governance, and, as we shall see, relationships between the two. They speak not just to the quality but also to the principles and potential merits of representative democracy. They are academic questions, to be sure, but they are academic questions with rather sweeping real-world implications.

The chapters that follow begin to provide some answers. We first set out expectations for public responsiveness and policy representation, varying as a function of issue salience and political institutions, and applying, we believe, across the democratic world. Our theoretical scope thus is rather broad. Our empirical focus is necessarily more narrow. "Policy" is captured using budgetary data; public preferences are measured using opinion polls. The empirical analysis is limited to the three countries for which extended, reliable time series of both opinion and spending are available: the United States, the United Kingdom, and Canada. We shall argue that these three countries provide a quite strong "most similar systems" research design. Additional leverage is gained by looking at multiple policy domains within the three countries, for a total of nineteen individual domains, across which institutional characteristics differ. The comparative reach nevertheless is limited, as we cannot explore the full range of political institutions with the data at hand. We can take an important step forward, however. We also can consider – as we do in the final chapter – what the broader implications of our findings may be for policy domains and regimes not directly assessed here.

The story that emerges is one in which representative democratic government in some cases works surprisingly well. There is strong evidence that the public actually adjusts its preference for "more" or "less" policy in a thermostatic way, as policy itself changes. There also is evidence that policymakers respond to changes in public preferences over time. The thermostatic model works. The magnitude and nature of both public responsiveness and policy representation do vary across policy domains and countries, and this variation is systematic. As we will show, varying degrees of responsiveness and representation can be explained at least in part by factors such as the salience of various policy domains, as well as by the design of government institutions, that is, by the vertical and horizontal division of powers. That this is true means that we can begin to make some generalizable predictions across different policy domains and political contexts. It means that we can begin to capture, empirically speaking, "degrees" of democracy.

POLICY REPRESENTATION

The relationship between public preferences and policy has been the central concern of the literature on representative democracy at least since Jean-Jacques Rousseau's *The Social Contract* (1762).[5]

---

[5] Rousseau's "general will" is clearly quite different than the "public preference" we are interested in here. His discussion of the reliability with which representatives

This was among the first considerations of the connection between representatives and their constituents, and many others have examined the opinion-policy connection since. The first explicit consideration of public opinion *per se* appears roughly fifty years later in the work of Jeremy Bentham. His writings reveal a view of representative democracy very similar to the one we are concerned with below: Bentham conceives of a reactive public that monitors government activities, and to which governments are held accountable (see Cutler 1999). Bentham was an elitist, to be sure, just like Edmund Burke one generation earlier, and John Stuart Mill one generation later. Each believed that certain people's opinions were more worthy than others. But each also focused on essentially the same question: What conditions or institutions are required to produce a representative democracy in which policies reliably reflect the interests of citizens – citizens, that is, whose interests are sufficiently informed to justify representation?

Political scientists are now much closer to answering that question. Or, at least, we are accumulating a body of evidence on when representation seems more or less likely, and under what conditions citizens are more or less informed on political and policy matters. But what exactly do we mean by "policy representation"? There are several different kinds of representation we might look for in a democracy. Drawing in large part on the theoretical literature above, as well as Pitkin's (1967) classic work on representation, our paramount concern is policy representation: policymakers' active representation of citizens' (aggregated) preferences. Indeed, while other versions of representation have garnered considerable attention, we suggest that most are valued in large part because they are likely to enhance the connection between what people want regarding policy and what governments provide.

Descriptive Representation

Take, for instance, discussions of "descriptive" representation. These typically focus on representatives' characteristics, specifically, on the extent to which representatives resemble the represented, particularly

would reflect the preferences of their constituents is nonetheless among the first considerations of how a system of government might be designed to reflect the preferences of its citizens.

with respect to demographic characteristics. Race, ethnicity, gender, language, sexual orientation – any number of characteristics can be salient. "Shared experience" (Mansbridge 1999) can also be critical – experience as a farmer, for instance, or of having grown up in a particular region. According to this view, a representative legislature should be a microcosm of the larger society. Indeed, a number of theorists refer to this type of representation as "microcosmic representation" (e.g., Birch 1971, 2001).

Support for descriptive representation comes in both symbolic and substantive forms. A symbolic argument for descriptive representation focuses on the representation of historically under-represented groups (e.g., women, or racial or ethnic minorities), and stresses the significance of seeing oneself represented in government, and of consequently seeing politics as something that you are or can be involved in. Results include the possibility of increased participation in politics by previously under-represented groups, and – often viewed as more fundamental – the enhanced symbolic legitimacy of a government seen to encompass diverse individuals or groups (e.g., Sapiro 1981, Phillips 1995; Kymlicka 1993). Descriptive representation may also facilitate communication between constituents and representatives, particularly in historically conflictual contexts (Mansbridge 1999). Indeed, there is evidence that some individuals are more likely to contact their representative if they share certain demographic characteristics (Gay 2002).

Proponents of descriptive representation have also argued that it can be a useful proxy for policy attitudes: "When interests are uncrystallized, the best way to have one's most important substantive interests represented is often to choose a representative whose descriptive characteristics match one's own on the issues one expects to emerge" (Mansbridge 1999:644). That demographically similar groups will tend to have similar policy attitudes is thus the heart of the substantive argument for descriptive representation. Bentham's support for microcosmic representation in Britain was based on the concern that a legislature dominated by the upper class would advance only upper-class interests, for instance. Bianco (1994) emphasizes race as a kind of cue for representatives' values and interests (see also Phillips 1995), a fact that is confirmed by representatives' own views on how and who they represent (e.g., Fenno 1978; Kingdon 1981; Mansbridge 1986). And the link between demographic characteristics is evidenced in the empirical literature on legislative behavior: day-care coverage is greater in Norwegian municipalities where there are more female representatives, for instance (Bratton and Ray 2002); black and female representatives in the United States are consistently more likely to introduce or sponsor black or women's interest bills respectively (Bratton and Haynie 1999); the voting records of Hispanic members of the House of Representatives are distinct in ways that may be culturally attributable (Welch and Hibbing 1984; Hero and Tolbert 1995; Kerr and Miller 1997).

That said, the extent to which demographic similarities are a substitute for policy attitudes is unclear, and using a proxy of dubious reliability is less than ideal. Note first that *preferences* and *interests* are not the same thing. Many people have a preference for a level of redistributive policy that clearly is not in their best interest, for instance – they are wealthy themselves but support politics that favor the less advantaged.[6] Similarly, many white (majority) respondents support policies that benefit visible minorities. In neither case are their preferences in line with what would seem to be their interests.

This gap between preferences and interests is confirmed in work on the actual behaviour of demographically "representative" elected officials. Some work on female legislators argues that women who successfully gain office are not necessarily representative of women's interests – that is, they may provide some kind of symbolic and descriptive representative function, but the extent to which their policy preferences are similar to women's (aggregated) policy preferences can be relatively limited (e.g., Gotell and Brodie 1996).[7] A number of authors have expressed further concerns about the way in which descriptive representation encourages the belief that certain groups can be represented only by certain people (in those groups), and alternatively that certain people can only represent certain groups (e.g., Kymlicka

[6] Indeed, the difference between preferences and interests is perhaps clearest in the literature on support for redistributive policy, where there are two conflicting expectations about the relationship between macroeconomic conditions and support for welfare policy: one, that worsening conditions lead to a general increase in support for government policies that help those in need, or two, that worsening conditions make self-interest more salient, and support for redistribution thus decreases for those concerned about the economy but unlikely to require government assistance. See esp. Blekesaune 2007.
[7] Survey research offers some supporting evidence. See, e.g., Kelly et al. 1991; Erikson 1997.

1995; Phillips 1995; Mansbridge 1999). Descriptive representation may actually be destructive to political community; some also charge that "Socially descriptive representation is pernicious because it makes recourse to constituencies unnecessary" (Morone and Marmor 1981:437). We view these problematic features of descriptive representation as in some sense supplementary – supplementary, that is, to the fact that demographic or experiential characteristics will only intermittently and unpredictably be relevant to the representation of policy preferences. Descriptive representation may thus be important in terms of providing role models, connecting to politics, or engendering a feeling of belonging in the political community. Where policy is concerned, descriptive representation falls short.

Electoral Representation

More common in the empirical literature is a version of representation which we will refer to as "electoral representation." Electoral representation is not always distinguished from descriptive representation, since theories of representation focusing on electoral systems are often motivated primarily by an interest in descriptive representation – the work arguing for proportional representation tends to focus on those systems' capacity to better represent subsets of the population that are demographically different, for instance. (See, e.g., Lijphart 1977; Katz 1997; see also the work on proportional representation and women's representation, e.g., Norris 1985; Matland and Studlar 1996.) Electoral systems themselves have played a particularly prominent role in the comparative literature on representation, however (see esp. Powell 2000). Indeed, the comparative study of representation is mostly based on a concept of representation that prioritizes the vote-seat function over everything else. That is, the electoral representation literature is often agnostic about the representation of groups defined by anything other than their vote. It equates the quality of representation with the efficiency and exactness of the vote-seat function. Lijphart's *Electoral Systems and Party Systems* (1994) begins with what we regard as a paradigmatic statement of electoral representation theory:

Except in very small communities, democracy necessarily means *representative* democracy in which elected officials make decisions on behalf of the people. How are these representatives elected? This indispensable task in representative democracies is performed by the electoral system – the set of methods for translating the citizens' votes into representatives' seats. Thus the electoral system is the most fundamental element of representative democracy. (1994:1)

Lijphart's working hypothesis is echoed in much of the comparative institutional literature. For a particularly succinct statement, see Sartori (1997:3): "In the beginning is how a people is made to vote." But also see much of the literature on vote-seat functions, in which the electoral system is paramount (e.g., Taagepera and Shugart 1989; Cox 1997). Indeed, this work largely reduces democracy to the method by which representatives are selected, not unlike Schumpeter's oft-cited and decidedly narrow view of democracy: "the democratic method is that institutional arrangement for arriving at political decisions in which individuals acquire the power to decide by means of a competitive struggle for the people's vote" (1942:269).[8]

The particular significance of electoral systems for democracy and representation is relatively clear, of course, and in fact has quite deep theoretical roots. One of the central debates in democratic theory regards the tension between individual equality – leading to majority rule – and the protection of minorities.[9] The tension is central in the *Federalist Papers*, where the American system of checks and balances is laid out with the primary objective of avoiding a tyranny of the majority in the face of individual political equality, a difficult and pretty much unattainable task. It is also prominent in J. S. Mill's argument for proportional representation, for instance, and Toqueville's concerns about democracy in America. The preoccupation with electoral systems follows almost directly from the fundamental concern with the equality of individuals in liberal democratic systems (see, e.g., McGann 2006).

Like descriptive representation, however, electoral representation only captures a part of what we might like in representative government. If descriptive representation is about the representation of (mainly)

---

[8] Notice that from this simple assumption about competition one can derive powerful implications for democratic representation (Downs 1956).
[9] For more complete discussions of equality in democracy, see, e.g Mill 1991; Dahl 1956, 2000; for theoretical work on equality as it pertains to electoral systems, see especially Rogowski 1981; Still 1981; Rae 1981.

demographic characteristics, electoral representation is principally about the representation of votes. In both cases, representation is – in Pitkin's terminology – "standing for." Electoral representational theory is interested in the extent to which a legislature mirrors the electorate, where the most salient characteristic of voters is for whom they voted. It thus focuses on how the distribution of seats reflects the distribution of votes. This is not to say that representation as "acting for" is entirely ignored; as with descriptive representation, electoral representational theory is premised on a connection between the representation of votes and the resulting representatives' legislative activity.[10] Some of the preceding work has demonstrated such a link, and our own models will provide further evidence of the connection between electoral representation and policy representation.

Policy Representation

In spite of the role that both descriptive and electoral representation have played in the empirical literature on democracy, they capture just a small part – and neither a sufficient nor a necessary part – of what we require of representation in a democracy. What we ultimately are interested in is policy representation, whereby the policy decisions of elected representatives are broadly reflective of some aggregation of public preferences, or – to draw on Rousseau – something like a "general will."[11] The quality of representation should be indicated not by shared belief, demographic proximity, or the accuracy of a vote-seat function, but by the extent to which representatives' actions are related to the preferences of those being represented.

[10] Hence, the related literature on whether the partisanship of government has an effect on policy outcomes. See, e.g., Schmidt 1996.
[11] Although Rousseau's "general will" is in many ways quite different from the "public preference" that we focus on here – see note 5 – there are also some striking similarities. Consider the following passage from Book 2, Section 3 of *The Social Contract*, which suggests a calculation of the "general will" that is very similar to our own measure of net preferences: "There is often a great deal of difference between the will of all and the general will; the latter considers only the common interest, while the former takes private interest into account, and is no more than a sum of particular wills: but take away from these same wills the pluses and minuses that cancel one another, and the general will remains as the sum of the differences."

There have been several bodies of literature that address policy representation – or at least aspects of policy representation – more directly. (For a thorough review, see Wlezien and Soroka 2007.) One body of work compares the attitudes of representatives and constituents as a means of testing the potential link between public opinion and policy. The typical research design is to take surveys of both the public and of policymakers and compare the two (e.g., Verba and Nie 1972; Uslaner and Weber 1979; Erikson et al. 1987; Herrera et al. 1992; Hill and Hinton-Anderson 1995). This design has been particularly popular in the foreign policy literature (e.g., Oldendick and Bardes 1982; for a review, see Holsti 1996). Policy positions are the focus for some scholars; others concentrate on the ways in which the public and policymakers understand issues; both are illustrated in a recent volume drawing together work in this field (Miller et al. 1999). In neither case is policy itself evident in the analysis, however. The work is premised on the notion that representatives' attitudes will influence policy. But it is perhaps more accurately labeled "attitude" or "opinion" representation, examining as it does the extent to which representatives' attitudes are similar to voters' attitudes.

There are also related bodies of work exploring the relationship between public and government agendas (e.g., Soroka 2002), and opinion and presidential or government rhetoric (e.g., Cohen 1999; Rottinghaus 2006; Jennings and John n.d.), as well as a burgeoning literature on party manifestos (e.g., Budget et al. 1987; Klingemann et al. 2006). The latter sometimes directly addresses the link between public preferences and parties' policy commitments. This literature tells us much about party positions over time and across countries. Like policymakers' attitudes, however, party manifestos can be far removed from policy. Indeed, recent work suggests only a modest relationship between the two (McDonald and Budge 2005). Although each of these literatures has contributed to our understanding of representation, none directly addresses policy itself.

A literature focused more clearly on policy*making* was sparked, if not fueled, by Miller and Stokes's (1963) "Constituency Influence in Congress." These authors brought together data on public opinion by constituency and both opinion surveys and the roll-call voting behavior of members of the U.S. Congress for an analysis of the extent to which prevailing attitudes within a constituency guided representatives' behavior. This research played a seminal role in the study of roll-call voting, primarily in the United States where roll-call data are readily available, but also elsewhere.[12] The resulting literature seeks to establish links between the voting behavior of members of the House of Representatives and some combination of constituency opinion (measured by various means), constituency aggregate demographics, and each representative's own demographic traits and party affiliations.

Roll-call voting is actual representative activity, and thus offers a better indication of Pitkin's (1967) representation as "acting for" than does the work on opinion representation. Roll-call votes are also more proximate to policy formation than are representatives' attitudes. The study of these votes does not address the kind of system-level policy representation that Pitkin describes, however.[13] Referred to as studies of "dyadic" representation (Weissberg 1978), the literature on roll-call voting asserts that representation is to be found in the relationship between individual representatives and individual constituencies. From this perspective, we have representation when representatives and the preferences of geographic constituencies line up. Dyadic representation does not constitute policy representation.[14] Although a strong relationship between constituency opinion and individual legislators' behavior can be viewed as increasing the potential for policy representation, it is not a necessary condition. A great many individual representatives could vote against the majority opinion in their district; so long as the various district preferences were spoken for by other districts' representatives, policy outputs could still be representative of the (national) majority preference (e.g., Hurley 1982). We simply cannot address the existence of representation, or a lack thereof, without concerning ourselves with policy development and

---

[12] This literature is both vast and varied; it includes the classic roll call voting literature (e.g., Mayhew 1966; Clausen 1973; Fiorina 1974; Kingdon 1981; Stone 1979; Wright 1989) as well as the literatures examining roll call votes along various measures of constituency opinion (e.g., Erikson 1978 1990; Achen 1978; Kuklinski 1977,1978; McCrone and Kulinski 1979; Shapiro et al. 1990; Bartels 1991). Outside the U.S., see, e.g., Barnes 1977; Converse and Pierce 1986; Matthews and Valen 1999.

[13] This has also been noted by Eulau and Karps 1977.

[14] As we will see below, actually determining whether constituency preferences and roll-call votes actually line up is not straightforward.

policy outputs. Policy outputs are necessarily an aggregate, or system-level, outcome. (On this point, see also Eulau and Prewitt 1973; Weissberg 1978; Hurley 1982; Page and Shapiro 1983:176).

There is a small but growing body of literature – in large part building on opinion representation and roll-call voting research – focused on the systemic representation of citizens' preferences in actual public policy. (For reviews of the literature, see Burstein 2003; Brooks 2006; Manza and Cook 2002; Weakliem 2003; Wlezien and Soroka 2007). Some research demonstrates a correspondence between opinion and policy at particular points in time. In the United States the classic work is Erikson, Wright and McIver's examination of states (1993). Brooks and Manza (2007) provide the most important comparative work, and show a strong correspondence between attitudes and welfare policy across countries. Other scholars go a step further and show "consistency" between public preferences for policy change, as captured in a single polling question, and the direction of policy change in a following period.[15] Yet other studies capture opinion at two (or more) points in time, and compare changes in polling results with preceding, concurrent, and subsequent changes in policy. Page and Shapiro's (1983) study of what they (and Monroe, 1998) refer to as "congruence" provides the classic case.[16] By examining policy before and after shifts in opinion, this type of analysis more directly tests whether opinion change does indeed cause (or at least precede) policy change.

The dynamic relationship between opinion and policy is, however, best captured through an analysis of the relationships between extended time-series of both opinion and policy. Stimson, MacKuen, and Erikson's (1995) model of dynamic representation in the United States is one archetypal case, as is Wlezien's (1995, 1996a) initial explication of the thermostatic model, upon which this book is based.[17] This

---

[15] Monroe (1979, 1998) provides a good example. See also Brooks 1985,1987,1990; Petry 1999; Petry and Mendelsohn 2004; Brettschneider 1996.
[16] See also Belanger and Petry 2005; Isernia, Juhasz, and Rattinger 2002. Note also that this approach can be applied very effectively across space as well as time. A number of studies look at variation across U.S. states, for instance. See, e.g., Erikson, Wright and McIver 1993, Goggin and Wlezien 1993; Norrander and Wilcox 1999. For cross-national work, see Brooks and Manza 2006.
[17] For earlier work along these lines, see Devine 1970; Weissberg 1976; Burstein 1979; Hartley and Russett 1992.

kind of dynamic approach to the opinion-policy relationship has seen increasing attention in recent years. Eichenberg and Stoll (2003) have examined the dynamic relationship between preferences and defense spending in the United States and Western Europe; Johnson, Brace, and Arceneaux (2005) have done the same for environmental policy in U.S. states; Jennings (n.d), on border control and asylum policy in the United Kingdom; and Hobolt and Klemmenson (2005, 2008), across several policies in the United States, the United Kingdom, and Denmark. All of this work examines the relationship between public preferences and public policy, the final and most significant outcome of representative activity.[18] In so doing, it provides empirical evidence of the strength and nature of policy representation, the kind of representation that we believe is crucial in modern representative democracies.

PUBLIC RESPONSIVENESS

The representative function of democratic governance – the production of policy consistent with our preferences – comes with a crucial stipulation: we need to know what we want representatives to do. That is, representation requires that we have policy preferences. Preferably, those preferences will be consistently, rationally based on a number of real-world phenomena. Of critical importance is policy itself. That is, preferences need to be informed by what policymakers actually do.

The case for public responsiveness as a critical component in the functioning of democratic systems is perhaps made most clearly in work on "systems analysis," by authors such as David Easton and Karl Deutsch.[19] Both authors draw on a body of work on "cybernetics," developed during and following the Second World War by Norbert Wiener and colleagues, and first focusing on the difficulties in shooting missiles from moving airplanes (Wiener 1961[1948]:5–7).

---

[18] There are representative activities that are not adequately implicated in public policies, admittedly, such as informal international treaties, or symbolic but nevertheless important public statements abroad or at home. But the vast majority of important representative functions should be implicated in public policy in one form or another.

[19] Indeed, the model of representation and responsiveness that we describe in Chapter 2 owes much to Easton's "Dynamic Response Model of a Political System" (1965:110).

Wiener writes, "... when we desire a motion to follow a given pattern the difference between this pattern and the actually performed motion is used as a new input to cause the part regulated to move in such a way as to bring its motion closer to that given by the pattern" (1961:6).

Wiener, among others, suggested that cybernetic processes could be usefully applied to both machines and humans. They could also be applied to societies and governments, and work by Easton and Deutsch in the early 1960s took up the task. In his argument for systems analysis, Easton (1965) provides a theoretical model of political systems in which the system stands between inputs (demands and support) and outputs (decisions and actions). In our model, these are preferences and policy, respectively, and, as for Easton, the relationship between inputs and outputs is a reciprocal one. This "feedback loop" is critical to the ongoing functioning of a political system. It is through this feedback, or public responsiveness – we will use both terms in the chapters that follow – that a system is able to manage demands and maximize support; it is through monitoring public preferences that a system is able to develop a capacity for responsive outputs, or policy. The ongoing interaction between public preferences and policy is in this way fundamental to the functioning of a democratic political system. Indeed, the more the public responds to policy, and policymakers represent public preferences, the more "efficient" the system, that is, the more effectively – quickly and fully – changes in preferences translate into changes in policy.

The same dynamic is described in Deutsch's work, best represented by *The Nerves of Government* (1966). For Deutsch, the flow of information is paramount, and, again, feedback is critical to the ongoing successful functioning of the system. Deutsch's feedback is "a communications network that produces action in response to an input of information, and includes the results of its own action in the new information by which it modifies its subsequent behaviour" (88). Deutsch goes somewhat further than Easton in describing both a representative government and a reactive public. The first is evident in his description of "lag" – the time it takes for a system to react to information – and "gain" – the extent of that reaction. Lag has to do with whether governments react in a timely manner to preferences for change, and gain determines whether the extent of the change is

less, more, or exactly what the public wants. The latter is evident in
Deutsch's discussion of "goal-changing feedback," that is, feedback
allowing for the goal to change over time based on new information.

Whether this feedback *can* exist is of course another matter. There
is of course a considerable body of literature questioning whether
citizens are sufficiently informed or reactive enough to play a role
in democratic decision making. The literature has a long and distinguished lineage, beginning with Plato and Aristotle.[20] J.S. Mill was
concerned about the relative ignorance of the average citizen (see Birch
1971:89–93). So too were the American founding fathers. For example, that just one third of U.S. senators is elected only every six years is
partly a defense against what the founders saw as an ill-informed and
sometimes irrational public. In *The Federalist* No.10, Madison writes
that the effect of representation is

> ... to refine and enlarge the public views by passing them through the medium
> of a chosen body of citizens, whose wisdom may best discern the true interest
> of their country and whose patriotism and love of justice will be least likely
> to sacrifice it to temporary or partial considerations.

In fact, Madison among others viewed representative government
as something quite different from and better than democracy, where
the latter was direct and thus more prone to the vulgarities of public
opinion (see Manin 1997).

The issue of public ignorance is also implicated in the literature
on what Pitkin (1967) calls the "mandate-independence" controversy:
the degree to which representatives must (a) do what they know their
constituents would do or (b) make educated decisions based on their
constituents' interests (see also, e.g., Fairlie 1940; Birch 1971:37–40).
Moreover, it is evident in the literature on whether representation
should be of individuals or "interests," most often associated with
Burke. Burke's argument for representation of interests was founded
in large part on his belief that a representative was capable of clearer,
more informed thought than his constituents. That representatives
were more capable of making beneficial decisions was partly because
debate and deliberation in Parliament was helpful; partly because
the purpose of Parliament was to develop and protect the national

---

[20] See, for instance, Plato's "Allegory of the Cave" in *The Republic*.

interest, rather than those local interests that the average citizen would be most interested and aware; and partly because Burke viewed the average citizen as ill-informed and largely incapable of rational decision making.

Schumpeter and Lippmann present perhaps the best-known treatises on the problems of an inevitably ignorant electorate. Schumpeter's (1950) argument against "the classical doctrine of democracy" rests on the belief that there is no "common good," nor is there a reasonable "will of the people" established by aggregating varying preferences. One objection has to do with the biases and difficulties inherent in aggregation (on this, see Arrow 1951; Riker 1982). But, even if this problem is overcome, "... we still remain under the practical necessity of attributing to the will of the individual an independence and a rational quality that are altogether unrealistic" (1950:253). Lippmann (1925) presents his case in more eloquent and stronger terms. Even if citizens were able to understand politics, they could not possibly have the time to inform themselves properly:

The individual man does not have opinions on all public affairs. He does not know how to direct public affairs. He does not know what is happening, why it is happening, what ought to happen. I cannot imagine how he could know, and there is not the least reason for thinking, as mystical democrats have thought, that the compounding of individual ignorances in masses of people can produce a continuous directing force in public affairs. (1925:39)

Lippmann's concerns about the ignorance and irrationality of the average citizen were largely supported by early public opinion research, finding that citizens were for the most part uninterested in politics and uninformed about current affairs. Columbia School researchers suggested that demographic characteristics were the primary drivers of voting behavior (e.g., Lazarsfeld et al. 1968) ; Michigan School scholars suggested that party loyalties drove voting (e.g., Campbell et al. 1964). In both cases, citizens seemed to have only very limited capacities to understand current issues and independently form opinions (see esp. Almond 1950; Converse 1964; Miller 1967). Wahlke (1971:273) nicely summarizes the view at the time: elections are the primary means by which governments are held democratically responsible, but, "However logical and obvious such a conception of democratic representative government processes may seem, the observed behaviour of citizens is in almost all critical respects inconsistent with it." More recent work on individual citizens' attitudes is only marginally less pessimistic. We know from much previous research that people are not highly interested in politics, for instance, at least not in a very consistent way.[21] Interest does appear to increase approaching an election, and this makes a good deal of sense. In between elections, however, people care much less and pay much less attention (Zaller 1998). Most people are not passionate about politics and would rather spend their time doing other things. Not surprisingly, they also appear highly uninformed (Berelson et al. 1954; Campbell et al. 1964; Converse 1964; Ferejohn 1990). The failure of Americans to know the names of the members of Congress is often cited. In one study, only 30 % could name either of the senators from their state (Delli Carpini and Keeter 1996). Knowledge of party control of Congress is no better (Neuman 1986). Even familiarity with basic government institutions and how they work is low (Althaus 2003). Many people just don't know the basic facts of political life, at least based on surveys.

Of course, it may be that all of these results substantially overstate the case. A number of growing literatures – relying on increasingly sophisticated survey instruments – show that the average citizen may be at least slightly more consistent, attentive, and educable than we initially thought. Consider for example the burgeoning literature on election campaigns, which shows a considerable amount of voter learning about the positions of candidates and parties (e.g., Andersen, Tilley and Heath 2005; Arceneaux 2005; Brady and Johnston 1987; Gelman and King 1993; Johnston et al. 1992, 1996; for a review of the broader literature, see Erikson and Tedin 2004). This is not to say that the average citizen knows very much about politics, even on Election Day. Rather, it is to say that she (or he) may know enough to make "good" decisions (Lupia and McCubbins 1998). But does this mean that people can effectively manage representative democracy by our standard? Or is the thermostatic model just too much to ask?

---

[21] Consider, for instance, basic responses to questions about interest in politics. In the 2000 National Election Study, only 20% of those surveyed said they were interested in politics "most of the time," although it should be noted that another 36% said they were interested "some of the time."

There are at least three possible ways by which the public can fulfill the role that we set out here. First, it may be that citizens actually do not need much information to have sufficiently informed preferences, and the information may be fairly easy to get. The demands of the thermostatic model require that the public responds to changes in policy, to be sure, but only in a very simple way; they need only to know, for instance, whether government has increased spending in an area and whether by a little or a lot. This seemingly does not require a high level of information or cognition. Politicians also have strong incentives to offer cues that help citizens make decisions (see Sniderman and Theriault 2004; Chong and Druckman 2007).

Second, it may be that not all individuals are informed about policy, but that a sufficient number are. It is not necessary that all individuals respond to what governments do. What matters is that some nontrivial number respond, enough to produce the aggregate level signal necessary to guide politicians. This is not a perfect way to representation, of course. That is, differential public responsiveness raises the possibility of differential representation, for example, that policymakers pay closer attention to the preferences of informed responders than to the preferences of others. It is of consequence when the preferences of the "informed" and "uninformed" differ, as we will discuss later in the book.

Finally, the responsiveness of individuals can differ across issues. Not everyone will pay attention to policy in different areas, and some people may follow what happens in one area while other people follow what happens in other areas. Their responsiveness to policy should differ accordingly. Just as it is not necessary that all individuals respond to policy, it is not necessary that the same individuals respond in all domains. What matters is that the number of people who pay attention is large enough to signal policymakers. Again, this way to representation is not perfect, at least to the extent the preferences of the "issue publics" and the rest of the population differ.[22]

---

[22] Note also that, regardless of how many people are responding, there can be errors in individuals' responses. As has been noted by numerous scholars, and most famously by Benjamin Page and Robert Shapiro (1983, 1992), such errors will be canceled out through aggregation if they are approximately random. If errors do largely cancel each other out, the mean preference will be an accurate indication of the mean individual. Even if errors in preferences do not cancel each other out,

Of course, it may be that not even significant issue publics notice what government does in many areas. We actually expect this, and theorize that public responsiveness varies substantially in understandable ways, being imperceptible in some domains and quite pronounced in others. We consider the underlying structure of public responsiveness in more detail in forthcoming chapters. For the meantime, suffice it to say that we – along with many others, most notably Bentham (1989; see Cutler 1999), Page and Shapiro (1983), and Converse (1990) – are some of Lippmann's (1925:39) "mystical democrats." We believe that an informed public interest is possible, at least in some areas. This belief is buttressed by a growing body of evidence that publics respond in the ways that justify policy representation as we described it earlier (like Page and Shapiro, but see also Durr 1993; Erikson et al. 2002 Wlezien 1995, 1996a, 2004). Examining the degree, extent, and nature of this public responsiveness is a central goal of forthcoming chapters.

SYNOPSIS AND PROGNOSIS

These are the ideas that guide our investigation, and it proceeds as follows. Chapter 2 provides an outline of the theoretical model on which our investigation is based – the thermostatic model of opinion and policy. Chapter 3 extends this model, suggesting ways in which the characteristics of issues and political institutions may mediate the links between public preferences and public policy. Chapter 4 describes our data on preferences and policy in Canada, the United States, and the United Kingdom. These data require some discussion, since we are trying to build models of preferences and policy that are as directly comparable as possible, across both policy domains and countries. Testing of the thermostatic model then begins in Chapter 5. This chapter includes the basic models, comparing the magnitude of public responsiveness across countries and policy domains. In so doing, it assesses the thermostatic model and how it varies with differences in issue salience and the level of federalism. Chapter 6 explores

those errors may be consistent over time in a way that makes the bias markedly less important to the examination of dynamic representation and public responsiveness. We discuss this further in Chapter 8.

responsiveness further – it considers whether publics respond to policy decisions (appropriations) or policy outputs (outlays), the timing of this responsiveness, and the degree to which it is really driven by the results of spending on the broader environment. Chapter 7 then examines policy representation, particularly the degree to which representation varies systematically in magnitude alongside issue salience and political institutions. Chapter 8 offers final analyses of both public responsiveness and policy representation, this time with an eye on the possibility that certain segments of the public are more responsive, or better represented, than others. Chapter 9 reviews our findings and interprets them in light of the preceding theoretical discussion, and introduces a measure of system efficiency to characterize the representational effectiveness of democratic institutions.

2

The Thermostatic Model

Imagine a time series of public preferences for policy in a particular area. Let us assume that we have regular annual readings of public preferences. To keep things simple, let us assume further that our readings are perfect; in other words, that there is no bias or sampling error. What happens when public preferences change? What are the consequences for policy? To what extent do changing policies then affect preferences? Our expectations are captured in a general model of opinion-policy dynamics.

THE MECHANICS OF PUBLIC RESPONSIVENESS

The representation of public opinion presupposes that the public actually notices and responds to what policymakers do. It means that the public must acquire *and* process information about policy, and adjust its preferences accordingly. As we have noted, without such responsiveness, policymakers would have little incentive to represent what the public wants in policy – without public responsiveness, expressed public preferences would contain little meaningful information. There not only would be a limited basis for holding politicians accountable; registered preferences would be of little use even to those politicians motivated to represent the public for other reasons.

A responsive public will behave much like a thermostat (Wlezien 1995), adjusting its preferences for "more" or "less" policy in response

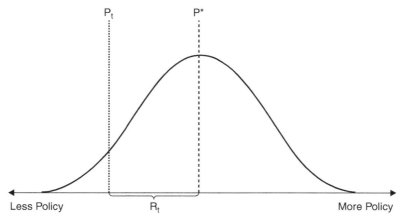

FIGURE 2.1. Preferences for Policy

to what policymakers do. When policy increases (decreases), the preference for more policy will decrease (increase), other things being equal. Consider the public as a collection of individuals distributed along a dimension of preference for policy activity, say, spending on defense. One hypothetical distribution is shown in Figure 2.1, depicted as a normal curve, following convention.[1] The figure is not meant to imply that individuals actually have *specific* preferred levels of policy in mind, which presumably is untrue except for a small number of people in particular policy areas. (This is discussed further later in this chapter.) Rather, it is intended to reflect the fact that people's underlying preferences differ, where some people want more than others. In the figure, those off to the right want more and those to the left less. This is straightforward.

What of the collective "public preference"? This is some summary of the overall distribution of preferences. It is difficult to perfectly summarize a distribution, of course, but we can fairly easily describe the central tendency. For instance, we can represent the public preference (P^*) as the median preference, the point that literally splits the public, where half want more and the other half less. This summary

---

[1] The characteristic shape of the distribution, e.g., its modality, really is not relevant to the analysis that follows, though the symmetry of the distribution is. We return to this issue later in the chapter.

of the public preference can be taken to imply a certain "ideal" level of policy – specifically, the level of policy the median citizen wants.

The public's relative preference (R_t) – the preference for policy change – is the difference between the current level of policy (P_t) and the public's preferred level of policy (P^*). If policymakers respond to R_t and provide more (but not too much) policy, the new policy position will more closely correspond to the preferred level of spending. One such possibility is depicted in Figure 2.2, where the new policy in the subsequent period, P_{t+1}, is closer to P^*. If the public responds thermostatically to this policy change, net public support for more spending will decrease: the new relative preference (R_{t+1}) will be smaller than the previous one (R_t), reflecting the upward shift in policy. In Figure 2.2, the public still favors more spending, on balance, but not as substantially as in the prior period.

Of course, the actual size of the shift in preferences will vary. It will depend on the distribution of underlying preferences, the location of P at time t, and the size of the shift in P at $t+1$. Indeed, if policymakers overshoot the public's preferred level of spending, the public will then favor less. In general, following the thermostatic metaphor, a departure from the favored policy temperature – which itself can change – produces a signal to adjust policy accordingly and, once sufficiently adjusted, the signal stops. As discussed in Chapter 1, this

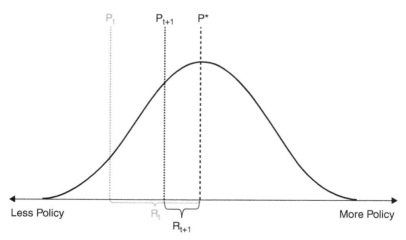

FIGURE 2.2. A Thermostatic Response in Preferences for Policy

conceptualization of public preferences has deep roots in political science, including Easton's (1965) classic depiction of a political system and Deutsch's (1963) models of "control."

These expectations can be expressed more formally. In our model, the public has both a relative preference for policy and an absolute preference. The former is a function of the latter, and it captures thermostatic public responsiveness. That is, the public's preference for "more" policy – its relative preference, R – represents the difference between the public's preferred level of policy – its absolute preference, P^* – and the level it actually gets, P:

$$R_t = P^*_t - P_t \tag{2.1}$$

In the model the thermostatic signal is not the dichotomous one that governs the heating (or air conditioning) units in our homes. It is more fine-grained, and captures both direction and magnitude. As the preferred level of policy (P^*) or policy itself (P) changes, the relative preference (R) signal changes accordingly. Changes in the preferred level obviously have positive effects: as P^* increases (or decreases), the gap between P^* and P widens (or shrinks), and R increases (or decreases) accordingly. In contrast, changes in policy (P) have negative effects: when policy increases (decreases), the preference for more policy decreases (increases). Notice that the public is expected to respond to current values of P, at time t. Of course it is possible that the response is more delayed, which can be tested directly – see Chapter 6.

This negative feedback of policy on preferences is the real crux of the thermostatic model. It is what distinguishes a reasonably informed public – one that knows something about what policymakers actually do – from an uninformed public. Observing it out in the world would mean that the signal that the public sends to policymakers contains meaningful information. Ultimately, it would tell us that effective accountability and control are possible, that the public is in a position to reward or punish the incumbent government for its actions.

Although we have thus far characterized responsiveness across time, notice that an identical expectation applies across space as well. Consider, for example, the fifty states in the United States. We know that the preferred level of policy in a particular area, say, education, differs across states. We also know that the level of policy differs across states. If the thermostatic model applies, the public's relative preference would reflect the difference between the two across states j:

$$R_j = P^*_j - P_j \qquad\qquad (2.2)$$

The preference for more (or less) policy in each state will depend on whether the public's preferred level is greater than policy itself in the different states. (For one empirical application, to opinion and policy about abortion in the different U.S. states, see Goggin and Wlezien 1993.)

Public Preferences in Theory and Practice

Most people do not have specific preferred levels of policy in most policy areas. This is true for two reasons. First, simple, precise options do not exist in most policy domains. Most policy objectives are not adequately captured by simple, categorical items, but rather by *ranges* of support or opposition, as depicted in Figure 2.1. Second, policy will often be far too complex for individuals to prefer – independent of current policy – a specific level of policy. Imagine asking people how much health or education spending they want; indeed, consider how you yourself would respond. The behavior of survey organizations is confirming, as they typically do not ask how much policy people want.

Indeed, there are very few domains in which we can reasonably expect people to have preferences for a specific level of policy. There are some apparently dichotomous policy choices where specific preferences might be more likely, such as abortion policy, or desegregation, or school busing. In abortion, for instance, the choice is apparently relatively simple, legal or illegal;[2] for desegregation,

---

[2] For this issue, people regularly are asked about the specific circumstances under which a respondent thinks abortion should be legal or illegal. For instance, the General Social Survey (GSS) traditionally has asked "whether or not you think it should be possible for a pregnant woman to obtain a legal abortion" under six conditions: a. There is a strong chance of serious defect in the baby; b. She is married and does not want any more children; c. The woman's own health is seriously endangered by the pregnancy; d. The family has a very low income and cannot afford more children; e. She became pregnant as a result of rape; f. She is not married and does not want to marry the man.

survey organizations have asked about "desegregation" or "strict segregation"; and for school busing, until 1984 respondents were asked whether they preferred "busing children" or having them go to school in their "own neighborhoods."[3] In each case, however, the dichotomous choice masks what is surely a range in preferences. There is almost always a middle ground – indeed, a middle ground that is as viable a policy option as either extreme. Preferences about going to war will have similar characteristics: a middle ground is possible, such as not supporting the war in principle but supporting one of the combatants, and wartime commitment knows a variety of degrees.

For many policy domains, then, a dichotomous choice is more apparent than real. Not surprisingly, good survey organizations have attempted to sort people whose preferences fall along a range between two polar options. The National Election Study (NES) uses 7-point scales on many issues. For instance, the NES has asked:

Some people feel that the government in Washington should see to it that every person has a job and a good standard of living. Others think the government should let each person get ahead on his/her own. And, of course, other people have opinions somewhere in between. Where would you place yourself on this scale?

Although this may do a good job differentiating individuals, it is not clear what the numbers mean in policy space. What exactly does a 4 on a 1–7 scale represent? Where do we place the policy status quo? This clearly makes it difficult to draw comparisons from responses to questions about different policies or bills at different points in time. While we may be able to tell that the public wants more at one point than another, we cannot tell how much it wants at either point in time, or whether it wants more or less policy than is currently in place.

Even more fundamentally, at every point in time the meaning of support or opposition to a particular policy is at least partly unclear. Does an opponent of a particular policy want more or less than the policy contains? How much more or less? We can't really tell, at least with the kind of precision we would like. Survey data thus necessarily offer

---

[3] The NES still frequently asks about whether "the federal government in Washington should see to it that black and white children go to the same schools."

only very limited insight into the public's absolute policy preferences. This makes it difficult to assess whether the public's preferences and government policies line up.

Fortunately, the public's relative preference (R) is much more adequately captured. Survey organizations quite regularly ask about relative preferences. Most commonly, respondents are asked about whether we should "do more," whether we are spending "too little," or whether spending should "be increased." There is good reason for asking about relative rather than absolute preferences: this is likely how most people think about most policies.[4] The resulting public preference is necessarily relative, of course: it captures support for policy *change*, that is, change from the current policy status quo (P). This is very convenient for our purposes, as we have a measure of the thermostatic signal the public sends to policymakers in different domains. *Without the measure we could not test the thermostatic model.* The question is, then: Do people adjust their relative preferences in response to policy change itself?

Because we do not directly measure the public's preferred level of policy (P^*), we need to rewrite the model of R (Equation 2.1) as follows:

$$R_t = a + \beta_1 P_t + \beta_2 W_t + e_t \tag{2.3}$$

where a and e_t represent the intercept and the error term respectively, and W designates a variety of exogenous drivers of R. The public's relative preferences regarding welfare policy may be conditioned in part by public concerns about economic security, for instance; relative preferences for defense spending may be driven by perceived security threats. Note that these variables, W, can be viewed not just as "controls," but alternatively as instruments for P^*. That is, in lieu of having measures of preferred levels of policy, these are factors that we believe are associated with P^*. The most critical part of Equation 2.3 is, however, β_1. If people do respond thermostatically, β_1 will be negative, and we will observe the result suggested in Figure 2.2.

---

[4] For similar reasons, presumably, survey firms commonly ask about relative assessments in regards to outcomes as well, e.g., whether the economy has gotten worse, crime is getting better, the environment is improving.

Positive Feedback

Although the thermostatic model posits negative feedback, it may be that policy feeds back positively on preferences – an increase in spending could lead people to want more spending in that domain (Baumgartner and Jones 1993, 2002). There actually is some suggestion of this tendency in Page and Shapiro's (1983) early work on opinion-policy covariation.

There appear to be two primary explanations for such positive feedback. First, people could react favorably to the outcomes of increased (or decreased) government role in a policy area. They might see that increasing government intervention improved the situation and conclude that more intervention will improve things even more. Second, people could be adjusting their preferences based on the behavior of political elites, becoming more (less) supportive of additional policy change. These dynamics presumably are most likely in policy domains of emerging salience, where government intervention is relatively new, for example, environmental policy in the 1960s and 1970s (see Franklin and Wlezien 1997). In these domains people's opinions are least crystallized and thus susceptible to new information and cues. (For similar reasons, we might also expect elements of positive feedback in domains of moderate or even high salience, at least for those individuals whose opinions are less well formed.)

We do not gainsay these possibilities; indeed, we explicitly entertain them in our analyses. Consider that positive feedback will be directly captured in Equation 2.3. That is, there is nothing in the equation that requires β_{1} to be negative. The parameter is the net effect of positive and negative feedback. If positive feedback is dominant, then it will overwhelm negative feedback and β_{1} will be positive; if negative feedback is dominant, as we expect, then β_{1} will be negative. The proof is, as they say, in the (empirical) pudding.

There is one further variant on positive feedback that we need to consider, one that also involves the actions of political elites. That is, it may not be that the public reacts positively to policy changes or even to the cues that correspond to these changes. Rather, politicians may effectively mobilize opinion in advance of policy change, in effect to create the support that they then can represent. This is not a new concern; it was argued most cogently in Jacobs and Shapiro's

(2000) *Politicians Don't Pander*. It is an engaging possibility and an important one to consider.[5] It also is relatively easy to test. Specifically, we can analyze the timing of changes in preferences and policy. This we do in our analyses of policy representation in Chapter 7.

On the Flow of Information

The thermostatic model is a simple one, but it sets out what may seem to be very high expectations for the public. In the extreme, we might imagine voters continuously monitoring the world, looking for evidence of policy activity. Even a sober portrait would appear more demanding than what Page and Shapiro (1983) propose in their famous book, *The Rational Public*. There, the public is conceived to have meaningful preferences for policy that tend to change sensibly, typically very deliberately, in response to real-world events. This is an important insight, and it marks an important step in the direction of our thermostatic model. Using Zaller's (1992) familiar reception-acceptance model, people appear to both receive and *accept* relevant information and update their preferences appropriately. Indeed, Page and Shapiro's analyses reveal that opinion change is largely uniform across a wide range of subcategories, including income, education, and gender (also see Soroka and Wlezien, 2008). This tells us that people with widely differing characteristics react in much the same way to new information over time. This is a striking finding. Still, the thermostatic model requires more – that people acquire and process information about policy.

We know that people don't have copies of the federal budget on their coffee tables. Only a handful even page through the *Congressional Record* or the magazines (*Congressional Quarterly* and *National Journal*) written largely for the inside-the-Beltway (Washington, D.C.) crowd, or those political junkies from elsewhere. Few people read the *New York Times* or the *Washington Post*, and even these papers really only give us a glimmer of insight into what government is doing. Indeed, most Americans don't read any kind of newspaper, and the situation is only a little better in Canada and the

---

[5] The process by which this might happen ultimately could be quite complex – see Chong and Druckman (2007).

United Kingdom (see, e.g., Norris 2000).[6] Is it reasonable to expect public responsiveness to policy?

The short answer is "yes." A growing body of work suggests that public responsiveness to policy is within the realm of possibility. To begin with, the policy decisions citizens are required to make are typically very simplified. This is not an artifact of close-ended survey questions, but a fact of everyday politics. The logic of party competition for votes encourages the structuring of policy alternatives – at least where citizens' decision-making is concerned – in relatively simple ways (Jackman and Sniderman 2002). Citizens are able to use cues or heuristics to help them make decisions with only very basic information (see, e.g., Lupia and McCubbins 1998; Popkin 1994). Politicians and parties also have a strong incentive to provide these cues (Sniderman and Theriault 2004; Chong and Druckman 2007).

More specifically, the thermostatic model only requires that people can tell whether policy has gone "too far" in one direction or "not far enough" given their preferences. This is not a sophisticated judgment. It does not require great detail about policy – just fairly basic information about what policymakers have done. Individuals need to have some sense of the direction and magnitude of policy change – for instance, that Reagan "really cut social programs," or that Clinton "increased taxes." With only these very general impressions of policy, relative preferences will change. In the wake of a cut in policy, those people who said we were doing "too much" but were close to saying "about right" will be more likely to give the latter response; those saying "about right" but were close to saying "too little" will be more likely to indicate the latter. This does not presuppose a high level of information. It also is the kind of information that is widely available. Even if we don't read the paper or watch television news or listen to the radio or hear about it from a friend, we could pick up the information by overhearing a conversation by the water cooler, in an elevator, at a bar, or on the train ride home.

---

[6] Of course there are other sources of information, and they have been on the rise while newspaper consumption has declined. Even so, recent work (e.g., Prior 2007) suggests that political knowledge has remained relatively steady (and low) over time.

Take, for instance, Bush's first package of tax cuts, in 2001. How did the public respond? In April 2001, only three months after Bush took office, Gallup asked a national sample of more than 1,000 adults: Do you consider the amount of federal income tax you have to pay as too high, about right, or too low? The public's response was perhaps all too much as we would expect, as 65% responded "too high," 33% said "about right," and only 1% offered "too low." Clearly, there aren't very many people who think that their own taxes should be very high.[7] During the summer of 2001, Bush's tax cuts passed through Congress and then went into effect in 2002. In January 2003, Gallup again asked a similar sample the same question.[8] Here, 47% responded "too high" and 50% "about right." This is a striking change. A good number of people evidently noticed what policymakers did, presumably many more than those whose relative preferences actually changed as a consequence of the tax cut.

Of course, not everyone notices. This is true even in areas such as taxes, where we expect many people to have a pretty good sense of whether there has been policy change and whether it is a little change or a big one. In other areas, such as the environment, fewer people may notice. In yet other areas, say, foreign aid, only a very small fraction of people may be able to tell what politicians are doing. And even among those who do detect policy change, some may take more notice than others. Attentiveness varies across individuals and across issues, with important consequences that we take up again in subsequent chapters.

How do people know when things are "about right"? Or that we're doing "too little" or "too much"? It's one thing to pick up signs of change and even the size of the change. But how do we know it's enough? How do we determine that it's not too much? This is important, since if people respond imperfectly, by undershooting or overshooting, then preferences will be less meaningful to politicians.

---

[7] Of course, this doesn't mean that people think that other people's tax rates shouldn't be higher. And, relatedly, surveys indicate that people from all income levels are much more likely to say that taxes on those with "low" and "middle" incomes are too high; people tend to be more evenly divided about taxes on those with "high" incomes. See Soroka and Wlezien (2008).

[8] Note that this poll was conducted well before Bush's second set of tax cuts, which were proposed and passed later in 2003.

That is, if we respond only a little in response to a big change in policy, or a lot in response to a little change, then the signal will be not be particularly meaningful to politicians at any particular point in time. To provide a clear, reliable signal, therefore, we seemingly not only need to know the direction and magnitude of change; we also need to have some idea of how the endpoint compares with our own ideal. This is true in theory but less so in practice, as we will see, because it is difficult for the public and scholars to tell whether preferences and policy match.[9] It nevertheless is useful to consider how it might work.

Determining how preferences and policy compare clearly would require a high level of information, but not necessarily for everyone. At minimum, some nontrivial segment of the public needs to be able to make the determination. The rest could overshoot or undershoot at random, e.g., those who should say taxes are "about right" instead say "too high," others who should say "about right" offer "too low." These cancel out in the aggregate, and what remains is the central tendency – in the preceding models, R.[10] This is a minimalist concept, of course, and it may be that the rest of the population does more than randomly guess. Many people have some information, after all, and cue-taking is pervasive in political life, which we discuss below. The

---

[9] As noted in Chapter 4, it just is not clear that we can provide valid measures of individuals' preferences for spending *at particular points in time*. That is, we cannot be sure that the "about right" response really taps a preference for keeping spending the same in a spending area. Part of the problem is the meaning of spending categories to the public, e.g., whether we should ask about spending on "welfare" or spending on "the poor." The problem also reflects differences in thermostatic responsiveness to policy across domains and countries, which makes preferences in some domains and countries more informative than others. (In domains where the public does not adjust preferences in response to policy, it is not clear what expressed preferences for "more" or "less" policy reveal.)

[10] As noted in Chapter 1, the argument that aggregate rationality can exist even in the face of individual-level error has been best summarized by Page and Shapiro (1983, 1992). These authors consider the issue in great detail, so we offer just a very brief synopsis here. Imagine that each individual, i, has a stable but reactive and rational policy preference, P^*_i, the measurement of which includes a certain amount of error, ε_i. Now, ε_i need not be distributed randomly for each individual; some individual preferences, P^*_i, may be more frequently biased upward or downward. But the distribution of errors across individuals at any given time is expected to be random; that is, the mean of individual errors at t is 0. Provided this assumption is correct (and we address this further in Chapter 8), aggregated preferences may well show a "rationality" that is not apparent at the individual level. Of course, this rationality may be evident at the individual level as well.

informed segment nevertheless drives the process (see, e.g., Stimson 1989).

But how does this group make an informed judgment? Generally, even the very well informed only have limited information about government. Some are experts in a particular area, say, the environment, and know a lot about what is happening in that area (Krosnick 1990; Hutchings 2003). They read a lot on the subject and frequently search for relevant information on the Web. Some may belong to interest groups. Some may even make their expertise their livelihoods. Of course, other people know a lot about other areas. This level of expertise is of obvious importance, but it is not the whole story. After all, most of us do not look at policy detail as a consumption good *per se* – that is, we are not policy wonks.

This contrasts somewhat with elections, as many of us enjoy – or are addicted to – the horse race of the campaign (Iyengar, Norpoth, and Hahn 2004). There are lots of election wonks. But the number of people actively following policy in any single domain is going to be too small to generate a rational, dynamic response to government policy all on their own. Many individuals use heuristics, of course (Popkin 1991; Sniderman *et al.* 1991; Lupia 1994; Lupia and McCubbins 1998; Lau and Redlawsk 2006; Gabel and Scheve 2007). Indeed, it may be rational to do so (Lau and Redlawsk 2006). We do not have to actually know what policymakers are doing – we can rely on what others say and do. Traditionally, political parties played this role; interest groups have too. Now, with the explosion of Internet outlets, sources abound.

We also have politicians themselves, who provide important information. They have been shown to be extremely reliable over time, at least in their voting behavior. Although we cannot always trust what they promise during election campaigns, we can for the most part count on what they'll actually do in office. According to Poole and Rosenthal (2007), politicians effectively "die with their ideological boots on." Very liberal members of Congress tend to stay liberal, conservative ones conservative, and moderate ones moderate. This allows us a lot of information. For example, when liberal members of Congress say we need more defense spending, we probably do need more, and attentive members of the public will take notice. When they say that we have enough, we probably don't have enough. When conservative members say we have enough, however, we most likely do, and probably then some. Of course, one's opinion will depend on where one sits.

We can choose specific politicians to serve as cue-givers. We can use them to tell us whether things are about right or whether we need to do more (or less). We presumably choose them because we trust them, and we rely on them more the more we trust them. It is a little like what we do with restaurant or movie critics. We are more likely to follow the advice of particular critics when their previous advice has served us well. The better the advice has served us, the more likely we are to follow it, of course. When the advice doesn't deliver, we take note. If it happens again and again, we may find someone else. In politics, things are more subtle, and we do not typically experience what happens the way we do with restaurants and movies. The internal logic is much the same, however (see Lupia and McCubbins 1998).Competition is critical. Alongside a free press, political competition is central to the flow of information from governments to citizens. Were there not competing interests among our politicians, that is, to spend more or less on different programs, it would be difficult for us to get information. Indeed, there would be reason for concern, as we would face the equivalent of a cartel. Fortunately, we do have competing parties vying for power. Preferences within parties also differ, and people compete for our votes to be party leaders and the like. Much as in the marketplace, there is an invisible hand of sorts in operation; as in the marketplace, things don't always work out perfectly. In democratic politics, of course, the payoff is in votes (and money).

THE MECHANICS OF POLICY REPRESENTATION

We have gone some way toward a model of public responsiveness to policy. Let us now turn to the flipside – policy responsiveness to public opinion. By comparison with public responsiveness, we know a lot more about policy representation, both theoretically and empirically. We know that representation can occur in one of two familiar ways.

The first way is indirect, through elections, where the public selects like-minded politicians who then deliver what it wants in policy. This is the more traditional pathway to representation, and is deeply rooted in the literature on responsible parties (see, e.g., Fiorina 1981; Key 1966; Mayhew 1974; Powell 2000; Ranney 1954). In effect, the public chooses among alternative policy visions and then the winning parties put their programs into place after the election. The second way to representation is direct, where politicians who are in office literally respond to what the public wants. This pathway reflects a more active political class. Here, politicians endeavor to stay attuned to the ebb and flow of public opinion and to adjust policy accordingly.

The two ways to representation are in a broad sense related. That is, the first way implies the second, at least assuming incumbent politicians are interested in remaining in office: elected officials are expected to respond to public preferences, even between elections, because of the threat of electoral sanction. Note that it is not necessary for voters to vote on the basis of their preferences and government action, rewarding and punishing politicians at each and every turn. It is necessary only that there be a reasonable probability that they will do so on any particular decision. That is, politicians must have a reason to think that they will pay a price for their behavior – that there is some level of risk for defying the public will. Of course, politicians also must value the risk – they cannot be too risk-acceptant.[11] There are other possible motivations for opinion representation, however. For instance, politicians may consider themselves public agents and endeavor to represent our preferences in policy.

Regardless of the specific motivations, we expect responsiveness to be dynamic. That is, responsive politicians should follow preferences as they change. We can express this expectation formally. To begin, if policymakers are responsive to public preferences, changes in policy (ΔP) in year t will be associated with lagged (year $t-1$) levels of the public's relative preference (R), its preference for "more" or "less." Policy will thus be a positive function of preferences, as follows:

$$\Delta P_t = g\,\{R_{t-1}\}. \tag{2.4}$$

---

[11] This is a minimalist model and differs from the usual formulation, including our own in previous work, wherein policy voting is explicitly required. This revised model sets out an expectation that is much easier to satisfy, at least in certain policy domains.

When the public wants more policy it tends to get more policy; when it wants less it tends to get less. Of course, as we have discussed, there are two specific pathways to represent: the indirect and direct. The indirect linkage involves two sequential connections: (1) between public opinion and party control of government and (2) between party control and policy. Thus, if there is indirect representation, we first would observe that party control (G_t) in year t is a function of the public's relative preference (R_t) in that year:

$$G_t = h\{R_t\}. \tag{2.5}$$

We then would observe that policy change (P_t) is a function of (G_{t-1}), controlling for preferences (R_t):

$$\Delta P_t = m\{R_{t-1}, G_{t-1}\} \tag{2.6}$$

or, alternatively,

$$\Delta P_t = \rho + \gamma_1 R_{t-1} + \gamma_2 G_{t-1} + \mu_t, \tag{2.7}$$

where ρ and μ_t represent the intercept and the error term, respectively. To be absolutely clear, if representation is indirect, γ_2 will be significantly different from 0. Party control may effectively mediate the influence of opinion on policy.

If policymakers are directly responsive to public preferences, then policy will follow preferences independent of government party control. This responsiveness is evident in the coefficient γ_1 in Equation 2.7 – if this coefficient is greater than 0, policymakers "respond" to preferences. This of course need not mean that politicians literally respond to changing public preferences; it may be that politicians and the public both respond to something else, for example, changes in the need for spending. All we can say for sure is that the coefficient (γ_1) captures policy responsiveness in a statistical sense – the extent to which public preferences directly influence policy change, other things being equal. We do note, however, the large body of qualitative research demonstrating politicians' attention to public opinion, much of which follows in the footsteps of John Kingdon's (1973) important work on members of the U.S. Congress.[12]

---

[12] Even more critical treatments (Jacobs and Shapiro 2000) acknowledge a substantial role for the public in politicians' decision-making.

We also can to some extent explore the exact nature of this responsiveness, as we will see in forthcoming chapters.

Note in Equation 2.7 that policy change for year t is a function of opinion (and government control) in year $t-1$. This specification is not meant to imply that policymakers do not respond to current opinion. Rather, it is intended to reflect the reality of policymaking, which is dominated by the cycle of budgeting, and largely happens over the course of the previous year (see Wlezien 1996b; Wlezien and Soroka 2003). Consider, for example, that policy for fiscal year 2006 is actually made in 2005 and is thus expected to reflect opinion in that year. The specification in Equations 2.4 through 2.7 consequently captures responsiveness to opinion when most budgetary decisions are made. So the new policy, determined by opinion in 2005, then affects opinion registered in 2006. This is current responsiveness, though the resulting output lags by one year.

The temporal relationships between opinion and policy are depicted in Figure 2.3. Here, we can see how the causal connections spill out over time. Notice that, although opinion and policy do affect each other over time, the effects of each on the other are not simultaneous – this year's preferences influences policy for next year, which influences next year's preferences. The effects also are oppositely signed; opinion has a positive effect on policy and policy has a negative effect on opinion. This is the ongoing process that characterizes our dynamic model. It is also the timing implicit in Deutsch's electrical engineering-inspired model of policymaking: a servomechanism converts an input to an output, compares actual output with the preferred output, adjusts input accordingly, compares the new output with the preferred output, adjusts input accordingly, and so on.

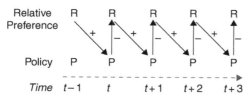

FIGURE 2.3. Preferences and Policy Over Time

Political Parties and Policy

Policy is not just about public preferences, of course. Other things matter, and perhaps most important is the party control of government. This is clear from our equations and surrounding discussion. It nevertheless is useful to consider exactly how political parties and representation combine to influence policy.

Figure 2.4 depicts one scenario. It shows a hypothetical timeline of social policy. Over the timeline, the public's preferences for policy change. For expository purposes, the figure shows the public's hypothetical level of policy (P^*), and not its relative preference (R). (This is because the relative preference is expected to respond to policy changes that result from transitions in party control, and this complicates presentation.) The party control of government changes as well, indicated by "D" and "R" along the bottom axis of the figure – these are used to designate "Democratic" and "Republican" control in the United States. For this illustration, the effects of party transitions on policy change are expected to be greatest early on and diminish over time, as policy approaches the party's ideal point. This is consistent with empirical research (Alt 1985). The parties' ideal points are assumed to be equidistant from the public's preferred level of policy.

In the figure, policy follows both public preferences and party control. Notice, however, that policy does not converge on the public

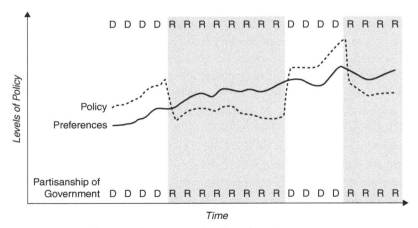

FIGURE 2.4. Policy, Preferences, and Political Parties

preference. Indeed, policy *never* matches what the public wants – it is always off to the left or right. It comes closest immediately after a partisan transition, for example, when a Democrat replaces a Republican, and then diverges over the course of the term. Policy still reflects public preferences, though in our depiction here party control matters more, and by a lot. Whether this is true depends on the degree of difference between the parties and also the variation in preferences over time. If the former is larger than the latter, then party control will tend to have larger effects. This may be especially true where executive and legislative control are unified, that is, in parliamentary systems, and when the same party controls both branches in a presidential system. The point is that the thermostatic model does not imply policy convergence on the public's preferred level. Even with high levels of public responsiveness and policy representation, policy can diverge significantly simply because of party control of government.

PUBLIC PREFERENCES AND THE POLLS

In our minds, politicians respond to public preferences. This does not mean that they respond to *polls*, however. To us, polls provide measures of preferences – they summarize national-level public opinion. They are important to us because we are interested in measuring opinion at this level and in doing so in a reliable way over time. We also have no other option – if we do not use polls, how can we measure the public preference for policy? Politicians do have other sources of information, however, and always have. This is what Congress scholar Richard Fenno has taught us so well over the years. Members of Congress rely on communications networks within their constituencies, and these work very well – they help explain how the members got into office in the first place, and why they're still there. The same is true in other countries (see, e.g, Cain et al. 1979; Heitshusen et al. 2005).

Politicians may still rely on polls to gauge opinion – indeed, there may be good reason to do so (Geer 1996). This is true even for legislators representing districts. Polls can provide a useful check on information the legislators get from other sources; they might also provide new information.[13] Legislators may be more likely to rely on

---

[13] But see also note 3, Chapter 1.

polls of people living within their districts rather than national polls, although some politicians, particularly those representing national constituencies, such as the president of the United States, may rely on national polls. Cabinets in parliamentary democracies may do much the same – although members of the cabinet may be elected from geographic constituencies, as in Canada and the United Kingdom, there is reason to suppose that as executive officials they consider public opinion more generally. This might lead them to consult polls of national samples. And the same may be true for leaders of legislatures in presidential systems.

That said, we remain agnostic about politicians' use of polls. Whether and to what extent politicians actually use polls is largely irrelevant to us, and it is not critical to what we argue or show. To be clear: we are interested in policymakers' responsiveness to public opinion, not polls *per se*. The latter provide information about the former, but they are not the same. And it may ultimately be that politicians generally do not follow the polls in decision-making but do follow public opinion. Although the former has been the focus of some researchers (e.g., Jacobs and Shapiro 2000), it is the latter that matters to us.

THE REASONABLENESS OF THE THERMOSTATIC MODEL

The thermostatic model is a relatively simple one. The model posits that relative public preferences will react negatively to policy change – specifically, that preferences will adjust downward (upward) as policy moves increase (decrease). In addition, the model posits that policy will respond positively to public preferences for more spending, shifting policy upward (downward) when the public prefers more (less) policy. Indeed, we maintain that the two relationships are theoretically interconnected. Without public responsiveness to policy, there is little basis for policy responsiveness to public opinion. Politicians not only would have little incentive to represent preferences in policy; they would have little information to go on, as public opinion would be an essentially meaningless signal.

The thermostatic model also is not highly demanding of the public. People are not expected to have clearly defined and well-reasoned positions on various issues. People also are not expected to be fully informed about the actions of policymakers. All people are not expected to respond. All that is required is that some meaningful portion of citizens have a basic preference for policy change in one direction or the other and that they adjust this preference over time in reaction to what policymakers do, based on the information those citizens receive through mass media, political groups, or friends and family, as well as through daily experiences with government services, and with society more generally. We believe that this responsiveness is possible, at least under certain circumstances. It of course is a testable proposition, and the subject of forthcoming chapters.

For the meantime, this chapter has set out the theoretical groundwork for the chapters that follow – the basic mechanics of the thermostatic model of opinion and policy. The nature and magnitude of both public responsiveness and policy responsiveness should vary across both policy domains and countries, however. We turn to this issue in Chapter 3.

3

Adding Issues and Institutions

Thus far, our expectations have been very general. We have posited that the public is responsive to policy change and that policymakers represent public preferences. We do not expect the model to apply in all policy domains in all countries, however. Indeed, we expect that the model will vary systematically with both issue salience and institutional characteristics.

ADDING SALIENCE

In its simplest sense, a salient issue is one that is politically important, one that people care about, and one on which they have meaningful opinions that structure party support and candidate evaluation (see, e.g., Miller, Miller, Raine and Browne 1976; Abramowitz 1994; van der Eijk and Franklin 1996). Candidates are likely to take positions on the issue and it is likely to form the subject of political debate (Graber 1989). People are more likely to pay attention to politicians' behavior on an important issue, as reflected in news media reporting (see, e.g., Brody 1991) or as communicated in other ways (Ferejohn and Kuklinski 1990). Politicians, meanwhile, are likely to pay attention to public opinion on the issue – it is in their self-interest to do so, after all (Hill and Hurley 1998). In issue domains that are not important, conversely, people are not likely to pay attention to politicians' behavior. Politicians, by implication, are expected to pay less attention to public opinion in these areas. This reflects a now classic perspective. (See, e.g., McCrone and Kuklinski 1979; Jones 1994; Geer 1996; Hill and Hurley 1998; Burstein 2003.)

The implications for our analysis are fairly straightforward. Consider first public opinion. In salient domains, a relatively large number of people are expected to respond to policy, by adjusting their relative preferences downward (upward) when policy increases (decreases). This is not to say that *all* individuals behave in this way; even in those domains that we normally consider to be salient, many people may not respond to policy at all. In non-salient domains, however, few, if any, people are expected to respond to policy change.[1]

These individual-level effects should sum up rather neatly and find expression in the coefficient for public responsiveness, or "feedback": in non-salient domains, where few people respond to policy, the coefficient tends toward 0; in salient domains, where most people respond, the coefficient tends toward 1. From this perspective, public responsiveness to policy is dependent on the level of salience. We can rewrite Equation 2.3, then, letting I designate importance. Across a set of policy domains j, the resulting equation is as follows:

$$R_{jt} = a_j + \beta_1 I_{jt} P_{jt} + \beta_{2j} W_{jt} + e_{jt}, \tag{3.1}$$

where I ranges between 0 and 1. Here, the influence of policy (P) on preferences is interactive and depends on the level of I – it is $\beta_1 * I$. If I equals 1, then the effect of policy is equal to β_1; if I equals 0, conversely, then the effect of policy is equal to 0. In that circumstance, the public simply does not at all notice what policymakers do. (In practice, of course, I seemingly always takes a value between 0 and 1.)

Policymakers may be more likely to notice and pay attention to public opinion for policy in a particular area when the public views that issue as important. Here policy responsiveness is expected to be

---

[1] Note that the literature on issue publics is relevant here. In particular, it makes clear that issue salience varies across individuals (or, to be precise, groups). See, e.g., Krosnick 1989; Hutchings 2003.

dependent on importance, implying another interactive specification. We can thus rewrite Equation 2.7 as follows:

$$\Delta P_{jt} = \rho_j + \gamma_t I_{jt} R_{t-1} + \gamma_{2j} Z_{t-1} + \mu_{jt}, \tag{3.2}$$

where Z designates the various other influences on policy, including the party control of government. Much as for public responsiveness, policymaker responsiveness to preferences depends on the level of I. The effect of opinion (R) increases as importance increases and peaks when I equals 1. When importance is nil, however, policymakers do not pay attention to public preferences.

Notice that these equations not only imply variation in responsiveness across domains, but they also imply variation in responsiveness within domains over time, as salience evolves. When an issue is new and not very salient to the public, its effect is expected to approach zero; as salience increases, representation and responsiveness can be expected to increase.

Introducing salience into our models provides substantial theoretical purchase. It suggests that the pattern of representation across policy domains will be symmetric to patterns of public responsiveness: where the public notices and responds to policy in a particular domain, policymakers will notice and respond to public preferences themselves; where the public does not respond to policy, policymakers will not represent public preferences. As has been much noted in preceding chapters: a responsive public is a central motivation for responsiveness on the part of election-seeking representatives. This line of thinking should help us understand certain patterns of policymaker behavior. For instance, it might tell us why one government is more responsive to public preferences in a particular domain than another government – because the public is more responsive to policy. It also may tell us why one government is more responsive to preferences for policy in some domains but not others – because the public is more responsive to policy in those domains.

ADDING INSTITUTIONS

Polities differ in many ways, and some of these differences should have significant implications for the nature and degree of public and policy responsiveness. Of fundamental importance are mass media openness and political competition, for instance. Though we do not examine it here, the role of mass media in democracy has been highlighted by both political theorists (e.g., Dahl 1970) and media analysts (e.g., Abramson et al. 1988). Without an open media, people cannot easily receive information about what government actors do, and are less able to respond to policy change. This in turn has implications for representation. Mass media openness may thus be a necessary condition for effective democracy.

Governments also have less incentive to respond to public opinion in the absence of some level of political competition; or, at the very least, the incentive is less reliable. This is widely recognized (e.g., Manin, Przeworski, and Stokes 1999).[2] Of course, elections are no guarantee of competition (Golder 2005), and even where we have a degree of competition in modern democracies the level varies nontrivially. How much competition do we need? We probably don't need perfect competition – even within the oligopolistic framework, where there are few sellers, we may have enough. That is, there is reason to think that a little competition may go a long way. Recall our discussion of risk in Chapter 2.

Note, however, that it is not clear that electoral competition is a *necessary* condition for representation. Following Achen (1978), representatives may represent because they are, broadly speaking, representative of the population. They may also represent not for office-seeking purposes, but because they are genuinely interested in doing a good job for their constituents (e.g., Fenno 1978). Perhaps we should not place too much emphasis on the need for competition. Even so, the absence of competition quite clearly removes a critical incentive for policy responsiveness. (We consider the effect that electoral competitiveness has on the strength of policy representation in Chapter 7.)

Even where we have basic levels of media and political competition, political institutions also may be important. Indeed, the literature on comparative institutions suggests that they are very

---

[2] Political competition also may be essential for the flow of information to the public as well. That is, in the course of election campaigns and policy debates, people learn about what politicians actually have done and are doing. Consider the now voluminous literature on negative campaigning in the U.S. – see Geer (2006) for an excellent review and assessment.

powerful mediators of opinion-policy connections. There are two broad categories that are especially significant: electoral systems and the division of powers.

Electoral Systems

Electoral systems are the emphasis of most of the existing relevant literature. Most of this research focuses on differences between majoritarian and proportional visions, using Powell's (2000) language, and mostly on how these differences matter for policy representation. Let us briefly review the literature in the area, focusing on the two leading exponents.

Lijphart (1984) provides the first direct statement on the subject. In his classic and influential book, *Democracies* (and again in a follow-up fifteen years later, Lijphart 1999), he assesses the performance of different types of democracy on different dimensions, including democratic quality. He finds that some "consensual" democracies tend to provide better descriptive representation and general ideological congruence than majoritarian systems. The consensual democracies are characterized by, most notably, proportional representation, multiparty systems, and coalition governments, exactly as Duverger would predict. In addition, these countries tend to be federal, have a constitution, and exhibit executive-legislative separation. Majoritarian systems, conversely, are characterized by simple plurality election rules, a two-party system, and single-party government, also as Duverger would predict. These countries also tend to have unitary or centralized government and an uncodified constitution. The differential performance of the systems, according to Lijphart, shows that the consensual approach is clearly superior to the majoritarian one.

Powell (2000) provides further empirical support, focusing specifically on differences between majoritarian and proportional election rules and their implications for representation. Relying on expert surveys relating to party positions and opinion surveys of the public in different countries, he shows that proportional representation tends to produce greater congruence between the government and the public. Specifically, the general ideological complexion of policy and the ideological bent of the electorate tend to better match in proportional systems.

According to Powell, this reflects the greater direct participation of constituencies the vision affords. The mechanism is the bargaining required to form a majority. Whereas majoritarian rules lead parties to coalesce in advance of a election, thus producing a clear majority on Election Day, proportional rules disperse power, thus requiring a set of parties to come together after an election to form a government. In reaching agreement, the resulting coalition effectively averages across the component party positions, thereby producing moderation. In majoritarian systems, in contrast, governments tend to be further off-center. Perhaps parties in these systems do not reliably move to the ideological center but instead tend to position themselves off to the left and right. It also may be that parties do compete for the center but that voters do not consistently select the most centrist party – that is, election outcomes may reflect other things, such as economic growth. Regardless of the exact underpinnings, the main result is fairly clear: Proportional elections tend to produce more representative governments than do majoritarian systems.[3]

Powell's results pertain to elections and their immediate consequences. But what about in the periods between elections? What if public opinion changes after an election? Are coalition governments more responsive to the change in opinion? Or are single-party governments in majoritarian systems equally, if not more, responsive?

During the periods between elections, there are good reasons to think that governments in majoritarian systems actually are more responsive. First, it presumably is easier for a single party to respond to changes than a multi-party coalition. Simply put, the coordination required to respond is more difficult and costly in the latter. Coalition agreements seemingly only make things harder. Second, majoritarian governments may have more of an incentive to respond to opinion change. This hypothesis generalizes Rogowski and Kayser's (2002) argument relating to comparatively higher votes-seats elasticities in majoritarian systems, namely, that governments in those systems are

---

[3] There are recent naysayers, however. Blais and Bodet (2006) argue that while proportional systems do encourage coalition governments, thus pulling the government more to the center, they also encourage a greater number and diversity of parties in the first place, which promotes representation of more extreme positions. The various scholars do focus on different periods of time, and it may be that both are right but that conditions changed.

more responsive to consumer interests than to producer interests. Because a shift in electoral sentiment has bigger consequences on Election Day in majoritarian systems, governments there are likely to pay especially close attention to the ebb and flow of opinion.

It thus may be that both proportional and majoritarian systems work to serve representation, but in different ways, where the former provide better indirect representation via elections and the latter better direct representation between elections. This is clearly an important avenue for further study, though it is well beyond the empirical reach of this book, which focuses on three majoritarian systems.

Divisions of Power

As electoral systems may matter, so too may government institutions. In particular, we expect that divisions of power – both vertical and horizontal – may structure relationships between opinion and policy over time. In short, we argue that:

(1) a vertical division of powers, or federalism, makes it more difficult for the public to gauge and react to government policy change, and thus dampens public responsiveness; and,

(2) a horizontal concentration of powers, or parliamentary government, makes politicians less responsive to changes in public opinion.

Vertical Divisions of Power

Let us first consider the vertical division, or federalism, and its consequences for public responsiveness to policy. We know that thermostatic public responsiveness requires that the people acquire accurate information about what policymakers are doing. This clearly depends on the supply of information, as we have discussed. It also depends on the clarity of that information. More precisely, it depends on the extent to which responsibility for policies is clear, and this is in part a function of how government itself is organized. Federalism increases the number of different governments making policy and thus makes less clear what "government" is doing (see, e.g., Downs 1999). Put differently, the government policy signal may be confused – or, rather, there may be different signals from multiple sources – at least in policy domains

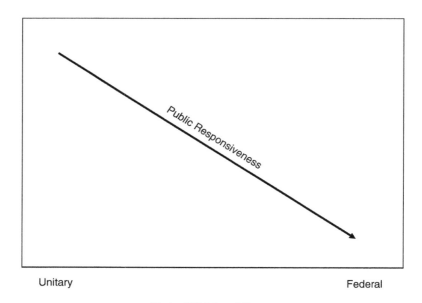

Unitary   Federal

Vertical Division of Powers

FIGURE 3.1. The Vertical Division of Powers and Public Responsiveness

for which different governments have responsibility. This clearly can dampen public responsiveness, as depicted in Figure 3.1.

Consider a unitary system, where there is but one government making policy in all areas. In such a system, there is no mistaking the source of policy change. The signal is clear, and we would expect a comparatively high level of public responsiveness, at least in salient domains. Now, consider a federal system. Here we have multiple governments, and there are consequently multiple sources of policymaking and policy information. There may still be considerable variation in decentralization among federal systems (Rodden 2004), and across policy domains within a single system. This has consequences for public responsiveness, we argue. (Also see Powell and Whitten 1993; Anderson 2006.)

It may be that governments have complete control for different domains; this is what in the American context is referred to as dual federalism (textbooks often invoke the image of a layer cake). In this design, different governments have different responsibilities and there are no interactions between layers. Much as in the unitary system, there is no mistaking the source of policy in each policy area; it is just that the source differs. We thus might expect a comparatively high level of responsiveness on the part of the public in politically important domains, regardless of which level of government is in charge. This presumes that the availability of information about the behavior of governments is fairly equal across levels of government, however, and this may not be true for at least two reasons: the behavior of the national government may receive more attention than that of lower-level governments, and the flow of information about lower-level governments may vary meaningfully across counties, states, and municipalities. Information on policymaking in a federal system may thus be more available in some domains than others, depending on which government is responsible, and responsiveness may vary accordingly.

More commonly, federal systems involve different governments sharing responsibilities in policy areas; this is often called cooperative federalism (the textbook image is of a marble cake.) There are two main ways in which different levels of government can be involved. One involves direct involvement by multiple levels. In this arrangement, there are different sources of policy change and implementation, which can create fairly obvious complications for the public, especially if policy change over time is not parallel across levels of government. It may not be that the public is less informed about the sum of policy across levels of government, though this is a possibility. There is very good reason to think that the public will be less informed about the behavior of specific levels, however, as this would require keeping what is happening at each level perfectly straight. Where there are overlapping jurisdictions, then, we expect a dampening of public responsiveness of preferences for policy *at any particular level of government*. For instance, we might expect that individuals' preferences for more policy at the national level would be less responsive to changes in national policy, independent of state or provincial or local policy. We would expect the same at these lower levels of government.

Things may be worse where one government transfers money to other governments. Here, multiple governments are involved but the actions of one government are not directly visible, at least in the actual delivery of services. In some cases, the recipient government still may not have much policy discretion. For instance, the recipient government may simply be the conduit for the transfer of public money, as is the case with grants-in-aid in the United States. Even where the recipient is not a mere go-between, there may be little discretion, as with some conditional grants. In these cases, federalism may make relatively little difference to the public, as change in policy at one level largely – although imperfectly – drives changes in policy at another level. Things are potentially quite different with block grants or revenue sharing. These mechanisms allow lower-level governments substantial discretion; indeed, revenue sharing comes with absolutely no strings. This situation is not very common in the United States, at least since 1986. While the national government may provide a broad direction for policy change at lower levels, what happens at these lower levels may differ quite a lot from place to place.

Largely unconditional block grants remain very common in Canada, where provinces have ostensibly exclusive jurisdiction over many policy domains but quite limited taxing power. The Canada Health and Social Transfer (CHST, 1996–2005), for instance, was a massive block grant from the federal government to provinces to help cover the cost of healthcare and education, and had relatively few strings attached. In a situation such as this, it is very often not clear to the public which government is responsible for what policy. Policy in one province may have gone up a lot, but does this mean we want the national government to do less? Or do we think that lower-level governments should do less? Or both? Indeed, the truth might be that we should think that the national government needs to do less and the local government more. Making such an assessment is, however, rather difficult – citizens simply cannot tell which government is principally responsible for a given shift in spending.

We thus have reasonably clear expectations about the effects of federalism on public responsiveness to policy. First, responsiveness to policy at any particular level of government should be generally lower in federal systems than in unitary systems. Second, in federal systems, this responsiveness should be especially low in domains where multiple governments are involved in policy. There may be a reasonable degree of responsiveness to policymaking by national and subnational governments combined, of course. But regarding any one level of government, preferences will be less meaningful.

This has implications for opinion representation itself. As we have discussed, there is good reason to think that we will have clear policy responsiveness only where we observe clear public responsiveness to policy. Some have argued that federalism actually increases net representation of broad policy preferences, as multiple levels of government provide greater opportunity (e.g., Trudeau 1968; Downs 1999). This possibility is perfectly consistent with our conjecture regarding representation at particular levels of government: It may be that representation of preferences for all levels taken together is greater even as the representation of preferences at each level is lesser. Given lower public responsiveness, the pressure for representation at each level of government may be reduced. That is, the public cannot as readily hold either level of government accountable.

Horizontal Divisions of Power

Now let us consider the horizontal division of powers between the executive and legislature and its implications for government responsiveness to public opinion. There are two general forms of executive-legislative organization: parliamentary and presidential. In the former, which is much more common among advanced industrial democracies, the executive is traditionally chosen from within the parliament and it serves only with the confidence of the latter. That is, the government depends on the support of the parliament to stay in power – in effect, the executive and legislative branches are fused. This concentration of powers is the defining characteristic of what is often called "responsible government." When put together with a majoritarian electoral system, we have "responsible party government."

In the presidential model, conversely, powers are divided into separate executive and legislative branches, each separately elected and endowed with separate powers. The separate institutions thus share power, where each can "check" or "balance" the other, at least with respect to statutes. The degree to which power is shared varies considerably across presidential systems, however. (This is in contrast with parliamentary systems, which show more similarity.) In the classic Madisonian version, neither branch can effectively act without the other, except where the legislative support is overwhelming – and even then, implementation is in the hands of the executive. In other presidential systems, power is not so evenly balanced. Typically the executive enjoys an advantage, and in some systems this is a decided one (Linz 1994; Cox and Morgenstern 2001). Although this variation in the balance of powers in presidential

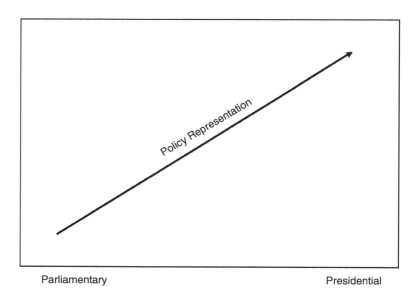

FIGURE 3.2. The Horizontal Division of Powers and Policy Representation

systems has consequences, we focus primarily on the classic Madisonian case. Doing so anchors our theoretical analysis and provides specific expectations for our empirical analysis.

Differences in these institutional arrangements may matter for government responsiveness to public opinion. In short, there is reason to suppose that parliamentary governments are less reliable in their attendance to public opinion, as shown in Figure 3.2. Scholars have long noted that dominance of cabinets over parliaments (see, e.g., the classic statements by Bagehot 1867 and Jennings 1959; also see Laver and Shepsle 1996). These scholars portray a world in which cabinet governments exercise substantial discretion. Cox (1987) attributes the role of cabinets to heightened electoral competition for seats over time. Other research provides a more institutional motivation for the lack of attendance to opinion in parliamentary systems, including Tsebelis (2002). First, in contrast with most presidential systems, the executive in parliamentary systems typically is the proposer: the government puts its legislation to the commons. Second, the legislature has only a limited check on what the executive does. It has what Lupia and Strom

(1995) call a "doomsday device," the no confidence vote. This is a very big check, obviously, but it can be very costly for the majority party; undertaking such a vote requires that governing party legislators be willing to face an early election. Huber (1996) finds that the threat of a no confidence vote can be used to the cabinet's advantage, and allows it effectively to control the legislative process. Strom (2003) highlights another doomsday device – the dissolution power – that allows the prime minister or cabinet to threaten the parliament with an immediate electoral competition. Because of these powers, Strom concludes that parliamentary government deals much better with adverse selection than it does moral hazard.

Once established, then, the cabinet can be difficult to control on a recurring basis. When there are differences between what the cabinet and parliament want, the latter cannot effectively impose its own contrary will. It cannot even easily veto. Perhaps most important of all, the legislature cannot consistently undertake "error correction," that is, adjusting the government's position where it may be going too far, or not far enough, given public preferences. This is a matter of particular relevance given the independence of individual ministers, and prime ministers, in the policymaking process (Laver and Shepsle 1996). Of course, it is not that the legislature has no influence. Backbench rebellions do occur (Cowley 2002) and can work to influence government. (These rebellions are telling indicators of executive independence from the legislature.) Less public expressions of dissent can too (Brand 1992). The executive still retains the advantage, and the discretion this affords has fairly clear implications for government responsiveness. Policy surely can be changed quickly, but perhaps not neatly in response to changing public opinion.

The situation is quite different in the Madisonian system. Here, the executive cannot act effectively without the legislature. The legislature proposes, and bills are the result of compromise within and, usually, across assemblies. The executive can veto legislation, but, with sufficient support, the legislature can impose its will. Of critical importance is the fact that the legislature and executive are elected separately. Each has an electoral incentive to represent; and, in contrast with parliamentary systems, elected members are not dependent on the executive for their jobs. So, although the separation of powers makes presidential systems much more deliberate in their actions, competition may make them more reliably responsive to changes in public opinion over time. That is, "errors" in responsiveness by one actor can be at least partly corrected by the other. A Congress can alter a president's request. A president can veto or threaten to veto if Congress proposes too much. Congress in turn can override the president's veto. The ability to check and balance makes dynamic policy representation more reliable in these presidential systems than in the parliamentary ones, we argue. There is already some support for this supposition from the United States – that is, Congress has been shown to alter presidential proposals to better reflect changing public opinion (Wlezien 1996a).

Of course, checking and balancing can vary among presidential systems. Presidents are advantaged in some presidential systems. There the executive has more discretion, and we would expect opinion to be a less significant predictor of policy change. Checking and balancing can vary even within Madisonian systems. Perhaps most notably, government can be divided or unified, and this may make a difference for how these systems work. When party control is divided – when different parties control the executive and legislative branches – there is a clear basis for disagreement between branches and thus more reason to check each other than when party control is unified. This of course is true. By implication, we also would expect to see more middling policies under divided government (Wlezien 1996a). Yet this does not mean that the Madisonian system works better when party control is divided. For this to be true, disagreement, when it does emerge under unified government, would go unaddressed, and one branch would triumph. If this were to happen and the executive were the consistent victor, the Madisonian system under unified government would function much like a parliamentary system. There is no reason to suppose this is true *a priori*, however.

All of this said, while we predict that parliamentary systems will be less responsive to public opinion than Madisonian systems, we still expect representation in parliamentary systems. Parliamentary governments are held accountable for their actions, after all, and there actually is more clarity of responsibility, at least in a majoritarian context. Although cabinets may not be as easy to check or their errors easy to correct, it does not mean that policymakers do not follow opinion. It just means that their responsiveness is less reliable. In statistical terms, the standard error is higher.

The horizontal division of powers may be important to public responsiveness itself. There are two distinct possibilities. On the one hand, past work suggests that executive-legislation separation confuses responsibility for government action (see esp. Franklin 2004). There is little gainsaying this point, but it is not clear that this separation increases the public's information about policy decisions – that is, people may notice policy change without knowing who is responsible, and feedback may be no different than if responsibility was clear. On the other hand, some scholars argue that horizontal separation actually makes it easier to elicit information (Persson, Roland, and Tabellini 1997). In this argument, separation induces competition among institutional actors.[4] Strom (2003) echoes much the same point, focusing on parliamentary systems and the collusion that copartisanship in those systems encourages. Here, information is concealed. Following this line of argument, we might expect greater public responsiveness in presidential systems, as information about policy change should be more readily available. We cannot be sure that the additional information clarifies more than it confuses, however, as different political actors – and, in a presidential system, *more* political actors – can advocate quite different positions as the process unfolds.

Institutions, in Sum

There are various reasons to expect patterns of public responsiveness and policy representation to differ across countries. We have hypothesized that public responsiveness will reflect the division of government powers, particularly the vertical division. Public responsiveness should be greatest in unitary systems and least in highly federal countries, especially in those policy domains where multiple governments are involved. We also have hypothesized that policy representation will reflect the division of powers, especially the horizontal separation. Government representation of public preferences should be greatest

---

[4] Persson et al. (1997) argue further that this can improve political accountability.

in Madisonian presidential systems and weakest in parliamentary systems. Electoral systems also may matter, as we have discussed above.[5]

Our expectation about presidential and parliamentary systems may appear to contrast with recent institutional models of policy change. Consider Tsebelis's already near-classic book, *Veto Players* (2002). He addresses the potential for policy change and argues that a system's capacity for change declines as the number of veto players increases. So, in a presidential system such as the United States where we have two (or more) players, he would expect less policy change than in parliamentary systems. He would predict the greatest change in the wake of elections, particularly when party control changes, in parliamentary systems. He also might predict more change between elections. Although Tsebelis poses expectations about the likelihood of policy change, however, he does not make predictions about the correspondence between policy change and public preferences.[6] It might seem, because the model predicts more change, that parliamentary systems are more responsive to preferences, but that is not quite right. After all, as we ourselves argue, prime ministers and cabinet members may exhibit more discretion in different policy areas (also recall Laver and Shepsle 1997). Thus, even as there may be more policy change in a parliamentary system (following Tsebelis), we expect it to be less associated with changes in public opinion per se, precisely because of the discretion parliamentary governments enjoy.[7]

---

[5] Following Powell, we might predict that a Madisonian system with proportional representation, a highly unusual combination, would work particularly well. The more typical majoritarian parliamentary system would work particularly poorly. The other two, much more typical, cases – majoritarian presidential and proportional parliamentary – should lie somewhere in between. It is not clear in what order, however. Given Powell's work, we might expect that the latter better serves representation. In effect, proportionality would powerfully mitigate the autonomy of cabinet governments.

[6] To be clear, he does not explicitly address the effect of public opinion, even with respect to elections.

[7] Note also that Tsebelis's predictions for federal systems seem relatively consistent with ours in that he expects comparatively less change in federal than in unitary systems. Although we find Tsebelis' predictions highly intuitive, they do not follow directly from our model, which concerns policy responsiveness to opinion, not change *per se*. After all, it is possible for federal systems to be less responsive, as we argue, and yet more changeable, contrary to what Tsebelis argues.

SYSTEM EFFICIENCY

The effects of political institutions are relatively straightforward when we consider policy representation and public responsiveness independently. Let us consider a combination of representation and responsiveness, however. Following the discussion in Chapter 1, let us take a combination of representation and responsiveness as a measure of the overall efficiency of a political system, where efficiency – following Deutsch – is a measure of the speed and degree to which a political system adapts to a shock and returns to a state of equilibrium. That is, efficiency is a combination of policymakers' reactions to preferences and the public's capacity to recognize this policy shift and adjust relative preferences accordingly.

Efficiency thus requires both policy representation and public responsiveness, affected as they are by a combination of issue salience and political institutions, particularly divisions of power. Figure 3.3 presents the general structure of efficiency, based on the discussion above. Here, policy systems – or policy domains within systems – can be plotted on two horizontal axes, one for the horizontal division of powers (at the back), and the other for the vertical division of powers (on the left). A given system's location on each axis has bearings on our expectations regarding representation and responsiveness. Representation will tend to decline as a system becomes more parliamentary, and responsiveness will tend to decline as a system becomes more federal. The product of responsiveness and representation – "system efficiency" – is depicted as a curved surface in Figure 3.3, shifting alongside both institutional variables.

The combined effects of horizontal and vertical divisions of power, plus salience, are somewhat more complicated than their effects considered independently. For instance, we expect that federalism has an indirect negative effect on representation because the decreasing public responsiveness in federal systems removes an important incentive and basis for policy representation. This is partly captured in Figure 3.3, where overall efficiency declines most rapidly along the left axis. Salience should also be important. As we have argued, a highly salient issue should exhibit greater degrees of both responsiveness and representation. This should result in an overall shift in the plane depicted in Figure 3.3 – a shift upward or downward, as illustrated by the arrows labeled "salience"

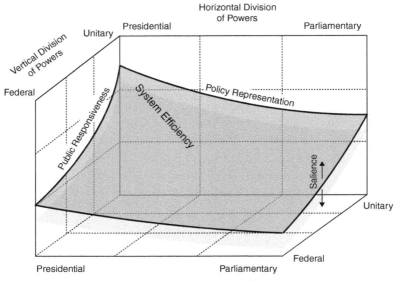

FIGURE 3.3. Divisions of Power and System Efficiency

on the right side of the figure. Note that when issue salience is taken into account, a centralized parliamentary system may show as much representation in a high-salience domain as a presidential system does in a low-salience domain. Public responsiveness and policy representation are driven by divisions of power and salience combined.

   In sum, system efficiency declines as we move both from unitary to federal, and from presidential to parliamentary. It shifts downward as we move from high to low salience. It is thus greatest when a domain is salient (meaning that the public pays close attention), in countries that are unitary (allowing for strong feedback) and presidential (encouraging strong responsiveness by policymakers). It is weakest when a domain is of low salience, in countries that are federalized and parliamentary, where feedback is dampened and dynamic representation less reliable.

FROM THEORY TO PRACTICE

In principle, we can explicitly test the different hypotheses outlined above. The problem is that data exist for only a handful of countries, namely, Canada, the United Kingdom, and the United States. These countries are not randomly drawn – to a large extent, they are "most similar." This may work in our favor. To begin with, in each of these countries we observe a similarly high level of media competition and openness.[8] The same is true for political competition.[9] The three countries are also majoritarian systems; that is, each uses single-member districts and plurality voting.[10] In effect, the case selection controls for electoral system.[11] Salience also varies widely across policy domains; these three countries pose no particular limitation on our ability to examine the effects of salience.

There are also important differences with respect to government institutions. First, the countries differ greatly on the federal dimension (Joumard and Kongsrud 2003). The United Kingdom is a highly unitary system, among the most unitary modern democracies at least until recent moves toward devolution (which occur after the period for which we have U.K. data, as we shall see). The United States and Canada meanwhile are highly decentralized systems, especially Canada, which (along with Switzerland) may be most different from the United Kingdom. Second, our countries also differ greatly with respect to separation of powers. The United Kingdom and Canada are classic parliamentary systems with unified powers; the United States, the classic Madisonian presidential system with separation of powers.

We thus expect public responsiveness and representation in Canada, the United Kingdom, and the United States to differ quite significantly. Our expectations are most clear for the public side of

---

[8] Indeed, the three countries examined here have high – and virtually identical – scores on the Freedom House's (freedomhouse.org) 2008 Freedom of the Press World Ranking.

[9] There are of course many different ways to conceptualize and measure political competition. The Polity IV project (http://www.systemicpeace.org/polity/polity4. htm) offers several different options, measured across most countries over time. The three we investigate here are, not surprisingly, all characterized as highly competitive, "institutionalized electoral" systems.

[10] Though the rules obviously do not produce a pure two-party system in each of the countries, as the Liberal Democrats continue in the United Kingdom, and there have been three or more competitive parties in Canada for some time.

[11] We do note that Powell (2000) actually characterizes the United States as between majoritarian and proportional; because of the separation of powers, he regards the U.S. federal government as an average across (party control of) Congress and the presidency. The separation of powers is a government institution, however, not an electoral one. We thus view it as both conceptually and empirically separate from the electoral system.

the equation. We expect that feedback will be greatest in the United Kingdom, lesser in the United States, and lesser still in Canada.[12] The patterns should vary across domains, however. Welfare is relatively centralized in Canada, for instance, while the other major social domains exhibit far greater degrees of federalism and quite different fiscal-federal arrangements. More federalized domains should exhibit less public responsiveness. Of course, the salience of the domains to the public also should matter.

For policy representation, things are slightly more complex. To begin, the pattern of public responsiveness will tutor policy representation itself, so that federalism has an important indirect effect. On this basis, representation of opinion over time will be greatest in the United Kingdom and weakest in Canada. We also expect that this representation will reflect the horizontal division of powers; specifically, it should be enhanced in the U.S. presidential system by comparison with the Canadian and U.K. parliamentary systems. "System efficiency" will thus be greater in the United Kingdom and the United States, and lower in Canada. The United Kingdom benefits from being a unitary system and the United States from being a presidential one; Canada benefits from neither.[13]

Although we cannot fully examine the effects of all the various electoral and legislative institutional differences, an analysis of the three counties does offer insights into the structuring roles of institutions on the application of the general thermostatic model.

---

[12] It is also possible that the horizontal separation of powers could change things dramatically. If separation decreases information, we would expect differences between countries to increase, especially between the United States and the United Kingdom; if separation increases information, we would expect relatively little difference between the three countries. Feedback in the United States would, for instance, decrease because of federalism but increase because of presidentialism; in the United Kingdom, the effects of unitary government and parliamentarism would similarly cancel each other out.

[13] Things may be more complex if federalism has *direct* effects on dynamic representation, that is, above and beyond its effects on public responsiveness. If it does, we may find that the differences between the countries are seriously attenuated. The heightened representation in the U.S. presidential system, for instance, might be reduced by that country's federal structure. In the extreme, where only federalism matters, government responsiveness will perfectly parallel public responsiveness.

4

Public Preferences and Spending

A Preliminary Analysis

Having outlined the general thermostatic model and the structuring influences of salience and institutions, we now turn to the model's implementation – that is, the way in which we make this model empirically testable. To assess the interrelationships between policy and opinion over time, we need to examine domains where policy activity is clearly defined and occurs regularly, and where reliable time series of public preferences across a wide range of programs are available. Budgets serve these purposes very well.

All budgets register policy commitment clearly, in terms of the money actually spent on something. In addition, at the national level, budgets occur annually, providing time series of policy commitment. Although they don't tell us everything about government policies, they do tell us quite a lot; after all, almost everything the government does requires money, either as an end to itself, as for entitlement programs, or as a means to an end, as for regulation. There also are (fairly) regular surveys that sample opinion about federal spending in various categories, at least in a handful of countries – Canada, the United Kingdom and the United States. (These three countries are, as far as we know, the only countries for which there exist long-term, directly comparable time series on public preferences for spending across a range of policy domains.) These opinion data capture relative preferences for spending – whether the public wants "more" or "less" than is currently in place. Using the data, we can begin to see whether and to what extent the public adjusts its preferences for more policy in response to policy itself across different policy areas in the three countries.

MEASURING PUBLIC PREFERENCES

Recall that, given the thermostatic model, we need a measure of preferences that taps the public's relative preferences for spending, its preferences for "more" or "less." Only with a relative measure can we directly assess whether and to what extent the public responds to policy change over time. (Of course, it would be nice to have a measure of absolute preferences too but, as we discussed in Chapter 2, this is in most cases not feasible.) Conveniently, as we have noted, survey organizations commonly ask about relative preferences for spending. The survey questions typically are of the following form: "Do you think the government is spending too much, too little or about the right amount on [health]?" An almost identical question has been asked in the United States, the United Kingdom, and Canada for various policy areas. This provides a strong basis for comparison across countries and domains.

There are some differences in question wording, however, and these are of some importance. To begin, in the United States the question is preceded by a preamble: "We are faced with many problems in this country, none of which can be solved easily or inexpensively. I'm going to name some of these problems, and for each one I'd like you to tell me whether we are spending too much money on it, too little money, or about the right amount." No similar preamble is used in U.K. or Canadian surveys. Perhaps more important, the question as asked in both the United States and the United Kingdom does not point to a particular level of government, and so the reference point is not clear. We thus cannot be sure whether responses register preferences about the national government or some lower level of government, or both. In Canada, there is no such problem. There is a slightly different preamble – "Keeping in mind that increasing services could increase taxes, ..." – more important is that people are asked directly about the "federal" government.

That no single level of government is implicated in the United Kingdom is not problematic, given that the country was essentially unitary for the period for which we have data (1978–1995) (Rodden 2003). Policymaking authority was concentrated in London, and so there was little basis for confusion about who controlled the level of spending in different regions and local authorities.[1] This is less true in the United States. There, policymaking is substantially decentralized across multiple levels, primarily national, state, and city levels. One might suppose, given its size and visibility, that most respondents in the United States are likely to think of the national government, and note that the preamble to the question actually prompts respondents to think about the "country." This may not be true, however, at least in all domains. To the extent that citizens do not think just of the national government, using responses to the question will lower observed public responsiveness to national policy in the United States. Preferences may change independently in response to state and local spending, for example. This is testable in theory, if more difficult in practice; it is addressed to some extent in diagnostic analyses discussed below.[2]

Public Preferences, Over Time

In each of the three countries, respondents have been asked about spending in various categories besides health – on a consistent basis, just three others in the United Kingdom, but eight more in the United States and five more in Canada.[3] The domains are as follows:

> U.S. Defense
> *Major Social*: Welfare, Health, Education
> *Other Domestic*: Environment, Cities, Crime, Foreign Aid,
> Space
> U.K. Defense
> *Major Social*: Health, Education
> *Other Domestic*: Transport

[1] Of course, while spending is controlled at the U.K. level, implementation does differ across regions and localities (Dowding and John 2007).
[2] If people really are thinking about the national level, of course, then responsiveness should decline as the level of decentralization increases, as we have theorized.
[3] Gallup has asked about "pensions" in the United Kingdom; in Canada, Environics has asked irregularly about several smaller domains, including the "arts." Survey organizations in the United States have asked about "drug addiction" and the "condition of blacks." These categories are not included in the analysis. Mostly, as for pensions and drug addiction and the condition of blacks, this is because the budgetary referent is not clear. For the arts in Canada, we exclude because it is of minor political significance.

Canada   Defense
Major Social: Welfare, Health, Education
Other Domestic: Environment, Transport

The question is asked with reasonable frequency in each country, to different cross-sections of the adult population in each year. In Canada, Environics asked the question between 14 and 16 times (depending on the spending domain) from 1984 to 2005, and some missing years can be filled in using similar data from Pollara;[4] in the United Kingdom, Gallup asked 18 times over a span of 21 years and not at all since 1995;[5] in the United States, the GSS included the question in almost every year from 1973 to 1994, and then every other year until 2004, and Roper asked in some of the missing years. In each country, respondents also are very likely to provide responses to the question; that is, there are comparatively few "don't know's," roughly 7% to 8% on average.[6] There consequently is relatively little concern about whether expressed preferences are representative, at least for the population taken as a whole.[7] Using the data, we can create time series in the three countries ranging from 16 to 33 years between 1972 and 2005, though note that there are some gaps in the series, which we address below.

While the survey item captures relative preferences, it is admittedly rather blunt. That is, responses provide only very general information about preferences, and actually conceal the intensity of preferences. Depending on the spending category and year, for instance, between 15% and 60% of the respondents in the United States express the opinion that we are spending "about the right amount." The median voter thus often lies within the middle category, indicating public

[4] Environics asked questions about most policy domains from 1984 to 2002. Data are missing in 1986, 1992 , and 1996; for domains in which Pollara also asked questions 1996 data are filled in using Pollara results. (For further details and a comparison of the Environics and Pollara series, see Soroka and Wlezien 2004.)
[5] Gallup did not ask the question in 1980, 1981, 1984, 1987, and 1994, but we are able to use measures from proximate periods for years 1981 and 1987. Data remain missing in the other three years. Note also that when more than one poll exists in a single fiscal year, results are averaged.
[6] The numbers are similar within domains, across domains, and across countries. See Appendix A for more detail.
[7] For treatment of "exclusion bias," see Berinsky (2004). Also see Brehm (1993) and Althaus (2003).

satisfaction with current spending levels. Responses in this category encompass variation in satisfaction, however, from those who are close to favoring less to those who are close to favoring more. The median survey response thus may remain the same, indicating satisfaction with current spending levels, even as the "true" underlying median preference changes over time. A similar situation exists for the few domains in which preferences are highly asymmetrical. In the case of crime, a majority always prefers that we spend more – again, the median response simply doesn't change. This is true in other domains as well. True preferences for spending really do vary over time, however. The trouble is that we cannot track this movement using the median survey response.

We nevertheless can characterize the change in public preference by aggregating across the set of responses. Again consider the distribution of unobserved true preferences along with the distribution of measured preferences, the latter defined by the proportion of respondents who want less, the same, or more spending (see Figure 4.1). Although we cannot observe the actual median value of the underlying distribution, we can use the mean preference in its place. This provides a nice measure of central tendency. Alternatively, we can infer the direction of preference by taking the difference between the percentage wanting more and the percentage wanting less – technically, the percentage saying we are spending "too little" minus the percentage saying we are spending "too much." This provides a more

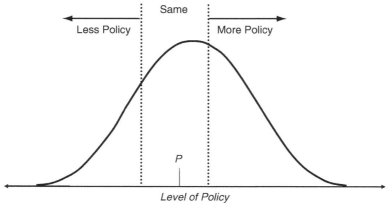

FIGURE 4.1. A Hypothetical Distribution of Preferences

intuitive empirical referent, that is, in terms of actual percentages of the public. At the same time the measure is virtually indistinguishable over time from the mean.[8] We thus use this "percentage difference" measure, what we prefer to call "net support" for spending.

The net support measure clearly indicates the direction of the spending preference. That is, to the extent there is any asymmetry in preferences, say, where a greater proportion prefers "more" spending to "less," this percentage difference measure indicates net support for more. Indeed, the measure not only indicates the direction of preferences, it reveals relative magnitude as well: the greater the net support, the greater the increase in spending the public wants, at least relative to other points in time. Shifts in the survey marginals will also be reflected in the variance in net support over time, even in domains where the median response continually indicates support for the same level of spending, i.e., that we are spending "about the right amount," or "too little."

Most important, the measure nicely reflects change in preferences over time. If a shock alters preferences in Figure 4.1, say, by shifting the distribution uniformly in the direction of more spending, net support will change predictably. Some of the people who said we should spend the same cross the threshold and express a preference for more spending; likewise, some who preferred that we spend less now say spending should stay the same; and the net support measure will shift upwards accordingly. This will be true whenever the distribution of preferences is symmetrical to the median, or even approximately so – regardless of the shape of the distribution.[9]

---

[8] Consider that for defense, the domain in which "about right" mentions vary most of all, the correlation between the two measures is over 0.99.

[9] The shape of the distribution in preferences does matter for reliability of the measure, however. With a flat (uniform) distribution, changes in preferences for more and less spending would perfectly mirror each other, as the number of people crossing from less to same will be identical to the number crossing from same to more, for example. For normal distributions, net support will work best over time when preferences are in the middle of the true underlying distribution, so changes are largely symmetrical. As preferences drift off to the far left or far right of the distribution, net support will be less reliable, as marginal changes in underlying preferences register less directly in our measure. This can be a serious problem at the outer reaches, when close to 100% want more or less spending. (At that point, only the small proportion of respondents in the tails of the distribution is crossing the response category thresholds.) Fortunately, we deal with no such series here.

The percentages preferring more and less spending actually do mirror each other quite closely in many domains. In defense, for instance, where roughly similar proportions prefer more or less spending, the "more" and "less" categories track each other very closely over time. This is less true for a domain such as crime, where almost no respondents favor less spending. (For crime, only the tail of the distribution of underlying preferences falls into the "less" category.) This has some implications for our analysis. A unit shift in net support reflects an increasingly larger shift in underlying preferences as we move away from the center of the distribution, and the effect of policy change on opinion (and opinion on policy) may vary accordingly. Specifically, we might expect a certain nonlinearity.[10]

One final note about net support: the measure does not explicitly take into account the responses of those who favor the spending status quo. That is, it ignores those who say the government is spending "about the right amount," and focuses only on those who say we are spending "too little" or "too much." This has minor consequences for characterizing the specific central tendency in public preferences. Just as with the mean of a distribution, however, two very different preference distributions can produce the same measure of net support. For instance, a distribution where 10% want less, 50% want the same, and 40% want more will have the same score as a distribution where 30% want less, 10% want the same, and 60% want more. In both cases, net support is +30%. Although the percentage of middling responses does not reveal anything about the central tendency, it does tell us something about variance. In this case, support in the second distribution is more variable than in the first; technically, just less than 50% more. This is not of direct concern given our interest in the central tendency, though it can be argued that variance influences the certainty of our estimates. There are several reasons we are not too concerned, however: The percentages of middling responses remain highly stable over time within particular domains, and this is true in all three countries. (See Appendix Table 1 for descriptives of all the data series.) We could continue to debate the point but prefer to focus instead on the data.

---

[10] Separate analyses (not reported here) indicate that allowing for a nonlinear form makes little difference for our analyses.

Public Preferences, Cross Sectionally

While the net support measure captures preference change over time, it does not provide a clear indication of preferences at any particular point in time. The fact that net support is positive, for instance, does not mean people really want more spending than is currently in place. The reason is that basic question wording makes a substantial difference to the responses we get. Consider the classic case of welfare in the United States (Smith 1987). When asked about "welfare," a majority of the United States public prefers less spending and a small minority favors more. But when asked about "the poor," the numbers are reversed, and a very large majority actually favors more spending. Which is correct? Does the public want more spending? Or does it want less? It is difficult to tell from survey marginals at any particular point in time, as the zero-point is not meaningful.[11] The problem is not isolated to the welfare domain, of course, though it may be more pronounced there than in other domains where differences in wording likely matter less. Whether we ask about "national defense" or "military, armaments, and defense" makes little difference, for example. It still matters some, though, and in other domains wording differences may matter more.[12]

That survey marginals are partly dependent on question wording is not because there are no real underlying preferences for spending in each domain. Indeed, we believe there are real underlying preferences – it's just that survey measures will capture them differently. Consider the difference between net preferences for spending when respondents are asked about "welfare" or "the poor," illustrated in Figure 4.2. From 1984 to 2004, the mean net preference for the former is –28; the mean for the latter is +55. The trends are very similar over time, however – the correlation between the two is over 0.80. The way in which the real underlying distribution of welfare spending preferences is captured by the two survey measures differs. Ask about "welfare" and we get one distribution; ask about "the poor" and we

---

[11] We may be able to infer the zero point in each domain from the existence and location of an equilibrium in preferences; this requires us to conduct our analysis of both preferences and policy and then solve the system of equations.

[12] Rasinski (1989) shows that other aspects of question wording can structure responses, for instance, when verbs such as "improving" or "protecting" are inserted before categories. Because of this, we rely on responses to questions using *identical* wording over time.

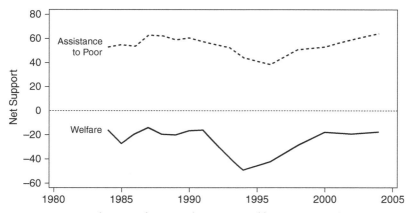

FIGURE 4.2. Preferences for Spending on "Welfare" versus "Assistance to the Poor"

get another. Perhaps the words do tap different things to people, e.g., the latter may include the working poor. It just is not clear.

The point is that at any single point in time it will be difficult to know exactly the relationship between our survey item and the underlying preference distribution. This complicates a strict interpretation of individuals' responses at particular points in time, i.e., what "about right" or "too much" or "too little" actually mean – also see the discussion in Chapter 2. Things are further complicated by the level of thermostatic public responsiveness itself in different domains. In domains where the public does not notice and respond to policy change, for example, measured preferences contain no information about whether the public really wants more or less spending.

These measurement problems limit the kinds of analyses we can do using measures of net support. Consider consistency analyses, which involve matching policy changes with expressed preferences for policy change (Monroe 1979, 1998; Page and Shapiro 1983; Gilens 2005). How can we tell that we actually are measuring true preferences for policy change? Consider Figure 4.2, for instance. Do people want more transfer spending or less? Although the measures have questionable utility as indicators of preferences at particular points in time, they do have a great deal of meaning over time. That is, we can tell whether support is increasing or decreasing. This is what matters to us here.

The "Mood" in Spending Preferences

Figures 4.3 through 4.4 depict the measures of net support for spending in the United States, the United Kingdom, and Canada. Recall that we do not have the same domains in all countries, which prevents a strict comparison. There clearly are big differences in the level of support for spending across domains, and across countries, though we cannot be sure what exactly these mean given the importance of question wording, discussed earlier. The time series patterns are revealing, however, and from this perspective the measures demonstrate considerable structure in public preferences across both programs and countries.

To begin, we can see that preferences in domestic domains tend to flow together over time in each country. That is, they drift largely in tandem, say, in a liberal direction and then in a conservative direction. This is not at all surprising, at least in the United States. Stimson (1991) has demonstrated such a pattern across a wide range of American policy domains, what he refers to as "mood." Figure 4.3 shows that the over-time relationship is especially pronounced for the clearly social domains in the United States, namely, health, welfare, and education. A comparison of the second and third frames of the figure suggests that preferences in a mix of other domestic domains, including the environment, crime, and cities, appear to be part of the general flow. Despite differences in the levels of support across programs, American preferences for various domestic spending programs change in very similar ways. Not surprisingly, the average net support for spending in the domestic categories closely tracks Stimson's measure of policy mood (Pearson's $r = 0.97$).[13]

The same also is true in the United Kingdom and Canada. First consider U.K. preferences in the top panel of Figure 4.4. Although there are fewer domains, mood still is evident, especially for spending on health and education, where preferences are almost indistinguishable. Net support for transport spending exhibits more independence. Meanwhile, preferences for defense spending largely mirror domestic preferences in the United Kingdom, moving in the opposite direction over time. In effect, there is a guns-butter trade-off in preferences. There is a strong hint in Figure 4.3 of such a trade-off for the United

---

[13] The results imply that Stimson's measure reflects, or is driven by, preferences for spending in these domains and, perhaps most importantly, that it captures a *relative* preference for policy over time.

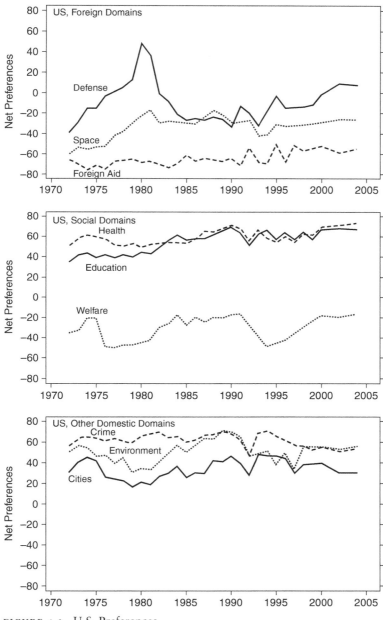

FIGURE 4.3. U.S. Preferences

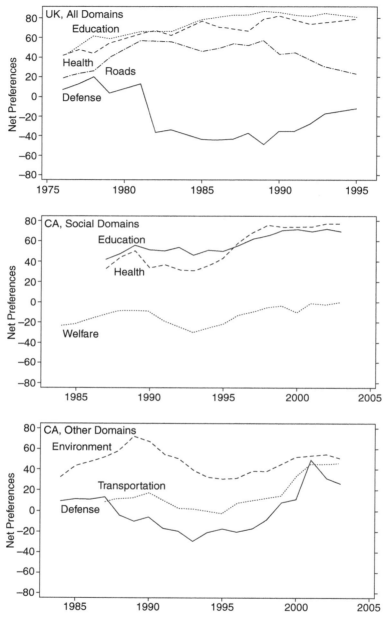

FIGURE 4.4. United Kingdom and Canadian Preferences

States as well. Indeed, public preferences across the different domains in the two countries appear to move in the same liberal–conservative direction over time. These results all are potentially quite telling for our analysis. The patterns imply a certain "global" movement of opinion that may drive politicians' behavior in various policy domains, even across different countries.

Canadian spending preferences in the bottom two panels of Figure 4.4 reflect even greater structure. There not only is a close positive association among social and other domestic spending preferences, but defense as well. That is, the guns-butter trade-off we detected in the United Kingdom and the United States does not hold in Canada, and instead preferences for more spending in *all* domains drift up and down together. The pattern implies that, although there is substantial structure in preferences in all three countries, the type of mood – the degree and extent of the "global" trend in preferences – differs in potentially interesting and important ways.

A Single Dimension?

The existence of a public mood is telling about the underlying determinants of preferences and their consequences for policy. It thus is important to examine the extent and limits of mood. Is preference change entirely global? Or are preferences partly specific to domains? To aid in our analysis, Table 4.1 presents the results of factor analyses of domestic and defense spending preferences in the different countries. The results provide information about the dimensionality of preferences, where the numbers in the table indicate the degree to which the different items load on, i.e., are related to, the different dimensions.

In each country, the first factor captures a major portion of the variance in spending preferences across most major domains. Indeed, in each country most major policy domains load on a single factor. The second and third factors capture just space, crime, and foreign aid in the United States; in the United Kingdom and Canada, just transport and environment, respectively, load on the second factor. Note that in both the United States and United Kingdom defense loads negatively on the same factor on which the major social domains load positively; in Canada, defense loads positively alongside the domestic domains. As we have noted earlier, there is a guns-butter trade-off in the United

States and United Kingdom, but not in Canada.[14] This may be because of the periods for which we have data in the different countries – when we restrict analysis of U.S. (and U.K.) preferences to the period when we have Canadian opinion data – after 1984 – we see no guns-butter tradeoff. Perhaps the decline and eventual disappearance of the Soviet Union fundamentally changed the structure of things.

Clearly, there are strong relationships between preferences across different policy domains. That said, there are real limits to this commonality. We see in Table 4.1 that some of the smaller domestic domains are largely separate from the dominant mood. Stimson himself identifies abortion as a separate dimension. The same may be true of other domains for which we do not have data.

Even the social and defense spending preferences themselves do not covary perfectly. This is evident from the factor loadings in Table 4.1, and the implied uniqueness – the proportion of variance that is specific to each particular domain – of each item. That the implied uniqueness in Table 4.1 is quite low for the smaller domestic domains is in large part a product of the second and third dimensions. If we restrict the analysis to a single factor – capturing just the "global" dimension – then the implied uniqueness ranges from 17% in the case of the environment, to 39% in the case of welfare, to more than 85% in each of crime, space and foreign aid. On average, about 31% of the observed change in preferences for major domestic domains is unique.

The average uniqueness of domestic domains in United Kingdom and Canada is somewhat similar (roughly 35% and 32%), though these averages are pulled upward by the smaller domestic domains (environment and transportation), and thus mask some important differences across countries. Considering just the major social domains in each country, for instance, the average uniqueness in the United States is 25%, in Canada 15%, and in the United Kingdom just 8%. The underlying structure of preferences thus differs across countries. Even in Canada and the United Kingdom, however, where preferences appear more "global," preferences in *all* domains exhibit specific change – they are not mere indicators of

---

[14] In Canada, defense and social spending preferences seemingly are driven by the same things. This implies that the variation in national security threat has been slight or that it has little direct consequence for spending in Canada.

TABLE 4.1. *The Structure of Public Preferences*

United States	Factor 1	Factor 2	Factor 3	Uniqueness
Environment	.909	−.199	.081	.128
Health	.864	.167	−.182	.192
Education	.851	.250	.221	.165
Welfare	.779	.132	.045	.373
Cities	.725	−.531	−.118	.179
Foreign Aid	.375	.803	−.169	.186
Space	.174	.649	.727	.020
Crime	−.103	−.698	.651	.078
Defense	−.673	.565	.073	.223
Eigenvalue	4.062	2.303	1.091	

United Kingdom	Factor 1	Factor 2		Uniqueness
Education	.905	.272		.108
Health	.888	.369		.075
Transport	.344	−.918		.039
Defense	−.894	.289		.117
Eigenvalue	2.525	1.137		

Canada	Factor 1	Factor 2		Uniqueness
Transport	.928	.130		.122
Defense	.887	.135		.195
Welfare	.886	.137		.195
Health	.880	−.418		.051
Education	.837	−.434		.111
Environment	.427	.854		.088
Eigenvalue	4.089	1.147		

Note: Results are based on a principal components factor analysis using un-interpolated preferences series. Domains are listed in descending order based on Factor 1 loadings.

a single, underlying preference for government action.[15] That there are specific components is easy to overlook given the dominant

---

[15] The specific movement in preferences is not mere sampling error. Given the frequencies and sample sizes of the actual polls, the amount of observed variance in net support that is caused by sampling error is relatively easy to compute (Heise 1969). The specific portion of net support exceeds the portion that is attributable to sampling error in every domain in each country. Because the sampling error actually is

structure, but of real importance given our investigation, as we will see.

MEASURING SPENDING POLICY

Having constructed our measures of public preferences for spending, we now turn to spending itself. Data on spending are much more readily available. They also offer higher, ratio-level measurement, where differences are comparable across both policy domains and countries. That said, it is – we were somewhat surprised to learn – rather difficult to assemble reliable measures of budgetary policy. This is true for three reasons that in hindsight are rather obvious: (1) differences between decisions and outputs, (2) problems with temporally consistent functional definitions, and (3) the difficulties of measuring spending in federal systems with overlapping jurisdictions. We discuss each of these issues in turn below; additional information on the sources of spending data is included in the Appendix.

Decisions versus Outputs

Budgetary policy is not the same thing as spending. The latter is relatively straightforward – the government spends what it spends. The problem is that the government does not completely control what is spent in a particular year. First, for various reasons – war, economic change, other unexpected developments – spending may be greater than or less than what the government budgets. This is well known. Second, spending in a particular year is a result of policy decisions taken in previous years. The classic story is about an aircraft carrier, where the budget authority specified in appropriations registers the single-year decision to purchase it and outlays are spread over the many years it then takes to build it.

In budgetary jargon, policy decisions are referred to as "appropriations" and actual spending outputs are called "outlays."[16] The empirical differences between appropriations (reflecting decisions)

---

shared (in some unknown way) between the common and residual components, this is a very conservative "test."

[16] Technically, appropriations specify an amount of "budget authority" that is available to executive agencies to enter into "obligations" to spend money.

and outlays (reflecting outputs) are rather easy to figure out. The top panels of Figure 4.5 plot inflation-adjusted measures of both appropriations and outlays in the United States. Notice that the relationship between appropriations and outlays varies across domains. For the social domains, outlays appear to be directly and currently related to appropriations; in contrast, defense outlays tend to follow appropriations at a one- or two-year lag. The implication is that spending defense appropriations takes longer than does spending social appropriations. These two cases are illustrative, and our own past work (Wlezien and Soroka 2003) reveals that the link between appropriations and outlays varies considerably across domains.

There are accordingly real differences between appropriations and outlays, and these differences may matter for models of the opinion-policy link. For instance, there is reason to suppose that outlays are more central for public responsiveness. That is, the public may be more sensitive to the flow of money into their localities and pockets than to policy itself, though the latter may matter to some people in certain domains. There is even stronger reason to suppose that appropriations are more central to policy representation, as they are more directly within the control of policymakers. These are testable propositions, and a focus of analyses in Chapters 6 and 7.

Note that even with appropriations there may be difficulties. That the level of defense outlays is consistently lower than the level of appropriations in Figure 4.5 is partly produced by the inflation occurring between budgetary decisions and actual spending. Outlays that are distributed over time, for example, in years $t+1$, $t+2$, etc., reflect inflation in those years, whereas the measures of appropriations in year t do not. Thus, inflation-adjusted measures of budget authority are themselves imperfect indicators of policy, at least to the extent that planned spending is long term. Unfortunately, this is not an easy limitation to redress.

Regardless, the extent to which we can distinguish between decisions and outputs in our own data is rather limited. The United States is the only country in which both appropriations and outlays are readily available. In both the United Kingdom and Canada, we only have outlays. The implication is that – given the weaker connection between policy-making decisions and outlays – analyses in these countries may be biased against finding opinion representation. Fortunately, we can (and do) rely on a combination of appropriations and outlays in the United States, and

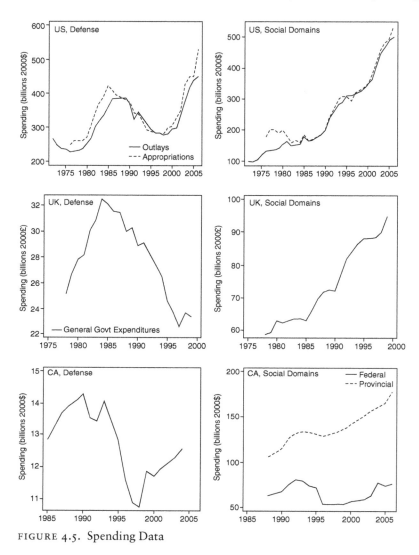

FIGURE 4.5. Spending Data

this helps a good deal not just for the U.S. analysis, as we shall see, but
also in comparisons with the United Kingdom and Canada.

Temporally Consistent Functional Definitions

Functional spending figures track spending over time not by
department but by function – health, education, defense, and so on. The

distinction is not unimportant, as the matching between departments and functions is not one-to-one. In the United Kingdom, for instance, an "Environmental Services" function can combine expenditures managed by the Department for Environment, Food, and Rural Affairs; the Office of the Deputy Prime Minister; the Office of Water Services; and various regional governments and agencies. In so doing, functions bring similar programs in different departments together under the same rubric. In effect, they capture the broad aims of policies and programs; they provide valuable information about the fiscal and policy priorities of governments that will often be masked or distorted when spending is examined simply by department.

Although departmental spending figures can be relatively easy to track, functional spending can be rather difficult. The functional definitions used by statistical or budgetary agencies can change slightly (or not so slightly) each year, so that a program may be included in health for one year and environment the next. A change in functional definitions accordingly has to be accompanied by a recalculation of spending figures for all previous years.

We do have fairly reliable spending data for the three countries. For the United States, we rely on outlays (and appropriations) measures from the *Historical Tables* published by the Office of Management and Budget (OMB), with temporally consistent functions back to 1972, the first year for which have opinion data (1976 for appropriations).[17] For the United Kingdom, there were greater problems with the existing data, and so we performed our own re-recalculations of spending back to 1980 (see Soroka, Wlezien and McLean 2006). When combined with two years of earlier data recalculated by HM Treasury for Public Expenditure Statistical Analysis (PESA), we have functionally consistent data from 1978 to 1995, the last year for which

---

[17] Strictly speaking, what we will call "appropriations" here in fact include appropriations, loan authority, and contract authority. Jones, Baumgartner and True (1998) have extended this "budget authority" series, using current functional definitions, back to 1947. Those data deal with certain accounting issues differently than the OMB data, and so differ marginally from the budget authority data provided in the *Historical Tables*. Because we wish to compare outlays and appropriations directly, we rely on the OMB data for both, even though appropriations are only available back to 1976. Note, though, that James True has more recently assembled a dataset for outlays that is directly comparable with the Jones et al. (1998) data: James True (2007), "Tracking the Purposes of Government: National Government Spending From Fiscal Years 1947–2006."

opinion data are available. For Canada, we combine two existing, functionally consistent matrices from Statistics Canada.[18]

The spending data for defense and the combined social domains are presented in Figure 4.5, for each of the United States, United Kingdom, and Canada. Combined social domains include health and education for the United Kingdom, and health, education, and welfare for the United States and Canada – the difference has to do with the availability of opinion data, discussed below. Note that the range for the y-axis varies considerably across panels solely because the differences in levels of spending across domains are too great to capture all spending on a common axis. In every case, data are inflation-adjusted, so all figures are in FY2000 U.S. or Canadian dollars or British pounds. And, importantly, all of these data are functionally consistent over time. There are additional measurement issues, however.

Federal versus Unitary Government

As outlined in Chapter 3, federalism is a critical mediating variable in our analyses. To revisit: we expect increasing levels of federalism to be associated with decreasing clarity of responsibility – that is, decreases in the ease with which citizens are able to identify what exactly a given level of government is doing. Where two different governments are spending money in the same domain, citizens may not be able to distinguish which government is responsible for what. Public responsiveness to spending by particular levels of government will likely decrease as a consequence, and this may also decrease the incentive for policy representation.

---

[18] To be more precise: there is a current Statistics Canada data matrix that is temporally consistent from the 1989 fiscal year (FY 1989–90), and another matrix from FY1965–66 to FY1994–95. These earlier data are also functionally consistent over time, but use slightly different definitions than the current series. Directly merging the data without any manipulation would create a strange punctuation in FY1988–89 for many series. Accordingly, in lieu of a single matrix that covers the entire period we are studying, we merge the two datasets as follows: the percentage difference from FY1988–89 to FY1987–88 is calculated based on the old series, and this percentage change is then applied to the new series. This is repeated back to FY1984–85, the first year for which we have public opinion data. That said, the pre-FY1988–89 data are used only intermittently in our analyses, due to the (un) availability of public preferences data.

While federalism is central to our comparative theory of opinion-policy dynamics, however, it represents a considerable problem where measuring spending is concerned. For the United Kingdom – a unitary system for the period we analyze here – there are few difficulties. The second pair of panels in Figure 4.5 show inflation-adjusted spending figures (in 2000 pounds) for the United Kingdom. In both the defense and combined social domains, a single government is responsible for programs and spending.

In the United States, things become more complicated: the federal and state governments will *both* be legislating and spending in certain domains. Fortunately, the structure of fiscal federalism is in many domains comparatively simple. For the most part, the federal government uses its own revenues to fund federal programs, while state local governments use their revenues to fund their programs (see, e.g., Rosen and Gayer 2008). While things are not perfectly straightforward in the United States, we have reasonable measures of what each level is doing. Even so, it is not clear that the public will be able to distinguish federal from state spending in any given domain. As a consequence, the capacity for the public to respond thermostatically, and thus the incentive for governments to provide policy representation, may be reduced.

The situation in Canada is even more complicated. The Canadian Constitution gives a vast majority of taxing powers to the federal government, but most of the costly social policy domains to the provincial governments. As a consequence, there is a spending gap – a federal government with large revenues and provincial governments with large budgetary obligations. The problem is (partly) solved through a system of transfers and grants from the federal to the provincial governments. Some of these grants are policy-specific, in which case the federal expenditures (via transfers) appear in the appropriate spending category. Some of these transfers are general- or combined-purpose transfers, however. The Canada Health and Social Transfer (CHST) was one example. For fiscal years 1996 through 2005, the CHST covered health, education and a number of smaller social programs, and provinces had considerable discretion regarding how the CHST was divided amongst policies. At the federal level, then, the CHST could not be included in any one domain; in the federal estimates, it appears in a separate "General-Purpose Transfers" category.

These funds are by no means negligible, and their exclusion from policy-specific spending categories means that in these cases "federal" spending estimates are quite poor measures of federal budgetary policy. (Indeed, in some cases "federal" spending does not capture even a significant minority of federal budgetary policy in a domain, since much of that spending occurs through fiscal transfers). The magnitude of provincial spending, which includes a good deal of federal transfers not otherwise included in the federal spending measure, is readily evident in the bottom-right panel of Figure 4.5, which presents inflation-adjusted social spending figures for Canada. (Note that all defense spending is federal, so only a federal spending line appears there.) As a consequence, budgetary policy in the social domains can only be accurately measured using consolidated spending data – data that capture federal funds spent by provinces along with provincial funds spent by provinces. Our Canadian data will thus in all domains except defense reflect a combination of federal and provincial policymaking, making the identification of policy responsiveness more difficult.[19] That we have difficulty sorting out spending estimates here is also notable: the complexity of Canadian fiscal federalism must surely reduce citizens' capacity to respond to changes in policy invoked by any single level of government.

The Structure of Spending

Despite the differences in measurement across countries, there is a good amount of structure in spending behavior. Descriptive statistics by domain (see Appendix Table 1) show that a lot more typically is spent on some programs, especially welfare, health, and education, than others. The most striking exception is defense spending in the United States, which on average is greater than spending on the three big-ticket social programs combined. The relative level of spending on the different social programs also is fairly similar across the countries. In the United States, spending on welfare is considerably greater

---

[19] That spending, particularly as citizens experience it, might be better captured using consolidated spending also could be true in the United States, particularly in highly federalized domains such as education. That there is no annual, functionally consistent measure of spending by the federal and state governments means that consolidated spending is difficult if not impossible to compute for the United States.

than spending on health, which in turn is greater than spending on education. (Indeed, welfare is nearly half of the average annual spending in the big three social domains.) In the United Kingdom, we don't have clean data on welfare, as welfare expenditures are difficult to separate out from other social services (see Soroka, Wlezien and MacLean 2006). Spending on health in the United Kingdom is greater than spending on education, as in the United States, though the differences are narrower.

In Canada, the ordering of federal spending is what we see in the United States, though spending on health and education is very similar. The relative size of welfare in Canada – a little more than 40% of average annual spending on the three social domains – is somewhat overstated in comparison with the United States. In the United States, we are able to isolate policy effects in the welfare domain by excising the "unemployment compensation" subcategory from our measure; in Canada, the welfare spending measure cannot be purged of Employment Insurance spending. As we shall see, that our measure of Canadian welfare spending includes Employment Insurance will matter for our analyses of opinion-policy relationships.

There still is a good amount of spending in the non-social domestic domains as well – not shown here (but see the Appendix Table 1 for descriptive statistics) – though recall that the domains themselves differ quite a lot across countries. We explore opinion and policy dynamics in these other domains depending on the availability of opinion data. That is, we only examine spending domains for which measures of public preferences are available, for example, foreign aid and crime in the United States but not in the United Kingdom or Canada, welfare spending in the United States and Canada but not the United Kingdom. Overall, though, spending in most of the non-social, non-defense domains is comparatively stable over time, exhibiting less ebb and flow. This is telling about the influence of politics and public opinion, as we will see.

Spending in virtually all spending domains does trend upward over time, documenting a well-known pattern of government growth. There are certain exceptions to the rule, however – spending on foreign aid and cities in the United States, defense and roads in the United Kingdom, and defense and transport in Canada.

TABLE 4.2. *The Structure of Government Spending*

United States	Factor 1	Factor 2	Factor 3	Uniqueness
Health	.974	.147	−.062	.027
Welfare	.966	.053	−.054	.062
Crime	.952	.175	−.041	.062
Education	.904	.242	.189	.089
Space	.791	−.330	−.297	.177
Environment	.688	.661	.147	.068
Defense	.505	−.649	.429	.140
Foreign Aid	.089	−.151	.944	.078
Cities	−.637	.678	.293	.050
Eigenvalue	*5.370*	*1.563*	*1.314*	

United Kingdom	Factor 1			Uniqueness
Health	.965			.070
Education	.960			.079
Transport	.284			.919
Defense	−.814			.338
Eigenvalue	*2.595*			

Canada	Factor 1	Factor 2		Uniqueness
Education	.943	.293		.025
Health	.912	.190		.132
Environment	.876	.368		.098
Welfare	.855	.128		.252
Defense	−.678	.667		.096
Transport	−.764	.561		.101
Eigenvalue	*4.263*	*1.033*		

Note: Results are based on a principal components factor analysis using outlays in the United States and consolidate spending in Canada. Domains are listed in descending order based on Factor 1 loadings.

We also observe a mood in spending. This is clear in Table 4.2, which presents a factor analysis of domestic and defense spending in the different countries. Much as for preferences, spending across various domains tends to move in the same liberal or conservative direction over time. As for preferences, spending on defense in the United Kingdom closely mirrors spending on social programs.

Likewise a connection is evident in the United States, although the trade-off is confined to spending on the environment and big cities. This is reflected in the second spending dimension in Table 4.2.

THE MEASURES SUMMARIZED

This chapter has taken a first step in making the thermostatic model of opinion and policy empirically testable. To test the model we need measures of relative preferences and over a reasonable length of time, and such measures do exist: Survey organizations have asked about preferences for "more" or "less" spending in different domains on a fairly regular basis in the United States, the United Kingdom, and Canada. Using these data we can capture public support for spending policy over time. Spending data allow us to measure policy.

Preliminary analyses of these data tell us much about the structure of opinion and policy across domains and countries. There is a clear guns-butter trade-off in United States and United Kingdom preferences and spending, and in Canadian spending. (This is not so in Canadian preferences, which we discuss further in Chapter 5.) The trade-off points to the interrelatedness across domains of both preferences and spending. So too does the evident mood, where preferences and spending in the large social domains (and other domains) exhibit a clear common component, moving up and down together over time. As much as half of the variance in some domains is specific to those domains, however. We argue below that issue salience and political institutions determine whether the public (and policymakers) respond to the more common trends, or those that are specific to particular domains. We start with the basic models of public responsiveness set out in Chapters 2 and 3.

5

Parameters of Public Responsiveness

Preceding chapters have set out the theory behind the thermostatic model, and our expectations of how public feedback and policy representation will vary across domains and political institutions. This is the first of four chapters that test these hypotheses.

We begin by looking at public responsiveness to policy change – the "feedback" critical to a functioning democracy. Across the next few chapters, our analyses proceed in four stages, corresponding roughly to these questions: (1) Does the public respond to policy change? (2) To what do they respond? (3) When do they respond? and (4) Who responds? The first question is of course relatively clear – we want to know whether the thermostatic model works, whether policy feeds back (negatively) on public opinion. The subsequent questions probe the issue of public responsiveness. In Chapter 6, we explore the difference in feedback to legislative action (appropriations) versus actual spending (outlays); we also examine there the timing of responsiveness – the point in the fiscal year when the public learns about changes in policy. We examine responsiveness further still in Chapter 8, which considers whether certain groups respond more than others.

We first want to know, Does the public respond? The chapter begins with a brief review of our model of public responsiveness. We then present models of defense spending alongside combined social spending, first in the United States and then across our three countries. These models set the stage for subsequent analyses. They demonstrate that public responsiveness exists, not just in isolated cases but across domains and countries. They force us to consider how to compare coefficients across domains and countries, where levels and variances in both preferences and spending differ greatly. And they confirm that political institutions do matter: feedback appears to be weaker in countries and domains where policy is made by multiple levels of government.

MODELING PUBLIC RESPONSIVENESS

Recall from Chapter 2 that the thermostatic model implies that the public's relative preference for policy (R) is the difference between the public's preferred level of policy – its absolute preference, P^* – and the level it actually gets, P:

$$R_t = P^*_t - P_t \tag{5.1}$$

As the preferred level of policy (P^*) or policy itself (P) changes, the relative preference (R) changes accordingly. Recall also that, because we do not directly measure the public's preferred level of policy (P^*), we need to rewrite the model of R as follows:

$$R_t = a + \beta_1 P_t + \beta_2 W_t + e_t \tag{5.2}$$

where a and e_t represent the intercept and the error term respectively, and W designates a variety of exogenous drivers of relative preferences. This is the equation we are interested in estimating. We are especially interested in the coefficient β_1. If the thermostatic model works, β_1 will be less than 0. That is, when policy increases, public preferences for more policy would go down; when policy decreases, public support for more spending would go up. Let us see whether this is true in practice.

Our measures of R and P were introduced in Chapter 4. Relative preferences (R) are captured using the percentage of respondents supporting more spending in given domain minus the percentage supporting less spending. Policy (P) is measured using spending levels in the different policy domains. We still need to identify measures of the public's preferred levels of spending (W). For instance, in the defense spending domain we need to locate variables that capture changes in security threat over time, e.g., the Cold War and then 9/11. In the various other domains things are less straightforward, as we will see.

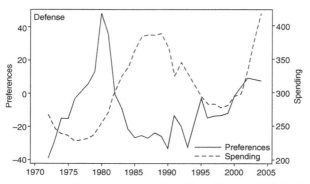

FIGURE 5.1. Preferences and Spending Change, U.S. Defense

A FIRST TEST: DEFENSE AND THE DOMESTIC
DOMAINS TAKEN TOGETHER

Do preferences react to policy change? Figure 5.1 suggests that, in defense at least, they might. The figure shows levels of defense spending alongside net preferences for defense spending in the United States. Preferences for spending increase dramatically in the late 1970s, peaking in 1980. At this point, defense expenditures begin to increase, and public preferences appear to respond accordingly – preferences decrease as spending increases until the mid-1980s. As spending decreases in the 1990s, however, net preferences for policy begin to rise again. This increase in preferences continues through 2000. Spending then shifts upward dramatically following 9/11. In 2004 our data show the beginning of a decrease in support for defense spending.[1]

Defense preferences appear to exhibit exactly the dynamic we expect, then – a thermostatic relationship between public preferences for spending and spending itself. When spending increases (decreases), net preferences for spending decrease (increase) shortly thereafter. This dynamic is examined more rigorously in Table 5.1, which presents results from an ordinary least squares (OLS) estimation of the thermostatic model of public responsiveness.[2] Following equation 2.3, preferences for policy

---

[1] Data from the 2006 GSS have recently been made available but are not included in our analysis. There is little change in most domains, although, fairly predictably given the Iraq war, defense spending preferences decline from a net support of about +9 in 2004 to a net support of –16 in 2006.
[2] Note that for this and all subsequent models we use interpolated public opinion data. Preferences are never missing for more than one year in a row; we use simple

at *t* are regressed on levels of spending (in billions of 2000 U.S. dollars) at *t*, along with two measures of perceived security threat. During the Cold War, U.S. defense preferences reflected attitudes toward Russia, captured by the "likes" and "dislikes" of that country (Wlezien 1995). Our measure of "net dislike" here represents the percentage of Americans who disliked Russia minus the percentage who liked the country; data are drawn primarily from the U.S. General Social Survey (GSS).[3] After the collapse of the Soviet bloc, we take the 1989 value and simply project it forward – that is, net dislike varies until 1989 and is constant afterward. A second variable, equal to zero until 2001 and equal to one from that point onward, captures the results of the shift in perceived threat following 9/11.

In Table 5.1 we see that the two control variables are positively signed (as expected) and statistically significant. The United States–Russia coefficient confirms that preferences for defense spending were connected with perceived threat from the USSR in the Cold War period. When United States–Soviet tensions increased during the late-1970s and through much of the 1980s, support for more spending increased; then, as relations improved and the Soviet Union collapsed, support for more spending decreased. Overall, a 1% increase in public likes (or decrease in dislikes) was associated with just about a 0.4% drop in support for more defense spending. The 9/11 coefficient captures the fact that, in the two years following 9/11, public support for spending increased even as spending moved upwards. Indeed, support was a

---

linear interpolation to fill in these missing data. Doing so tends to increase the autocorrelation in the series, of course, but has only a very marginal effect on results.

Our use of relatively simple OLS models, rather than more sophisticated time series techniques such as ARIMA or error-correction models (ECMs), is motivated by the fact that (a) the OLS model we use follows our theoretical model exactly, (b) the comparatively short length of the time series, and (c) the various gaps in our preferences data, the latter two of which preclude explicit time series modeling. We do explicitly test for time-dependency, of course, as noted below.

We are not concerned about cointegration in our data, as relative preferences in theory cannot be integrated, as they are a combination of two integrated series – the underlying preferred level of spending and spending itself. This is confirmed by diagnostic analyses.

[3] These GSS data were supplemented using American Institute for Public Opinion (AIPO) data in 1979 and 1981, when the GSS was not in the field. In 1992, 1995, and 1997, when GSS also was not in the field, we interpolate using data from adjacent years.

TABLE 5.1. *Complete Feedback Models, Defense and Combined Social Domains, United States*

	DV: Preferences	
IV	Defense	Social
Spending (Outlays)$_t$	−.258**	−.169**
	(.051)	(.043)
Preferences t-1		.624**
		(.105)
Counter [a]	1.175**	.066**
	(.524)	(.016)
U.S.-Russia	.360**	
	(.112)	
Post-911	31.684**	
	(9.246)	
Constant	−32.508**	−21.560**
	(11.975)	(5.136)
R^2	.594	.837
Adjusted R^2	.532	.819
DW	1.024	
Durbin's h (F-statistic)		.412
p value		.527
N	31	32

Cells contain OLS regression coefficients and standard errors (in parentheses), where * p < .10; ** p < .05. All variables are mean-centered.
[a] The counter variable is linear for defense, squared for the social domains.

whopping 32 points higher. Both the United States–Russia and 9/11 variables suggest a relatively simple fact: public support for defense spending is systematically linked to perceived security threat.

The critical test of the thermostatic model is the coefficient for spending. Recall that we expect this coefficient to be negative and significant. In this case it is, and it suggests that for each additional US$1 billion (2000) spent on defense, net preferences shift downward by about a quarter (0.25) of a point. To put this in perspective: the average absolute annual shift in defense spending over the period is roughly US$15 billion; this increase (or decrease) would produce, on average, just less than a 4-point shift downward (or upward) in preferences for spending. Of course, some years exhibit large shifts in spending while others do not. Figure 5.1 nicely illustrates the connection between large changes in spending and the correspondingly large shifts in net preferences.

The second column of Table 5.1 includes an analysis of the three major social domains (health, education, and welfare) combined. In this case, spending is the sum of spending in the individual policy domains and preferences are measured using the average net preference across those domains. The results using the combined measures need not simply summarize the by-domain results to follow,[4] but they do provide useful general parameters.

The models of social spending preferences do not include the measure of national security threat included in the defense model.[5] They also do not include measures of economic security. Although previous research (Durr 1993) suggests that a growing economy leads people to be more supportive of spending on social programs, this is not the case for our analyses. We find that a troubled economy also does not lead the public to be more supportive of spending on social programs. Canadian welfare preferences are the one exception. These preferences are quite strongly related to unemployment levels, and so

---

[4] It may be that feedback is specific to domains, where the public responds to spending on the particular areas. Alternatively, it may be that both feedback is more collective, and that the public responds more generally across domains. We have already seen in Chapter 4 that preferences for spending (and actual spending) in the different domestic programs move together over time. It thus may be that the public only notices the changes in spending for the different programs taken together, and not the changes that are particular to each domain. We consider the possibility of "global" versus "specific" responsiveness in more detail in the next chapter.

[5] This may seem an obvious decision, though there is reason for including the measures to assess the possible interdependence between defense and domestic spending preferences in the United States and United Kingdom. The factor analysis in Chapter 4 implies a guns-butter trade-off in preferences or spending itself in those countries. That is, it may be that the underlying preferred levels for spending on defense and domestic programs vary inversely over time or it may be that spending levels do so, which, because of negative feedback, cause preferences for more defense and social spending to move in different directions. Even so, preliminary models suggest that national security threat is not a reliable predictor of domestic spending preferences, and including it has no substantive impact on the other variables in these models. This contrasts with earlier research (Wlezien 1995) and implies that a guns-butter trade-off in U.S. spending preferences did not continue after the collapse of the Soviet Union.

we include a measure of unemployment rates in the Canadian welfare preferences models.[6]

The only systematic change in the underlying preferred level of domestic spending, across almost all domestic domains, is a trending increase over time. To capture this trend, we use a counter variable that begins at 0 in the first year of the analysis and then increases in a linear way year-by-year. We do not assume that the increase in spending is linear, however. Instead, we test a linear counter alongside both quadratic and cubed versions, and combinations thereof. In the model in Table 5.1, as in most subsequent models of social spending, the counter that provides the best fit is the quadratic version, suggesting that – everything else held constant – there has been a nonlinear, exponential increase in real public preferences for domestic spending in the United States. The same is true in Canada. In the United Kingdom, the increase appears to be linear (note that our U.K. data end in 1995). The causes of the underlying trends are not considered here, though they are consistent with patterns of broader preference change (Inglehart and Abramson 1994).

We also – and, again, this applies to all subsequent models of public responsiveness – include a lagged preferences variable where necessary, to account for residual autocorrelation, largely the effect of other exogenous variables not included in our basic model of feedback.[7] That a lagged dependent variable is not required in the defense model implies that it is more fully specified than our models of domestic spending.

Returning to Table 5.1: the most important result is that, as for defense, the coefficient for social spending is negative and highly significant. This coefficient suggests that a US$1 billion (2000) increase in spending is associated with an average downward shift in net support of about 0.17. The effect is less than what we observed for defense (-0.25). This suggests that public responsiveness is lower in the social domains, though we have to be careful when drawing such a conclusion. A US$1 billion shift can mean quite different things in

---

[6] For information on data sources, see the Appendix.
[7] This is simply a matter of including a lagged dependent variable in every model of preferences, and dropping this variable whenever (a) that variable is not statistically significant, and (b) a Durbin-Watson test suggests that no control for serial correlation is required (that is, that there is no significant serial correlation in the residuals from a model estimated without the lagged dependent variable).

different domains. This is true not only because the things purchased for defense are quite different from those purchased for healthcare, but also because there are quite different levels of, and variances in, spending in different domains. A US$1billion shift thus can represent a very large, out-of-the-ordinary shift in overall policy commitments in one domain and only a marginal shift in another. (There are systematic ways of comparing across domains and countries, which we turn to shortly.)

Table 5.1 makes clear that the U.S. public responds to spending on defense as well as on the set of social domains taken together, but what about our other countries – the United Kingdom and Canada? What about particular social domains – welfare, health, and education? Table 5.2 shows the results. This is the first of many tables in which we show only the feedback coefficients. That is, rather than present nine regression models in their entirety, we show just the feedback coefficient from each model. Complete results, and information on the particular specification of each model, are included in Appendix Table 2. To begin with, we focus on results in the first two rows, for defense and the social domains combined, in our three countries.

Raw coefficients are listed in the columns labelled *B*. These demonstrate that negative feedback is as evident in the United Kingdom and Canada as it is in the United States. Indeed, the coefficients are somewhat larger in absolute terms in Canada, and considerably larger in the United Kingdom, than in the United States. Again, some of this difference is a consequence of different spending levels and variances across domains. Looking across countries presents an additional difficulty, however: in each case the spending coefficient indicates the change in preferences given a $1 billion shift in national current units (NCUs) – that is, U.S. dollars, or Canadian dollars, or U.K. pounds. Because the pound is worth more than both the U.S. and Canadian dollars, U.K. spending figures will almost always be smaller than the other countries' – holding everything else constant, a 1-unit shift in U.K. pounds should matter more than a 1-unit shift in either U.S. or Canadian dollars. This is an artificial difference, of course.

Although the effect of using different currencies can be dealt with simply by transforming all spending data (or coefficients) into U.S. dollars, we need a transformation that can deal both with differences

TABLE 5.2. *Feedback Coefficients, Defense and Social Domains*

Domain	U.S.		United Kingdom		CA	
	B	Standardized	B	Standardized	B	Standardized
Defense	-.258**	-14.321	-9.542**	-22.080	-4.424*	-4.720
Major Social	-.169**	-17.885	-1.355**	-13.042	-.361**	-6.259
Welfare	-.627**	-25.767			-2.226**	-20.742
Health	-.284**	-15.924	-2.323**	-14.238	-2.143**	-26.102
Education	-.288*	-3.074	-3.497**	-12.456	-.716*	-4.079

B shows OLS coefficients, where * p < .10; ** p < .05. Standardized shows the effect of a one-standard deviation change in spending on preferences. Full models are listed in Appendix Table 2.

in NCUs and the different levels and variances in spending (which are not simply products of the different currencies.) We do so in Table 5.2 by showing the effect of a one standard deviation change in spending on preferences, in the columns labeled *Standardized*.[8] (The standard deviations themselves are included in the tables of descriptives for all variables in Appendix Table 1.) Using standard deviations clearly allows us to take into account the variances of the different spending series. It does not account for differences in levels of spending, however. This actually is of little consequence, as controlling for the variance or levels of spending has roughly the same effect from the point of view of comparing coefficients. Across most of our spending domains, variance is highly related to levels of spending; simply put, there tends to be more room for spending change when the level of spending is greater. This is highly intuitive.

Let us look more closely at results for the United States, in the first two columns of Table 5.2. The raw coefficients in the first column are the same as in Table 5.1, where we presented these models in their entirety. The effects of one-standard-deviation shifts in spending are listed in the second column. For example, a one standard deviation (or US$55 billion, 2000 dollars) change in defense spending in the United States produces an 11.4-point drop in net support for spending. Comparing the coefficients for the United States in the two columns, one change in results jumps out immediately: feedback for defense appears greater than for social spending in column one, but it is smaller in column two. Indeed, the American public appears slightly more responsive in the combined social domains (–17.3) than in defense (–14.3). That said, the differences are not statistically significant.[9]

---

[8] Note that our standardized measure is not the same as the more typical *beta* coefficient, which would express the effects of spending change in terms of standard deviations in preferences. Here, we look at the effects of spending change in actual units (percentage points) of net preferences.

[9] There also are some peculiarities where U.S. defense is concerned, so that public responsiveness in defense may be somewhat understated in Table 5.2. First, U.S. defense is the one major exception to the rule that levels of spending and variance are highly related. In spite of very high levels of spending, this domain exhibits low variance, comparatively speaking, in part because defense has not been subject to the steady upward trend in spending that is evident in the major social domains.

Keeping this in mind, how does the United States compare with the United Kingdom and Canada? Using standardized measures narrows the gap between U.S. and U.K. results – compare the raw coefficients for defense to the one-standard-deviation measures. The United Kingdom is still highly responsive across the board, especially in defense. In the social domains, responsiveness actually is slightly lower in the United Kingdom than in the United States, though we should keep in mind that the social domains we have for each country are slightly different. (Welfare is missing for the U.K.) Insofar as some domains are more salient than others, this is a difference that cannot be accounted for by using standard deviations or other transformations. It may thus be that the United States appears more responsive than the United Kingdom simply because the social domains we are using are not the same. We will see whether this is the case when we look at each individual spending domain, and compare, for instance, health spending across all three countries.

In Table 5.2, the Canadian feedback coefficient clearly is not as great as that for the U.S. and U.K. models – it is less than half the magnitude of that in the United States and one quarter that in the United Kingdom – but public responsiveness is nonetheless evident.[10] We also can see that public responsiveness is evident in the Canadian domestic domains, and that it is lower in Canada as well, about one half of the level in the United Kingdom and one-third of what is seen in the United States.

What do these first results tell us about public responsiveness to policy change? First and foremost, they indicate that the public in all three countries responds to spending on defense and for the set of domestic domains taken together. This is satisfying and important. They also hint at some real differences across policy domains and countries.

A different transformation of the coefficients, taking into account levels of spending rather than variance, suggests that public responsiveness in defense is at least as great as it is in the social domains. Second, we will see in later chapters that, in contrast with most other domains, defense preferences may respond more directly to policy change reflected in appropriations decisions than to actual expenditures.

[10] This contrasts with what we showed elsewhere – that Canadians were not *significantly* responsive in the defense domain (Soroka and Wlezien 2004) – the coefficient was negative but just missed statistical significance. The difference is due to the inclusion of additional data for 2003–2005.

For example, that responsiveness to defense spending is much less in Canada than the United States and United Kingdom may reflect the comparatively low salience of that domain in Canada. That responsiveness to domestic spending also is lower in Canada may reflect the high level of provincial autonomy there. We get more purchase on the effects of both salience and divisions of power when examining the domains individually.

PUBLIC RESPONSIVENESS, BY DOMAIN

In one important way the overall conclusions change very little when we look at public responsiveness in each individual domain: public responsiveness is still pervasive, across policy domains and countries. That said, feedback does vary across domains in systematic ways. And the ways in which it varies tell us much about how both salience and political institutions affect the opinion-policy link.

The bottom three rows of Table 5.2 present public responsiveness coefficients for the three major social policy domains, across all three countries. In the U.S. results, the feedback coefficient is negative in each case, as expected, and significant in every case. It is especially strong in the welfare domain, where a one-standard-deviation shift in spending leads to an average 26-point shift in preferences. This is fully 75 percent of the range in welfare net support over time. Clearly, results for combined social spending mask the extent of public responsiveness evident in welfare taken on its own.

Negative feedback is evident in the other major social domains as well, although it is more limited than welfare in terms of magnitude. There is strong responsiveness in healthcare, where a one-standard-deviation shift in spending leads to an average 16-point shift in preferences. The effect is considerably smaller in education – the effect of a one-standard-deviation shift in education spending leads to an average shift of about three points in preferences. Indeed, the magnitude of responsiveness in education is similar to that for space; environment, cities, and crime exhibit roughly similar degrees of feedback – about 2.5 times more than education, although still considerably less than defense and the other major social domains. (These coefficients are not presented in Table 5.2 but they are shown in figures below, and all results are presented in the

Appendix Table 2. All coefficients are statistically significant except for foreign aid.)

Feedback is similarly evident in by-domain results for the United Kingdom and Canada, all of which are negative and statistically significant (including domains not shown in Table 5.2). In the United Kingdom, defense exhibits the greatest degree of public responsiveness, roughly similar in magnitude to welfare in the United States. Health and education also show strong responsiveness. Feedback in Canada is rather small for defense and roughly similar to education in the United States. The two domains in Canada in which there is strong feedback are welfare and healthcare. Recall that the Canadian models use *combined* federal and provincial spending, however. We return to this in Chapter 6.

In the meantime, we suggest that some combination of issue salience and federalism may help account for the variation in public responsiveness across domains. This appears to be the case in Table 5.2. That there is strong feedback in healthcare in Canada fits with the extraordinary salience of this domain through much of the period analyzed here, for instance. Responsiveness in welfare in the United States may also be a product of issue salience. Comparatively strong feedback across all U.K. domains fits with the clear policy signal that should characterize a centralized system. These general observations can be examined more formally. What we need are comparable measures of issue salience and federalism.

Issue Salience and Public Responsiveness

Valid, reliable measures of issue salience are rather difficult to come by (see Wlezien 2005). That is, we don't have very good measures of the importance of issues to the public at any particular point in time, let alone over time or across countries. One option, and a standard measure of salience in the agenda-setting literature, is the open-ended "most important problem" (MIP) question used regularly in commercial omnibus surveys. Specifically, respondents are asked: "What do you think is the most important problem facing this country today?"

The question is not ideal for measuring the importance of issues. Most notably, it asks about *problems*, not issues or policy domains.

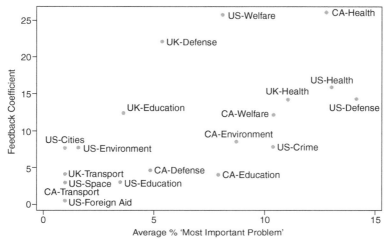

FIGURE 5.2. Salience and Feedback

Welfare may not show up much in MIP responses because it is not a problem to many people – at least not the most important problem – even as the issue remains relatively important to the public.[11] Another option for gauging salience would be to look to the literature on voting behavior for evidence of the weights different issues have had in different countries and years. This seems a fruitful direction, though it is difficult to produce comparable issue voting models across election years within countries. It is even more difficult to do so in the years between elections, and adding countries further compounds these difficulties.

The existing MIP data may at least provide a general sense of the effects of issue salience. To assess this possibility, Figure 5.2 shows standardized feedback coefficients from Table 5.2 (as well as for all other domestic domains) plotted against average percentage of MIP mentions for each domain in each country. The MIP question is asked

[11] There are numerous other problems with the measure, mostly deriving from the wording "most important." Asking about the most important problem (or issue) ignores the possibility that a wide range of issues can be of importance to some people and that issues can increase or decrease in importance together over time. It is not entirely clear that asking about the importance of individual "issues" would make much difference (Wlezien 2005).

in roughly the same way in the United States, the United Kingdom, and Canada; here, we rely on the average monthly percentage of respondents who cite the relevant policy issue (defense, health, and so on) as the most important problem, using all available polls from 1982 to 2002 – considerably more than 100 polls in each country. (See Appendix for details.) To be sure, these data provide an imperfect measure of the importance of these issues to citizens. Even so, for the domains for which data are available, MIP results may indicate some differences in salience across policy domains and countries that help us make sense of the varying extent of feedback in Table 5.2.

Despite difficulties with the MIP measure, Figure 5.2 suggests a strong relationship between it and feedback. As MIP mentions increase, the degree of public responsiveness does too. The correlation between the two is a healthy 0.60. The pattern also is suggestive about the nature of the causal relationship between salience and public responsiveness. That is, salience appears to represent a "necessary" condition. This is evident from the relative absence of observations in the upper left-hand corner of the table: without high salience, feedback is either nonexistent or relatively small in magnitude. There is nevertheless still considerable variance in public responsiveness at each level of salience. Consider the difference between U.K. defense, Canadian defense, and U.S. education, all exhibiting roughly the same level of average salience (approximately 5 percent).

High salience is not a sufficient condition for high levels of public responsiveness, however. This is clear from the presence of observations in the lower right-hand corner of the figure. The result is important, as it allows for the influence of other factors, including government institutions. Education and the environment in Canada reveal less feedback than we might expect given the apparent salience, for example. Federalism seems a likely culprit – education is the most federalized spending domain in Canada, and the environment is only slightly less so. Let us consider more directly the effects of federalism.

Federalism and Public Responsiveness

To examine the effects of federalism, we rely on one relatively simple measure: the percentage of total spending in a given domain that comes directly from the national/federal government. By "directly," we mean that spending in that domain must be from the national government, on policies for which the national government is responsible. Most block transfers to subnational governments – even most conditional grants – do not fall into this category because those funds are controlled (and spent) at least in part if not completely by subnational governments. This measure – percent national spending – thus captures, broadly at least, the degree to which there is a clear signal from a single level of government. For measurement details see the Appendix.

To what extent do our feedback results line up with the degree of federalism in each domain? Does federalism appear to diminish feedback? Or, to put it differently, does the clear policy signal in a centralized policy domain produce greater responsiveness? Figure 5.3 presents a preliminary test, plotting the standardized coefficients alongside percent national spending. For expository purposes the percent national spending is logged, which serves to spread out results in the middle of the x-axis. (That is, logging has no real effect on the relationship between percent national spending and the feedback coefficients, but it does make different domains more discernible in the figure.) Entirely centralized domains are included as well, greyed out somewhat on the far right of the figure, as 100 percent national.

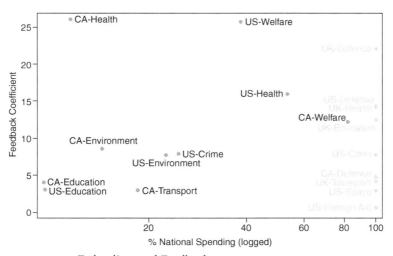

FIGURE 5.3. Federalism and Feedback

Looking across domains that are at least to some degree decentralized, the feedback coefficient does tend to increase alongside centralization; excluding Canadian healthcare, the correlation is 0.73. Canadian healthcare is a striking outlier, however – here we see extraordinarily strong feedback given a high degree of federalism in that domain. Issue salience is likely a factor here – note (Figure 5.2) that healthcare is the single most salient domain in the sample. The same is evident for U.S. welfare, which shows slightly higher-than-expected feedback given the degree of federalism in Figure 5.3, but also high issue salience in Figure 5.2. Like salience, centralization is not sufficient for public responsiveness; there is as much variation in entirely centralized domains as in more federalized policy areas.

Our relatively simple measure captures just one relevant dimension of federalism. Policymaking by multiple governments will produce different policy signals only to the extent that those governments are doing different things. In a domain such as healthcare in Canada, a considerable reliance on grants from the federal government, in some cases with conditions attached, restricts the range within which provinces are able to make independent policy, particularly where budgetary policy is concerned. If national (federal) and state (provincial) governments are all raising and lowering spending together, then responding to one government is – statistically, at least – indistinguishable from responding to the others, or all of them combined. We accordingly should consider not just the proportion of money spent by a single level of government, but the degree to which spending moves together across governments.

One option is to look at the average bivariate correlation across all pairs of time series for state or provincial government spending – that is, produce a matrix that includes correlations of spending series over time, for a single domain, across every single pair of states or provinces, and then look at the average of all those correlations. Doing so provides a summary measure of the degree to which every state or provincial spending series moves alongside every one of the others. It captures the extent to which trends in spending at the subnational level are similar, or not.

Among the U.S. domains, the average bivariate correlation across all state spending series (from 1972 to 2004) is lowest for welfare, at 0.83. Even this is relatively high, however: roughly 70 percent of the over-time variance in state welfare spending is common across all states, and the proportion of common over-time variance is even greater for all other U.S. domains considered here. The situation in Canada is quite different. Here, the average bivariate correlation across all provincial spending series (from 1989 to 2006; again, see note 13 for sources) is 0.31 for environmental spending, 0.45 for welfare, and 0.60 for education. As a consequence, the policy "signal" in each of these domains will vary considerably across provinces. The exception in Canada is healthcare. Here, the average correlation is 0.93. At least where federalism is about the degree to which there will be different policy signals across provinces, the extent of federalism in the Canadian health domain is rather overstated in the simple percent national spending measure. Public responsiveness in the Canadian healthcare domain is thus augmented in part due to very high issue salience, and in part due to the very high correlation amongst provincial spending series.

Salience and Federalism Taken Together

Both issue salience and federalism help to explain some of the apparent outliers in Figures 5.2 and 5.3. More precisely, federalism helps account for differences in feedback at different levels of salience. Consider first that feedback is consistently low for all domains that exhibit both comparatively low salience and comparatively high degrees of federalism (for example, environment or education in the United States, or transport in Canada). Consider also the difference in feedback from, on the one hand, Canadian education and environment, and U.S. crime, to, on the other hand, U.S. welfare and U.K. defense. Each of these domains exhibits roughly similar salience, but there is considerably more public responsiveness in the centralized domains.

Still, as we have seen with Canadian healthcare, there is more to federalism than simply the proportion spent by the national government. There are other factors to consider as well. U.S. defense shows somewhat less responsiveness then we might expect given its high level of both salience and centralization, for instance. Even with these outliers, Figure 5.2 and 5.3 present powerful illustrations of the relationship between public responsiveness, issue salience, and federalism.

Regression analysis nicely summarizes what we see here. In a model regressing standardized feedback coefficients on (linear) MIP results and (logged) percent national spending, both variables are positive and statistically significant and the model explains roughly 64% of the variance in feedback.[12]

PARAMETERS OF PUBLIC RESPONSIVENESS

This chapter sets out some initial empirical guideposts. We have seen that the thermostatic model works across many domains in all three countries. There is evidence of public responsiveness to policy in 18 of the 19 policy domains examined here – all but foreign aid in the United States. The magnitude of public responsiveness does vary considerably across policy domains, however. Issue salience has a powerful effect on public responsiveness. So too do political institutions, namely federalism. Taken together, we have seen that issue salience and federalism are powerful predictors of the magnitude of public responsiveness across policy domains and countries.

Though these results clearly are important and of potential consequence for what policymakers do, they only take us part of the way. That is, they provide a very coarse picture of public responsiveness. We know based on the results that the public behaves like a thermostat and that the tendency varies in predictable ways. We do not know to what exactly the public is responding. We also have not confronted possible alternative hypotheses. This requires more empirical work.

[12] In this model, MIP and percent national (% National) figures are included exactly as shown in Figures 5.2 and 5.3. The model includes two additional variables: (1) a dummy variable equal to 1 for all domains that are entirely centralized (where % National is restricted to 0 in these cases), and (2) a dummy variable equal to one for Canadian healthcare, to soak up the effect of large and restrictive federal transfers in an otherwise highly federalized domain. The estimated model is as follows: *Public Responsiveness* = −14.657 + .582*MIP + 6.660*%National(logged) + 20.818*Centralized + 20.832*CDNhealth. N=19; all variables significant at p <.10.

6

Public Responsiveness Explored

Chapter 5 demonstrated that public responsiveness to policy is pervasive. This is satisfying and important, and it provides a corresponding basis for policy representation. Before considering representation, however, this chapter probes further public responsiveness to budgetary policy, focusing on "to what" and "when" the public responds. It does so by addressing five issues related to public responsiveness, each an extension of the basic thermostatic hypothesis investigated in Chapter 5. The issues are in one sense rather disparate, and take the analysis of public responsiveness in different directions. But the results all do bolster the claim that what we have identified as public responsiveness to budgetary policy is actually that.

First, we examine the degree to which the public responds to policy decisions versus policy outputs, that is, to the making of budgetary policy versus to expenditures as they occur. Second, we explore when in the fiscal year the public responds; this also helps us understand to what the public responds, as we will see. Third, we consider whether the public is responding to the outcomes of spending policy rather than to spending itself. We examine, for example, the degree to which public responsiveness is focused on changes in crime spending or on changes in the crime rate. Fourth, we also explore the degree to which responsiveness in a federal context is focused on spending by a single government, versus the spending of multiple governments. Finally, we briefly discuss the degree to which responsiveness is focused on spending in particular domains, or the more "global" trend across domains.

The results of these various analyses add substantial detail to the general picture of public responsiveness portrayed in Chapter 5. Not only is there strong empirical evidence that publics respond to actual policy; there is further evidence that this responsiveness quickly follows policy change, and also that the focus of public responsiveness varies systematically with issue salience and the level of federalism.

BUDGETARY POLICY VERSUS ACTUAL SPENDING

Our analyses have thus far focused on the public's responsiveness to government expenditures. This may be appropriate, as there is reason to suppose that the public responds to spending as it makes its way into people's pockets. It may be, however, that the public responds more directly to budgetary policy – although expenditures are important, they are not policy *per se*.

The problem is that finding reliable measures of budgetary policy in most countries is not easy. Indeed, in most countries it is impossible, and we have no choice but to rely on outlays (often labeled "expenditures" outside the United States). This is true for both the United Kingdom and Canada, as discussed in Chapter 4. More proximate policy data are readily available for the U.S. federal government, however, which makes clear distinctions between the budget authority specified in appropriations, and outlays. (Recall that budget authority is the money on account that agencies then spend over time.) Moreover, as discussed in Chapter 4, data on appropriations are available over time, using exactly the same functional categories as the outlays data we have been using thus far. We consequently can test directly the degree to which public responsiveness is focused on budgetary policy (appropriations) versus actual spending (outlays).

We do so here by estimating models of public feedback identical to those in Chapter 5, first using outlays and then appropriations in each domain. Note that there is one minor difference in these models: appropriations data are only available from FY1976, and so these estimations are, for both outlays and appropriations, restricted to this period. Feedback coefficients for outlays will thus be marginally different from those in Table 5.2, but more directly comparable with the appropriations coefficients examined here.

TABLE 6.1. *Outlays versus Appropriations, United States (1976–2004)*

Domain	Feedback				Correlation b/w Outlays and Appropriations
	Outlays		Appropriations		
	B	Rsq	B	Rsq	
Defense	−.246**	.602	−.233**	.585	.942
Welfare	−.629**	.782	−.460**	.816	.874
Health	−.241*	.695	−.140	.675	.996
Education	−.266	.686	−.164	.670	.936

The first and third columns contain OLS coefficients, where * $p < .10$; ** $p < .05$.
Full models are listed in Appendix Table 2.

Table 6.1 presents results for defense and the social domains. The first column shows feedback coefficients from the models using outlays. These are the baseline models of by-domain public responsiveness. Results in the third column then show feedback coefficients from models that use appropriations rather than outlays as the measure of budgetary policy. The table also shows the R-squareds from each model in columns two and four.[1]

As we have seen before, the outlays coefficients in the first column are consistently negative, although the coefficient for education just narrowly misses statistical significance in this more restricted time period. The crux of our current test is a comparison of these coefficients with those resulting from the models using appropriations, shown in the third column of the table. There we can see that the appropriations coefficients also all are negative, though the estimate for health is less reliable – the same is also true for defense and education. (For more detail, see the standard errors reported in Appendix Table 2.) These differences are not statistically significant. They nevertheless indicate that, with the important exception of welfare, the public is at least as responsive to actual spending as to spending decisions themselves.[2]

[1] Note that we do not use standardized coefficients here because the variance in outlays and appropriations is in each domain very similar. And, as we shall see, the R-squared is for our present purposes more useful than the magnitude of coefficients in any case.

[2] For welfare, there even is some suggestion that appropriations work better, as the R-squared is slightly larger.

What explains the pattern across domains? One obvious suspect is the connection between appropriations and outlays. The closer the correlation between the two, after all, the more similar the results should be. This would explain the similarity in the results for defense, health, and education, where the correlations between appropriations and outlays all are .94 or higher. By contrast, in welfare, there is a greater disjuncture between the two. This allows for more difference in responsiveness, but why is the public seemingly more responsive to appropriations in this domain?[3] Issue salience may matter. In more salient domains we might expect people to pay attention to and to notice policy decisions as much as they notice actual spending. As we saw in Chapter 5, welfare is a fairly salient domain even using most important problem responses. Public responsiveness implies even greater salience. Indeed, public responsiveness to welfare exceeds feedback in every other domain, and not by a little – see Table 5.2. Perhaps it is not surprising, then, that the public is at least as responsive to appropriations as to outlays in this domain. Education is less salient, and here we observe that the public is more responsive to actual outlays. The same is true for the other domestic domains not shown in Table 6.1. (Full results are included in Appendix Table 2.) Health does not follow the pattern, however. It is salient to voters, and appropriations and outlays for health are highly correlated, but the public is much more responsive to outlays, as it is for low-salience domains. This implies that even to the extent the public notices differences in this domain between appropriations and outlays, it cares more about the latter – what is actually spent.

Overall, these results are quite satisfying. In general, public responsiveness appears to be directed less toward policy decisions (appropriations) and more toward actual policy outputs (outlays). This is especially true in domains where appropriations and outlays are less directly connected and in domains of lower salience, where less attention presumably is paid to what happens during the course of policymaking. That the public tends to be more responsive to outlays makes more meaningful, practically speaking, the feedback that we observe. In other words, the public's preferences are informed by what government actually does, which depends on both policy decisions *and* implementation.

---

[3] This is supported by regression analysis including the two measures together.

THE TIMING OF RESPONSIVENESS

Since the public is more responsive to outlays than to appropriations, responsiveness should be apparent only after the fiscal year has begun. If the public responded more to appropriations decisions, in contrast, we would expect the public to respond earlier, as appropriation bills are passed and signed into law. But when exactly during the year does the public respond? Does the public respond quickly, once spending has started to shift? Or does it happen over the course of the fiscal year, as the money is actually spent?

We can gain some initial insight into the timing of responsiveness from quarterly Trendex polls conducted in the United States from the first quarter of 1971 to the last quarter of 1982.[4] These polls, sponsored by General Electric, include questions asking about preferences to "do more, do less, or do about the same" on defense, health, and education in the United States. The resulting measures of net support are displayed in Figure 6.1.

The magnitude of change across quarters is not obvious in Figure 6.1, so Table 6.2 provides a closer look. The table shows the average absolute change in net preferences from the previous quarter to the current quarter. The top left cell thus captures the average magnitude of change in defense preferences in every first quarter for which we can estimate the change in preferences. (This requires data for the previous quarter as well as the one that precedes it, of course. There are some missing data in the series, so the sample size is somewhat reduced. See the notes to Table 6.2.) The average absolute changes in preferences, by quarter, allow us to examine whether there is one quarter in which preferences tend to change more than in other quarters. Results suggest that there is: the first quarter of the calendar year, January to March. Preference change in this period is greatest not just for defense, but also for health and education. Indeed, preferences for the latter remain, comparatively speaking, fairly constant after the first quarter of the year. Defense opinion shows a reasonable amount of change during the second quarter, but less thereafter.

These results are generally consistent with our analysis of outlays and appropriations. Just as the public shows more sensitivity to

[4] See Appendix for details.

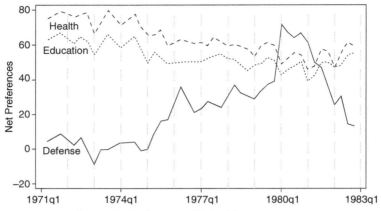

FIGURE 6.1. Quarterly Preferences, United States

TABLE 6.2. *The Magnitude of Change in Preferences, by Quarter*

| Quarter | Average Absolute Change in Net Preferences | | |
	Defense	Health	Education
1	8.8	6.6	5.7
2	6.8	2.9	2.2
3	4.9	3.4	2.9
4	3.6	3.0	2.4

Based on quarterly data from Trendex, 1971–1982. For Quarters 1 and 2, N=8; for Quarters 3 and 4 N=9.

spending, we see that preferences exhibit the most change after the fiscal year is under way and the public has begin to experience shifts in spending priorities. Recall that the U.S. fiscal year begins in October and that spending changes often take time to implement. Indeed, the budget often is not even complete until November or December, or even after the first of the year. But opinion change occurs for the most part after December. That said, it occurs quite soon thereafter – sometime between December and March.

The availability of polling data in U.S. data allows us to test further the timing of public responsiveness. Our analyses of public responsiveness have thus far relied on opinion data from the General Social Survey (GSS), which is conducted in March. The survey thus

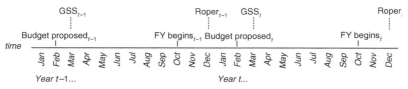

FIGURE 6.2. The Timing of Polls and Responsiveness

captures preferences at the end of the first quarter of the calendar year, at the fiscal halfway point. Trendex data suggest that may in fact be the best time to capture public responsiveness, but this can be tested directly. We also have data from Roper, from 1973 to 1999, and these Roper polls capture opinion in December, only two months into the fiscal year.

The difference in the timing of Roper and GSS polls allows us to assess the timing of public responsiveness explicitly. Figure 6.2 illustrates the timeline of the budgetary process and two regular polls capturing net preferences for policy. Budgets are proposed in February, during the second quarter of the previous fiscal year $(t-1)$. In theory, the budget is then implemented in October, the beginning of the next fiscal year (t); in practice it often takes until November or December, as we have noted.

To capture the timing of public responsiveness in these polls, we test when opinion changes: (1) over the time during which the new budget is signed into law and the fiscal year begins, that is, in Figure 6.2, between the GSS at $t-1$ (in March) and the Roper poll at $t-1$ (in December); and (2) over the remaining period, between the Roper poll at $t-1$ and the GSS at t. To so do, we use the measure of lagged preferences from the most recent poll; where the dependent variable is net preferences from the Roper poll at $t-1$, lagged preferences are from the GSS poll at $t-1$. Likewise, we estimate a model where preferences are from the GSS poll at t and lagged preferences are from the Roper poll at $t-1$. In both models, then, we effectively capture responsiveness to spending, controlling for the level of preferences in the previous poll. If there is little change in the intervening period, current preferences will be overwhelmingly determined by past preferences and spending should have little impact. If there is change over the intervening period, and if this change is in reaction to spending, we should find evidence of public responsiveness.

TABLE 6.3. *Feedback Coefficients: The Timing of Feedback, United States*

Domain	DV: Roper (December)$_{t-1}$ IV: GSS (March)$_{t-1}$	DV: GSS (March)$_t$ IV: Roper (December)$_{t-1}$
Defense	.003	−.175**
Major Social	.043	−.274**

Cells contain OLS coefficients for each IV, where * p < .10; ** p < .05. Full models are listed in Appendix Table 2.

Results are shown in Table 6.3. For the sake of simplicity, we show results just for defense and the three major social domains combined. The first column captures effects between the GSS poll in March and the Roper poll in December of the previous year, when budgetary decisions for the current fiscal year (usually) are made. Here we can see that there is no evidence of thermostatic responsiveness during the period, as the coefficients for spending are not different from zero. The public simply does not respond as appropriations make their way through the policymaking process. The results in the second column show that the public does respond immediately thereafter. The spending coefficient in models capturing change between the Roper poll in the previous year and the current GSS poll is consistently negative and highly significant. The policy-responsive shift in public preferences that characterizes the thermostatic model occurs sometime between December and March, the period in which the new budget takes effect.[5]

The pattern of these results confirms both the pattern evident in Trendex data and the greater responsiveness to outlays, which change only after the fiscal year is under way and the new budget is in effect. It also contrasts with what we would expect if the public were responding only to the policy decisions of government – that is, we would expect greater responsiveness to appropriations and a much faster reaction,

[5] Note that there is also no evidence of feedback after the GGS at *t*. In a model using Roper results at *t* as the dependent variable, and GSS results at *t* as an independent variable, the spending coefficients for defense are insignificant (B=-.015, se=.045). For social domains, the spending coefficient actually is positive (B=.084. se=.031). There also is no evidence of feedback prior to the GSS at *t-1*, though this would be rather peculiar given how far in advance of spending this preference change would be.

during the course of the policymaking process.[6] We cannot be sure that the timing of public responsiveness is exactly the same in the United Kingdom and Canada. Nonetheless, our U.S. results provide strong support for the idea that what we capture statistically in Chapter 5 is indeed public responsiveness to policy change.

POLICY, OUTCOMES, AND PUBLIC RESPONSIVENESS

Does the public actually respond to spending, or do our spending measures just happen to capture responsiveness to the results of spending, or policy outcomes?[7] The foregoing results are suggestive. We have learned that public responsiveness is focused mostly on outlays (instead of appropriations), which tells us that the policy-making process is not the focus of responsiveness; the public reacts more to actual spending. Given that responsiveness occurs mainly in the second quarter of the fiscal year, however, it is unlikely that the public is reacting purely to the consequences of spending. This is because many people will not directly feel the impact of many spending changes by this point in time – that is, responsiveness at this time is just too quick. Three or four months into the fiscal year, there is simply not time enough to realize much change in outcomes in many policy areas.[8] Thus, based on these results, there is reason to think that the public responds to spending itself. Of course, the question is best settled empirically.

[6] Separate analysis that indicates little independent responsiveness to party control as well. See also note 7.
[7] Note that there is another possibility as well: that what appears here as responsiveness to spending is in fact responsiveness to the partisanship of government. That is, rather than react to changes in welfare spending, for instance, the public reacts to a government with a reputation for reducing welfare spending. While possible, it does not account for the annual responsiveness evidenced here – see note 6. Including the partisanship of government in our models also has little to no effect on the magnitude of the spending coefficients. The results are available upon request.
[8] Also keep in mind that responsiveness in some domains may be more global than specific. In a domain like transport in the United Kingdom, the public may not be responding directly to either transport spending or outcomes, but rather to the common global trend in outcomes or spending across domains. Identifying what exactly preferences are responding to here is especially difficult.

Directly assessing the relative effects of spending and outcomes is, unfortunately, rather difficult. The problem is that measuring policy outcomes in practice is not always straightforward. How do we quantify "national security," for example? Even assuming we could quantify it, how do we identify the portion that is due to policy *per se*? Similar problems obtain in other domains. We nevertheless can explore the relationship between preferences, spending, and outcomes in certain domains. One domain in which this is possible is crime, at least in the United States, the one country for which crime preferences are available. The reason for crime spending obviously is to address the rate of crime, a phenomenon for which there are a number of reliable measures. We thus can explore whether the public responds to spending independent of the crime rate. To do so, we examine the effects of the rate of (a) violent crime, (b) nonviolent crime, and (c) violent and nonviolent crime taken together, where each is the number of crimes per 100,000 residents. (See Appendix for details.) As we have no strong prior assumptions about which of these measures is most appropriate, we rely on the one that performs best in statistical models: nonviolent crime.[9] Results are shown in Table 6.4.

The first column of Table 6.4 shows the feedback coefficient from the original crime preference regression analysis in Chapter 5 (Table 5.3). The negative and significant coefficient tells us that the public adjusts its preferences thermostatically in response to spending. The second column shows results for a similar model in which the nonviolent crime rate is used in place of spending. Note that we expect the crime rate to have a positive effect – as crime increases, so too should demand for spending on efforts to reduce crime. This is the case here. A one-unit shift in the nonviolent crime rate is associated with roughly a 0.008-point upward shift in preferences. The coefficient actually is quite sizeable, since the standard deviation in nonviolent crime over the period is 495 (with a mean of roughly 4,600). Note, however, that this model using the crime rate explains less variance in preferences than did the original model using spending. (Consider the drop in the R-squared in the bottom row.) In the third column we see results for a model that includes both

[9] When preferences are regressed on both nonviolent and violent crime, the former is significant (.008, p<.01) and the latter is not (.001, p=.94), and the R-squared is consistently slightly higher when using nonviolent crime. Also see Table 6.4.

TABLE 6.4. *Feedback: Spending and Outcomes, Crime*

IV	DV: Crime Preferences		
	Model 1	Model 2	Model 3
Spending (Outlays)$_t$	-1.215**		$-.948$**
Nonviolent Crime$_{t-1}$		.008**	.003
R^2	.478	.397	.492

Cells contain OLS regression coefficients, where * $p < .10$; ** $p < .05$. Models also include linear counters. Full results are presented in Appendix Table 2.

spending and crime together. The finding is clear: spending remains a strong predictor, but the crime rate does not.

The same pattern holds in other domains for which this kind of comparison is possible. Table 6.5 shows results from a similar analysis for health, in which a standard measure of hospital investment – number of acute care beds per 1,000 residents – can be used, this time in all three countries. (See the Appendix for details.) We expect the effect of acute care beds to be negative – as the number of beds increases, net preference for more spending should decrease.[10] There is indeed evidence of responsiveness to the acute care beds measure in the United States and United Kingdom; in Canada, there appears to be positive feedback.[11] In each case, however, the spending model explains more variance in preferences, and, when the two measures are included simultaneously, the effect of spending overwhelms the effect of healthcare outcomes.[12]

What accounts for the apparently strong responsiveness to spending rather than to outcomes? One possibility is that spending figures capture a number of different outcomes to which preferences are responding. The advantage for spending in this case would simply be one of measurement – spending captures trends in outcomes better

[10] Note that due to data availability, the U.K. model here uses just 16 years rather than the 18 used in Chapter 5 models. The feedback coefficient presented in Table 6.5 is thus marginally different from that in Table 5.2.

[11] Note that the same is true if we adjust the timing of the outcome measure to account for the possibility that it takes longer for the public to observe and react to outcomes.

[12] Hospital beds are but one measure of health care outcomes, of course, and it may be that the public is more responsive to other indicators, including those relating more to caring than curing (see Newhouse 1977).

TABLE 6.5. *Feedback: Spending and Outcomes, Health*

IV	DV: Health Preferences		
R^2	Model 1	Model 2	Model 3
United States			
Spending$_t$	−.284**		−.284**
Acute Care$_{t-1}$		−4.113**	−.000
R^2	.685	.605	.685
United Kingdom			
Spending$_t$	−2.317**		−1.847**
Acute Care$_{t-1}$		−12.452**	−3.404
R^2	.946	.897	.951
Canada			
Spending$_t$	−2.143**		−2.533**
Acute Care$_{t-1}$		25.962*	−2.690
R^2	.931	.890	.935

Note: Cells contain OLS regression coefficients, where * $p < .10$; ** $p < .05$. Models also include linear and/or squared counters, and lagged preferences measure, where applicable. Full results are presented in Appendix Table 2.

than any single outcomes measure can. That responsiveness is focused purely on outcomes seems unlikely, however, given how early in the fiscal year responsiveness occurs. Responsiveness at this early stage must be driven in part by information about spending itself – about the ongoing and future developments in the domain that are presumed to be related to changes in spending.

Note that responsiveness of this type requires that people believe that there is a strong connection between spending and outcomes – they must believe that changes in spending have (or will have) predictable effects on outcomes, to reduce crime or improve healthcare, for example. It is this belief that makes sensible the reaction to budgetary policy early in the fiscal year. The belief may be rooted in reality, in which case the public's response to spending may be quite rational; and there is reason to think that spending does impact outcomes in a positive way, probably quite powerfully. There also is reason to think the relationship is not perfect, that spending does not always have a positive impact – indeed, what government does can make things worse. The point is that responding to spending, although important to the functioning of democracy, may not always be the most rational type of responsiveness.

FEDERAL VERSUS CONSOLIDATED SPENDING

Canadian data on budgetary policy present difficulties and opportunities in the study of public responsiveness. Both are a function of the same feature: the funding of major social programs under provincial jurisdiction through, in large part, semiconditional block transfers from the federal government. The exact form that these block transfers take has changed over time. The differences in these fiscal-federal arrangements are less important here than the similarities, however: each is a block transfer from the federal government to the provinces. To the extent that there are conditions, they are rather slight (Watts 1999), although the size of the transfer – even without conditions – will constrain provincial differences in some ways. The money is distributed to the provinces based on a formula decided by, and with minor conditions set by, the national government, but is actually spent by the provincial governments with some degree of discretion in policy design and implementation. In addition, provinces use some of their own revenues to support health, education, and welfare; and there is some direct federal spending in each domain as well. That there is disagreement even among experts on which level of government is responsible for budgetary change is not surprising. The clarity of the policy signal coming from either level of government is very low in these domains.

Spending in the major social domains in Canada is thus best captured at a "consolidated" level – specifically, consolidated (a) federal and (b) provincial, territorial, and municipal governments. That said, it is possible to measure spending at each level separately (see figures in Chapter 4), and doing so allows us to examine the effects of federalism on public responsiveness more directly. In Table 6.6, we present a very simple comparison: public responsiveness in Canada, by domain, using either the (1) consolidated or (2) federal measures of spending. (Defense is not included here because all defense spending is federal.)

Results for consolidated spending in the first column are the same as those in Chapter 5 – these are the baseline models of by-domain public responsiveness in Canada. The corresponding results using federal

TABLE 6.6. *Feedback Coefficients: Consolidated, Federal, and Provincial Spending, Canada*

Domain	Consolidated		Federal	
	B	Standardized	B	Standardized
Welfare	−2.226**	−12.194	−.891**	−4.659
Health	−2.143**	−26.102	−.918**	−5.290
Education	−.716*	−4.079	−1.690*	−1.989

Note: B shows OLS coefficients, where * p < .10; ** p < .05. Standardized shows the effect of a one-standard deviation change in spending on preferences. Full models are listed in Appendix Table 2.

spending are listed in the third column. Columns two and four, labeled Standardized, show the standardized measure of responsiveness, which takes into account the variances of consolidated and federal spending, respectively. Responsiveness to consolidated spending is greater than responsiveness to federal spending in all the major social domains.[13] This is true even when comparing the unstandardized coefficients for welfare and health, although consolidated spending is necessarily greater than federal spending – that is, although a CA$1 million increase represents a much smaller proportion of consolidated spending, responsiveness to this change in consolidated spending is greater. In education, the comparatively large coefficient for federal spending is halved when we take into account consolidated spending. Of course, direct federal spending in each of these domains pales in comparison with the spending that occurs through block transfers, and it is unlikely that the programs through which direct federal funding occurs produce results sufficiently distinct from the remaining spending to make federal spending very noticeable. Federal spending elicits much less responsiveness.

In environment and to a lesser extent transport (see Appendix Table 2 for results), responsiveness to federal spending is clearer.

---

[13] It is also the case that for these social domains the R-squared for models using consolidated spending is somewhat higher than for models using federal spending. (See full results in the Appendix.) Note also that when consolidated and federal spending are included in a model together, the coefficient on the former consistently overwhelms the latter.

Indeed, in these two domains, responsiveness is greater for federal spending than for consolidated spending. The difference is important. In the major social domains, characterized by conditional block transfers, using consolidated spending tends to enhance findings of public responsiveness; in the other domains, combining the spending behavior of multiple levels of government appears to depress responsiveness coefficients.

In the primary social domains, it is not clear that the Canadian public can distinguish between federal and provincial policymaking. Indeed, it appears that provincial policymaking can affect net preferences for federal policy. This makes some sense in the health and education domains, where so much of provincial funding is dependent on federal transfers. It makes less sense in welfare, perhaps, where slightly more provincial funding comes from the provinces themselves, and where the federal government practices a greater degree of direct spending.

We expect these differences to be evident not just in Canada but elsewhere. That Statistics Canada collects spending data at both the federal and provincial levels means that we can look at the effects of federalism in this country in some detail. But we expect the same dynamic to be true in other federations as well, including the United States. There, we have already seen somewhat dampened responsiveness in the highly federalized education domain, for instance. Federalism poses problems for public responsiveness.

"GLOBAL" VERSUS "SPECIFIC" RESPONSIVENESS

We have thus far assumed that public responsiveness is specific to domains – that the public responds to spending within particular policy areas. This reflects the traditional view of opinion, where preferences are presumed to capture information particular to each domain. (See Geer's 1996 review of the literature.) It may be that the public's response is more collective, however. Opinion may not be driven so much by spending in a single domain as by generalized trends in spending across various related domains. We have already seen in Chapter 4 that both preferences for spending and actual spending in the different domestic programs move together over time. Factor analyses in Table 4.2, for instance, show that a considerable amount of variance in the different domestic spending series is captured by a single factor. The connection between preferences and spending may consequently be more generalized, or "global." In the extreme, the public can be thought of as having a single, very general preference for government activity; from this perspective, measured preferences in various domains represent (multiple) indicators of a single, underlying preference for government action. This characterization of public opinion clearly implies a very different pattern of representation from the traditional, domain-centric perspective.

This more global version of public responsiveness has been explored elsewhere, most clearly in Stimson's work on "policy mood" – especially see Erikson et al.'s *The Macro Polity* (2002). There, Stimson and colleagues provide strong evidence of global trends in both public opinion and public policy in the United States, and of strong relations between the two. There is, however, good reason to suppose that not *all* responsiveness is global. We have seen in Chapter 4 that preferences exhibit independent movement in each domain, and substantial amounts in some. Preferences reflect things that are unique to the different domains, then, potentially including policy itself. This is more true in some domains than others. It may thus be that the focus of public responsiveness itself varies, being highly global in some domains and more specific in others.

Our own previous research suggests that issue salience is an important structuring factor. For example, in the United States we see that the public responds specifically to policy on welfare and health (Wlezien 2004). People appear to pay close attention to what happens within these high-salience policy domains. The same is not true in other, less salient domains. There the public responds more globally, to the overall direction and level of spending. A similar relationship between salience and domain-specific responsiveness obtains in the United Kingdom and Canada as well (Soroka and Wlezien 2004, 2005). Comparing across countries also suggests that federalism matters. For more decentralized domains, in which policy is made by multiple governments and for which the policy signal is less clear, public responsiveness appears to be more globalized. In the absence of precise information about a given policy domain, the public may use information about policy in various related domains as a substitute.[14]

The varying degrees of specific responsiveness shown in past work have implications for the way in which we interpret public responsiveness

[14] Or, put differently, due to complicated federal policymaking arrangments in each domain, the public may really only be able to observe policy in a more general way – as a general increase or decrease in spending across multiple domains.

in the models here. We know that in some domains the public clearly notices and responds to policy within the particular areas. It indicates a high level of public monitoring, and provides a strong basis for representation of public preferences within those domains. The same is not true for some of the other domains, but there a more general, "global" responsiveness may nonetheless exist.[15]

THE FOCUS OF PUBLIC RESPONSIVENESS

The foregoing analyses have explored the public responsiveness findings from Chapter 5. More precisely, these analyses have shown that the public responds primarily to spending, not the policy decisions that structure spending over time. The public thus appears a bit measured, awaiting the completion of the budget process to see spending change actually begin. It does not wait very long, however. Thermostatic responsiveness is complete before the fiscal year is half over, well before spending is complete and the effects of spending are felt on the broader environment. The public in effect anticipates outcomes, assuming that increases in spending will have predictable effects down the road. (These may not materialize, of course, which raises a range of questions regarding the design and implementation of policy.)

For the meantime, we should not lose track of the big story: there is public responsiveness across a wide range of policy domains. Chapter 5 found strong empirical evidence of public responsiveness to policy, and further tests in the current chapter support the contention that our feedback coefficients are indeed capturing the thermostatic adjustment of public preferences to real policy change. This finding begs the question: Who is driving the public responsiveness we observe? Do all citizens respond to policy similarly, or are there systematic differences across different groups based on age, or education, or income? We have already noted (in Chapter 2) that trends in net preferences need not be driven by preference change in the entire population, but by preference change in one or another relatively small proportion of the total population. Knowing who responds matters a great deal, not just because it begins to

---

[15] Our models may underestimate the magnitude of responsiveness, particularly in less salient domains.

flesh out the individual-level dynamics behind the thermostatic model, but because – if public responsiveness breeds policy representation – we might expect a more responsive group to be better represented. We accordingly examine the responsiveness, and representation, of different subgroups in Chapter 8. First, however, we examine the broader effects of public preferences on policy itself.

7

Policy Representation

We have seen that the public responds to policy change. This is true across many domains and across several countries. The finding is of importance unto itself, to be sure. It also provides the basis for policy representation. That is, public responsiveness provides the critical incentive and information for representation by policymakers. Whether policymakers respond in kind is the subject of this chapter.

We begin below by reviewing and then estimating our model of policy representation across policy domains. We discuss the results with a particular focus on how they relate to our findings in previous chapters. If public responsiveness is the incentive for representation, the two should covary – increased responsiveness should translate into increased representation. We test this hypothesis here. Recall that we have also posited that government institutions should matter for representation, even taking into account public responsiveness. Specifically, governments in parliamentary systems are expected to be less responsive to preferences than (Madisonian) presidential ones. This possibility is considered here as well.

Beyond these primary concerns, we explore additional issues in representation, following in part the analyses of feedback in Chapter 6. In particular, we examine the possibility that representation is stronger for budgetary policy (appropriations) than actual expenditures (outlays). We also examine the degree to which representation increases alongside electoral marginality – just as public responsiveness creates an incentive for representation by policymakers, so too may electoral pressure. We want to know whether representation is stronger when current politicians are more at risk of losing their seats.

MODELING POLICY REPRESENTATION

Recall first from Chapter 2 our basic model of policy representation. In the model, policy change in the current fiscal year (P_t) is a function of relative preferences for policy (R_{t-1}) and the partisan control of government (G_{t-1}) during the previous fiscal year. (The lag serves to reflect preferences and party control when the current year's budget is actually made.) The equation is:

$$\Delta P_t = \rho + \gamma_1 R_{t-1} + \gamma_2 G_{t-1} + \mu_t, \tag{7.1}$$

where ρ and μ_t represent the intercept and the error term, respectively. This model captures both indirect and direct representation: the former – representation through election results and subsequent government partisanship – is captured by γ_2, and the latter – annual adjustments to policy reflecting shifts in preferences – is captured by γ_1. The latter is the most critical for our purposes. It is the coefficient that captures responsiveness on the part of policymakers, the kind of dynamic representation that we expect (though to differing degrees across policy domains) where the public notices and responds to what policymakers do. Consequently, we focus our attention in this chapter on this coefficient.

The rest of the model requires some discussion. To begin with, we include variables capturing the partisan control of government (G_{t-1}). In parliamentary democracies we use a simple dummy variable. It takes the value "1" whenever the Conservative party holds the parliamentary majority in the United Kingdom or the Progressive Conservative party does so in Canada. Otherwise, it takes the value "0." The timing of G_{t-1} in both of these countries had to be checked carefully, since the schedule of elections is not fixed. In the United Kingdom, governments elected in spring elections will sometimes propose a budget later in the fiscal year (e.g., Thatcher in June 1979, or Blair in July 1997). Spending for that fiscal year is thus an amalgam of the previous and current governments' fiscal policies. This does not happen in Canada, though in that case a government elected early in one fiscal year may not produce a budget until the next (Trudeau in 1974, Martin in 2004).

The timing of elections is of course more straightforward in the United States but government partisanship has to be measured differently. Here, G_{t-1} is captured with two variables: (1) a dummy variable equal to 1 whenever the president is a Republican and 0 when the president is a Democrat, and (2) the percentage of Congress (averaged across the two chambers) that is Republican, which ranges from 35.9% to 53.8% over the period.[1] Again, the variables tap partisanship at the time the budget was passed, i.e., in the previous fiscal year.

Some domains require additional controls. First, it is necessary to control for President Carter's substantial spending add-ons – "supplemental" spending – to Ford's last budget upon taking office in FY1977 (Wlezien 1993). The impact of this change in party control on spending for cities was felt immediately, in the current fiscal year.[2] Second, it is necessary to control for economic effects in some domains in Canada and the United Kingdom (see Appendix Table 3), which are powerfully driven by unemployment rates. A similar pattern is evident in U.S. welfare spending, and to isolate policy effects there we simply excised the "unemployment compensation" subcategory from our measure (see Chapter 4). Canadian spending data are available in reliable, but quite general, functional categories, so our measure of welfare spending there cannot be purged of Employment Insurance spending. This is why we need to control for unemployment rates in the Canadian welfare models. In the United Kingdom the issue does not apply, as we do not even have a measure of welfare spending to begin with.[3]

---

[1] To be absolutely clear, we calculate the percentages of Republicans in the House and Senate and then take the mean.

[2] This is true for outlays, where dummy variables for both FY 1977 and 1978 capture the substantial spike in supplemental appropriations advanced by Carter. Note that when using appropriations, as we do late in the chapter, welfare and environment are affected only in the current fiscal year, and a FY 1977 dummy variable is included accordingly.

[3] Some past work has added other controls as well, which we do not use here, including national debt and other economic indicators (see, e.g., Blais et al. 1996, Durr 1993, and Stevenson 2001; as well as some of our own work, namely, Soroka and Wlezien 2004). None of these variables was significant in any more than a small minority of the models considered here, however, nor did the additional variables make much difference to the other coefficients in the model. Note also that in all cases but one there is no significant autocorrelation in the differenced spending series, and so we

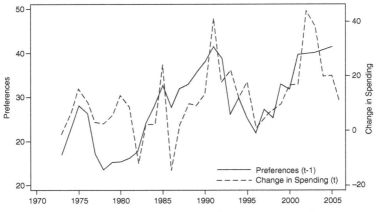

FIGURE 7.1. Preferences and Spending Change, U.S. Social Domains

A FIRST TEST: POLICY REPRESENTATION IN DEFENSE AND THE SOCIAL DOMAINS

Let us see whether and to what extent policymakers respond to public preferences. Figure 7.1 illustrates the relationship between preferences and spending in the combined social domains in the United States. The figure is adjusted somewhat by comparison with figures in Chapters 4 and 5, following equation 7.1. First, net preferences are lagged by one year. Second, we show *changes in* rather than levels of spending (in billions of FY2000 U.S. dollars). The figure thus captures both the timing and nature of policy responsiveness. Preferences (in year t-1) are lined up alongside the change in spending they may have affected (in year t).

This figure indicates a positive relationship between social preferences and spending change. When the public wants more social spending policymakers usually provide it. The pattern is not perfect, of course, and there are some obvious exceptions. The bivariate correlation nevertheless is sizable and robust (Pearson's r = .61, p < .001). We examine this dynamic more systematically in Table 7.1, which presents a first test of policy representation, focusing on spending on defense and the combined social domains in the United States.

Notice from the table that the partisanship of government clearly matters for spending in the United States. In the defense domain

do not include lagged spending in the model. The one exception is U.K. defense spending, where autocorrelation remains, and so lagged spending is included.

TABLE 7.1. *Complete Representation Models,*
Defense and Combined Social Domains, United
States

	DV: Spending	
IV	Defense	Social
Preferences $_{t-1}$	.705**	1.287**
	(.125)	(.249)
Party of President $_{t-1}$	14.577**	−5.551
	(4.878)	(3.950)
Party of Congress $_{t-1}$	1.088**	−.740*
	(.402)	(.354)
Constant	−58.748**	37.155**
	(18.896)	(17.114)
R^2	.596	.493
Adjusted R^2	.555	.441
Durbin-Watson	1.767	2.044
N	33	33

Cells contain OLS regression coefficients and standard
errors (in parentheses), where * $p < .10$; ** $p < .05$. All
variables are mean-centered.

(column 1), Republican president leads to an average increase in
annual spending change of about 14-billion (FY2000) US dollars. A
one-percent change in the Republican proportion of Congress has a
sizable affect as well – roughly a $1-billion change in annual spend-
ing change. The specific nature of the effects may seem counterintuitive – that is, the coefficients imply that the impact of party control
compounds over time, e.g., the party of the president influences
spending change year-after-year, not merely during transitions. This
is not quite right, however.

Because defense spending feeds back (thermostatically) on public
preferences, the actual change in spending owing to party control actually will tend to decline over time, at least to the extent
policymakers follow public preferences. For instance, upon replacing
a Democratic president, a Republican president is likely to propose
and get increased defense spending, which in turn causes preferences
for more defense spending to decrease. If the president is responsive to
these preferences, the change in spending in the next fiscal year will be

lower; it still might go up, but just not as much as in the first year, in transition. In practice, the *actual* spending change under Democratic and Republican presidents diminishes fairly quickly over time, i.e., presidents effectively bring policy in line with their preferred partisan levels. This is consistent with and could help explain the diminishing marginal effect of party control of government over time that Alt (1985) detected many years ago. Given feedback, the patterned effect of presidential party also makes the cyclicality of defense spending preferences more understandable, that is, as presidents drive policy off in one direction or another, the public support for more spending goes in the opposite direction. We consider this more explicitly in Chapter 9.

The effects of party on spending in the combined social domains are listed in column 2 of Table 7.1. Here the coefficient for the president is expectedly negative but insignificant; for Congress, the coefficient implies that a one percent change in the Republican percentage of Congress leads to an average 0.74 billion dollar decrease in social spending. This is as expected – *ceteris paribus*, Republicans should spend less on social domains. Interestingly, they spend about as much less on social programs as they do more on defense.

Most importantly, both models reveal relationships between public preferences and annual spending change. For defense, a one-point increase in support for more spending in year $t-1$ leads to a $0.7 billion increase in year t. For the combined social domains, a one-point increase in support for more spending in year $t-1$ leads to a $1.3 billion increase in year t. Both effects are highly reliable. This is important evidence of actual policy responsiveness; that is, spending changes in response to preferences independently of party control of government, which itself may reflect preferences.

How much policy representation do we observe? Is it a little or a lot? As with the coefficients for public responsiveness, the representation coefficients for defense and social spending are not necessarily directly comparable. We try to account for this in Table 7.2, which shows results for defense and the social domains across all three countries. As for public responsiveness, we focus in this table (and the tables that follow) on just the most pertinent coefficient, γ_1, the coefficient capturing direct representation; complete models are listed in Appendix Table 3.

TABLE 7.2. *Representation Coefficients, Defense and Social Domains*

Domain	U.S.		U.K.		CA	
	B	Standardized	B	Standardized	B	Standardized
Defense	.705**	4.316	.048**	3.592	.011*	1.768
Major Social	1.287**	4.701	.224**	2.928	.464**	2.918
Welfare	.326**	3.728			.322**	4.600
Health	.563**	4.540	.112**	2.925	.092**	2.675
Education	.207*	5.231	.075**	2.114	.110**	1.849

B shows OLS coefficients, where * p < .10; ** p < .05. Standardized shows the effect of a one-standard deviation change in preferences on spending, expressed as a percentage of the mean level of spending over the period. Full models are listed in Appendix Table 3.

The first two cells of column 1 in Table 7.2 show representation coefficients for defense and the combined social domains in the United States, as we have already seen in Table 7.1. These are transformed in the second column into a more comparable metric: the effect on spending of a standard deviation change in preferences, as a proportion of the mean spending level over the period. The measure thus accounts for differences in the variance in preferences, the level of spending, and the different national currency units across domains and countries. In the United States, this transformation effectively narrows the gap between results for defense and the social domains: the coefficients in column two are 4.3 and 4.7, respectively. Using this measure, therefore, responsiveness to defense and social spending preferences is indistinguishable.

Is a similar pattern evident in the United Kingdom and Canada? Both countries certainly show evidence of responsiveness – in both domains the coefficient is positive and significant. Transformed coefficients suggest slightly less representation in the United Kingdom, however, and lesser still in Canada. Within the United Kingdom, representation appears slightly stronger in defense; within Canada, representation is strongest in the social domains.

Recall that we expect representation to be linked at least in part to the strength of feedback. An attentive, responsive public is the major motivation and source of information for policy representation, after all. Figure 7.2 thus plots these standardized representation results alongside the standardized feedback coefficients (from Table 5.2). The relationship between the two is clear and strong – as feedback increases so too does representation, and the correlation is a healthy .73.

Institutional differences also matter. Recall that we expect representation to be driven in part by the horizontal division of powers. In the U.S. presidential system, both the President and Members of Congress are directly elected and accountable. Assuming an attentive public, there is in this system a strong incentive to represent, and each institution can correct representational errors by the other. This is less true in the U.K. and Canadian parliamentary systems, where the executive has a great degree of policymaking power and does not as reliably benefit from error correction by the legislature. (See Chapter 3.) Even as the unitary system in the United Kingdom

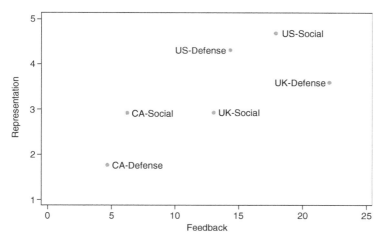

FIGURE 7.2. Feedback and Representation (Feedback measure is SD; Representation measure is SD[Pr]/Mean[Sp])

may facilitate strong public responsiveness in that country, in comparison with the United States and Canadian federal systems, the U.S. presidential system may create the strongest basis for policy representation. It follows that the United States may be stronger on the representation side, and the United Kingdom stronger on the public responsiveness side. This is borne out in Figure 7.2. So too is the fact that Canada should – as a consequence of being both parliamentary and highly federalized – be constrained on both fronts. In Figure 7.2, Canada shows the least degree of both policy representation and public responsiveness.

POLICY REPRESENTATION, BY DOMAIN

Results are presented for the individual social domains in the bottom three rows of Table 7.2. Just as with the social domains combined, there is strong evidence of policy representation in each individual social domain. The same is true for the other domains not shown here, with but a few exceptions: crime and foreign aid in the United States, and transport in the United Kingdom and Canada. (See Appendix Table 3 for details.) It is notable that transport in both countries also exhibited comparatively low public responsiveness as did foreign aid in the United States. This is more evidence of the connection between public responsiveness and representation.

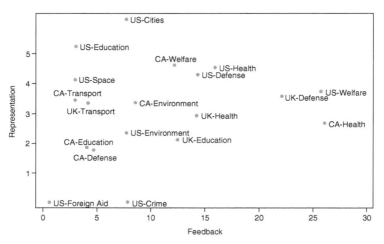

FIGURE 7.3. Feedback and Representation by Domain (Feedback measure is SD; Representation measure is SD[Pr]/Mean[Sp])

Figure 7.3 plots transformed responsiveness and representation coefficients by domain. Here we see that as public responsiveness increases so does policy representation, though there is less correspondence than we saw focusing just on defense and total social spending in Figure 7.2. There is still a statistically significant relationship between the representation and feedback coefficients plotted here.[4] That said, the relationship between public responsiveness and policy representation is rather weak in the left-hand side of the figure, where feedback is modest. There we observe a great range in representation, from very low to very high. This may surprise but actually is as we might expect given institutional differences across countries. Consider that most of the domains in the upper left-hand corner of the figure – those exhibiting very strong representation despite only modest public responsiveness – are in the United States, our one Madisonian presidential system, where we expect greater representation. The fact that we observe high levels of representation there in what evidently are low-salience domains implies that institutions, to the extent they do matter, encourage more representation than we expect based on public responsiveness alone.

---

[4] The correlation betweeen representation and logged feedback, where the latter is logged to capture the nonlinearity evident in Figure 7.3, is .39 (*p*=.09, N=19).

Even taking into account differences across countries, however, a good amount of scatter remains. This partly may reflect nonlinearity in the relationship between feedback and representation. Still, we must keep in mind that our measures of both public and policy responsiveness are not perfectly comparable – they provide only a very coarse indication of differences across countries and domains, and are better for indicating general patterns than specific ones.

What is clear from the foregoing results is that (a) representation of public preferences is evident in the budgetary policy, across different domains and countries, and (b) this representation covaries, as expected, with the degree of public responsiveness. As we have stated, our coefficients for both responsiveness and representation do not allow for very fine-grained comparisons across domains. There nevertheless is a relationship, if only a very general one, between the two, and it is in line with our theoretical expectations.[5]

REPRESENTATION IN BUDGETARY POLICY

Although the survey questions used to produce our measures of public preferences ask directly about spending, policymakers do not directly control exactly how much money is spent in different areas. Outlays reflect a variety of factors that are beyond political control, including changing economic conditions and national security threats. Even putting these things aside, expenditure decisions reflect implementation, which adds additional sources of difference. Although it may make sense that the public reacts to actual

---

[5] Just as public responsiveness can be "global" or domain-specific, so too can policy representation, and it also has been the subject of previous research (Wlezien 2004; Soroka and Wlezien 2004, 2005). There it was shown that the pattern of representation is largely symmetrical to the pattern of public responsiveness to policy itself: Where the public notices and responds specifically to policy in a particular domain, representation tends to be specific; where the public responds – in effect, more globally – to policy across a set of domains taken together, representation is more global; where the public does not respond to policy, representation tends not to occur. The pattern was shown to apply especially in the United States and to a lesser extent in the United Kingdom and Canada, where representation is more global. This is as we might expect, given that the United Kingdom and Canada are parliamentary systems, where governments can exercise greater discretion in responding to opinion change, that is, they may tend to pick and choose among different programs in response to shifts in the underlying public mood.

TABLE 7.3. *Representation Coefficients: Outlays versus Appropriations, United States*

Domain	Correlation b/w Outlays and Appropriations	Representation			
		Outlays		Appropriations	
		B	R²	B	R²
Defense	.942	.670**	.572	.854**	.561
Welfare	.874	.345**	.181	.860**	.388
Health	.996	.562**	.540	.572**	.277
Education	.936	.234*	.119	.006	.129

Cells contain OLS coefficients, where * $p < .10$; ** $p < .05$. Full models are listed in Appendix Table 3.

budgetary outputs, policy representation may be better captured by appropriations, which more accurately capture the decisions of poli-cymakers, unaffected by other things that happen later and cannot be anticipated.

As a consequence, models relying on outlays may slightly underes-timate the representation connection. We consider this possibility in Table 7.3, which presents representation coefficients for defense and the social domains in the United States, using both outlays and appro-priations. Recall that reliable measures of appropriations are available only from the 1976 fiscal year, and to ensure comparability, both out-lays and appropriations models are restricted to the same time period. Outlays coefficients here will thus be slightly different from those in Table 7.2. It is reassuring, however, that dropping a few cases makes little difference to the magnitude and significance of the representa-tion coefficients.

There are just two domains in which representation appears to be greater in appropriations than in outlays – defense and welfare – and only significantly so for the latter. In health, the coefficients are basi-cally indistinguishable;[6] in education, representation appears greater in outlays.[7] It is notable that the domain in which appropriations matter most is the same domain for which, in Chapter 6, we saw the public was

---

[6] The same is true for environment and cities. See Appendix tables.
[7] The same is true for the remaining domains, including crime, foreign aid, and space. See Appendix tables.

more responsive to appropriations themselves. Where the public is more likely to notice policymaking, capturing representation at the point at which policymaking occurs matters. (See also Wlezien and Soroka 2003.)

REPRESENTATION AND MARGINALITY: THE ELECTORAL CONNECTION

The United States exhibits a greater degree of policy representation than either the United Kingdom or Canada. This is true in spite of the fact that the U.K.'s unitary structure facilitates comparatively strong public responsiveness. It is a product, we have argued, of a horizontal division of powers that allows the legislature to act as an effective check on the executive, and vice versa.

Electoral incentives also vary over time. There is a considerable literature on the effects of electoral marginality on individual representatives in the United States, for instance. David Mayhew's *The Electoral Connection* is the seminal work here, arguing that members of Congress (MCs) are primarily office-seeking, and that the incentive to represent public preferences is achieved through the possibility of electoral sanction. That MCs are consequently more likely to be responsive to their constituents when they are at greater risk of losing the next election is a long-standing and commonly held expectation (Fiorina 1973; Macrae 1952; Froman 1963; Kuklinski 1977).[8]

The same may be true at the level of governments. That is, governments more likely of losing the next election may be particularly responsive to preferences, and recent work suggests that this is the case (Hobolt and Klemensen 2008). It follows that we may find a relationship between the magnitude of policy representation and marginality, not just across political systems but within countries over time.

Capturing marginality at the government level does present some difficulties, however. Standard measures include the "seat margin" or "vote margin," the percentage of seats or votes by which a government holds a majority. A government that wins 70% of the popular

---

[8] There is disagreement in the literature, however – see especially Fiorina 1974; Groseclose 2001; Gulati 2004.

vote is less at risk than one that wins 52%; a government that holds a legislative majority by 25% of the available seats is less at risk than one that holds a majority by 5% of the seats. That said, seat and vote margins are not equivalent, because the relationship between seats and votes will vary across institutions and over time.[9] It is possible for a government to hold a bare majority in the legislature, but for many of those seats to have been won by a wide margin. In a multiparty systems such as Canada, the share by which a government wins votes or holds seats also does not capture the degree to which the remaining seats or votes are divided amongst the other parties. When two parties regularly divided the "right" vote, for instance, the Liberal Party was less at risk of losing at least a plurality of votes across many constituencies. And in the United States, we need to take into account marginality for both the president and the legislature.

Even so, seat or vote margins present a relatively simple and possibly quite powerful measure of marginality. Is this marginality systematically related to the magnitude of representation? Put more formally, we can assess whether representation is dependent on marginality, as follows,

$$\Delta P_t = \rho + \gamma_1^R R_{t-1} + \gamma_1^M M_{t-1} + \gamma_1^{RM} (R_{t-1} * M_{t-1}) + \gamma_2 G_{t-1} + \mu_t \qquad (7.2)$$

where M, electoral marginality, is interacted with R, relative preferences for policy. If marginality matters, the coefficient γ_1^{RM} would be less than 0, indicating that policymakers are less responsive as the vote margin (M) increases.

Table 7.4 presents results testing this possibility for the combined social domains in each of our three countries. These models are specified exactly as in Table 7.1, except that the direct and interactive effects of marginality are added to each. (Note that we have no *a priori* expectations about the direct effect of marginality.) Marginality is captured using congressional vote margins in the United States – specifically,

---

[9] Indeed, the difference between seats and votes points not just to the need for a decision on measurement, but to the potential importance of electoral disproportionality. The marginality of a given government will be a function of both the margin by which they have won seats (votes), and the disproportionality of the system, which makes more or less likely the probability that a given shift in votes makes a difference in election outcomes.

TABLE 7.4. *Representation and Marginality, Combined Social Domains*

	U.S.	U.K.	CA
Preferences $_{t-1}$	1.764**	.051	.501
Vote Margin $_{t-1}$	−1.951	.001	.189
Vote Margin $_{t-1}$ * Preferences $_{t-1}$	−.158*	.018	.005

Cells contain OLS regression coefficients where * p < .10; ** p < .05. All variables are mean-centered. Full models are listed in Appendix Table 3.

the measure taps the share by which the winning party exceeded 50% of the two-party vote.[10] For the sake of clarity, only the coefficients for preferences and marginality are shown here. (For complete results, see Appendix Table 3.)

In the United States, the interaction between marginality and preferences has the expected effect. As the margin by which the vote share exceeds 50% increases, representation decreases. Indeed, with the inclusion of the interaction the coefficient for the direct effect of preferences is now slightly larger than it was in Table 7.1. This is because the coefficient now reflects the effect of a one-unit shift in net preferences under "perfect" electoral threat, that is, a vote margin of zero. The actual range of the vote margin variable over this period for Congress is .15 to 8.6%. The effect of marginality on representation is not slight, then: a five-point shift in congressional marginality reduces the representation coefficient for the social domains by 45%, from 1.76 to .97. At the maximum vote share (58.6%) observed over the period, responsiveness drops further still, to .40. Extrapolating beyond the data, we would estimate little-to-no representation if the vote share exceeded 61%, a very high number and one that we do not take seriously. We do take seriously the underlying pattern, however.

Models for the United Kingdom and Canada show no such pattern – neither the direct or indirect effects of marginality are

---

[10] We focus on the congressional vote margin here, but also tested a similar model using a presidential vote margin variable. Presidential vote margin had no effect in those preliminary tests, however, and for the sake of parsimony we exclude it from the analyses here. The results are available upon request.

significant and the preferences coefficient not longer is as well. It may be that governments in these countries really are sensitive to marginality but that it is not neatly captured by vote share. It may be, for instance, that governments are more sensitive to current readings of marginality that might be evident in trial-heat polls asking about citizens' likely vote.[11] It also may be that marginality does not adequately capture the effects of disproportionality, which varies considerably across countries and elections too. A 5% victory in one election may be more meaningful for government control in one place and time than in another.

Addressing these possibilities is well beyond the scope of this book. For the time being, we accept that our results may actually capture the effect of the electoral connection, both over time and across countries. Indeed, it might be that electoral pressure matters more in presidential systems, for instance, where constituency opinion plays a strong role.[12] Our findings are consistent with this expectation; whether it is a general pattern remains a subject for additional research.

REPRESENTATION OR MANIPULATION?

There is one nagging concern where representation is concerned: is the representation we observe the consequence of policy following preferences, freely determined, or mere artifice, where politicians mobilize preferences and then apparently act in line with them. This is of course not a new concern. It is apparent in Pitkin's (1967) consideration of representation in authoritarian regimes; it is also central to Habermas's (1962) discussion of manipulated public opinion in an increasingly media-dominated public sphere.

---

[11] These are available on a fairly regular basis in the three countries. The problem is that the polls do not mean the same things at different points in time. That is, polls from early in the election cycle are less informative about a distant election outcome than are those from later in the cycle. Even if we were to translate poll results into Election Day vote predictions, it then would be necessary to translate these predictions into the probability of losing government control. This is not straightforward in the United Kingdom, and it is even more complicated in Canada, where the effective number of parties approaches 4.0 (Johnston 2008). The possibility of government calls for elections, as in Canada as of late, complicates things further. It would make the subject of a good future book, we think.

[12] See, for instance, Cain et al. 1987. Note also that this expectation is consistent with comparative findings on constituency service (Heitshusen et al. 2005).

Most prominent in recent years has been Jacobs and Shapiro's (2000) *Politicians Don't Pander*. These authors argue that, in short, "The conventional wisdom that politicians habitually respond to public opinion when making major policy decisions is wrong" (xii). Rather, politicians increasingly use opinion polls to carefully select the theme, frame, or language that is most likely to engender support for a given proposal, and then set about creating an opinion environment that is conducive to the kind of policy that politicians want to pursue (Chong and Druckman 2007). The means by which this occurs is considerably more nuanced then simply arguing a point until a majority agrees – it involves the careful manipulation of preferences in a way that is imperceptible to the average citizen, but nonetheless has significant consequences for the apparent support for a given policy.

The Jacobs and Shapiro story is engaging. Whether it is true, and regularly so, is another matter, however. That is, it could be true that, while opinion is in some cases open to this kind of influence, the typical relationship is the kind which we have portrayed above. In our case, it is relatively easy to test. If preferences are first manipulated and then responded to, then changes in preferences should be apparent before policy change. In the following regression model, then,

$$\Delta R_t = a + \beta_1 \Delta P_t + \beta_2 \Delta P_{t+1} + \beta_3 W_t + e_t. \tag{7.3}$$

β_2 should be positive, suggesting that changes in relative preferences in the current period (t) are driven by – perversely – changes in the policy in the next period ($t+1$). That is, we should find (captured in β_2) that preferences first shift positively, either instead of or in addition to finding a concurrent thermostatic effect of policy change on preference change (captured in β_1). Of course, we need to take into account other factors, W, as per our analyses in Chapter 5.

Table 7.5 shows results of estimating this model, testing the timing of the relationship between preference change and policy change. Results are shown for defense and for the combined social domains in each country. (Recall that the thermostatic model predicts a negative coefficient in each case, and this is true for the change models just as it is for the models using levels of spending in Chapter 5.) For U.S. defense, for instance, the first cell shows the coefficient for future changes in spending (.173) – the test for manipulation – and the second cell shows the coefficient for concurrent changes in spending (−.322).

TABLE 7.5. *Do Preferences Change Before Policy?*

| | DV: Δ Preferences$_{t-1}$ | | | | | |
| | U.S. | | U.K. | | CA | |
Domain	ΔSp_{t+1}	ΔSp_t	ΔSp_{t+1}	ΔSp	ΔSp_{t+1}	ΔSp_t
Defense	.173	−.322**	1.474	−8.714**	−.183	2.663
Major Social	.072	−.149**	−.528	−1.100**	.061	−.503**

Cells contain OLS coefficients, where * p < .10; ** p < .05. Full models are listed in Appendix Table 3.

Here, and in all other cases, there is no evidence that the current preference change reliably reflects future policy change. None of the coefficients for spending at *t* +1 are signficant. This form of manipulation clearly finds no support here.

These models do not capture all possible forms of manipulation, of course. They capture only the possibility that, in the short term, current preference change consistently reflects prospective policy change. The long-term manipulation of preferences, supported by work on U.S. attitudes towards the Middle East, for instance (e.g., Said 1997), is not captured here. Neither is the possibility that preferences are mobilized in advance of desired policy change only for particular policy decisions, perhaps including very important ones. But – at the very least – we can be confident that our evidence of representation is not an artifact of such short-term manipulation.

RESPONSIVENESS AND REPRESENTATION

Budgetary policy responds to public preferences. Policy change is not just about preferences, of course, and we have seen the effects of party control of government. But preferences clearly do matter, albeit to varying degrees. That is, policy representation varies systematically across domains and countries. It is greatest when there is some kind of public responsiveness, which we have shown to be a function of both issue salience and federalism. Insofar as federalism limits public responsiveness, then, it also limits representation. Other government institutions may have different effects: the "check" or error correction provided by presidentialism may actually increase representation.

Electoral pressure may matter too – representation may be greatest when a lack of responsiveness is more likely to lead to electoral defeat. Indeed, this electoral pressure might be critical to our findings where presidentialism is concerned; in the absence of political competition, presidentialism may not matter much. Put differently, presidentialism may matter most when competition is strong.

Of course, as we have already discussed, we cannot be absolutely sure based on our analysis that policymakers actually respond to changing public preferences. All our models can tell us for sure is that there is policy responsiveness in a statistical sense – the extent to which policy changes follow public preferences, other things being equal. It may be that politicians and the public both respond to something else, for example, the perceived "need" for spending. Both defense spending and preferences for defense spending may react to the actual security threat, for instance. In this case there would be representation insofar as spending followed preferences, but that representation would be rather indirect, even spurious. Testing this possibility is difficult, as we rarely have reliable and comprehensive real-world measures for a policy domain. The existing literature on the use of polls by governments does nonetheless suggest that politicians do respond to public opinion, at least in high-salience domains (see, e.g., Jacobs 1993; Kingdon 1995). This literature is particularly strong where the U.S. president is concerned – see Jacobs and Shapiro 1995; Eisinger 2003; Druckman and Jacobs 2006; Murray 2006; Murray and Howard 2002).[13] Although we cannot entirely rule out the possibility that both the public and policymakers are reacting to something else, there is reason to think that a good deal of what we call representation here is exactly that.

Moreover, although there are differences across domains and contexts, we should not overlook the fact that representation is evident in every policy domain examined here. This surely is good news. There is reason to think it may be too good, perhaps. Paul Burstein has warned that to focus just on the major policy domains means

---

[13] Our own tests using these data also suggest that spending does indeed react to preferences independent of available real-world measures. See, e.g., Soroka and Wlezien 2005; Wlezien 1996a.

that we probably overestimate the proportion of policy domains in which there is representation (2006; see also Page 2002). Put differently: there are a great many smaller policy domains for which no polling data exist, and for which there is unlikely to be much representation at all. Our own results point in this direction – as salience declines, so too does representation. This may come as a disappointment to those looking for strong representation in all domains. But strong representation across all domains is too much to expect. We cannot require that citizens have informed preferences in all domains. Even taking into account issue publics (discussed in Chapter 2), there may not be informed preferences in many smaller policy domains. This is acknowledged in the theoretical literature on representation – in Burke's discussion of the representation of "interests," for instance, and Pitkin's (1967) review of the "mandate-independence" controversy. In some policy areas, politicians may rely on more "global" trends in preferences across domains; they may also simply have a greater degree of independence. Even so, we find evidence of some degree of representation even in domains of rather moderate size and salience – transportation in Canada and the United Kingdom, for instance, or cities in the United States. That representation extends even to these domains is of real importance.

8

Disaggregating Public Responsiveness and Policy Representation

Preceding chapters have demonstrated that policy does represent preferences, and that preferences in turn respond to policy change. We have thus far not examined exactly *who* is responding and being represented, however – we have been concerned almost entirely with the public taken as a whole, the "macro" public. We consequently know relatively little about what is happening beneath the surface. Take public responsiveness to policy: Do all people respond? Or does the tendency vary across groups? Does the pattern vary across issues? These questions are not only interesting in themselves; they are also especially important because of their potential consequences for opinion representation. If only certain segments of the public are paying attention, after all, then there is reason to think that policymakers may only represent the opinions of those segments. Just as for public responsiveness, we know relatively little about heterogeneity in policy representation. Do governments respond to all citizens equally? Or are some groups better represented than others? Does the representation of subgroups vary across domains? Each of these questions is addressed empirically in the current chapter.

ON EQUALITY

"Procedural equality" – where "the political preferences expressed by each citizen receive equal weight in the decision-making process" (Beitz 1990) – is a central tenet of democratic theory. Indeed, considerations of equality and democracy have been critically intertwined at least since Rousseau's treatises on government, in large part because while most versions of democracy require a certain degree of equality, exactly how much and what kind of equality is open to debate.

The issue most pertinent to our current objective relates to the difference between "formal" and "substantive" political equality (Brighouse 2002) – in Rawlsian terms, the difference between "basic liberties" and their "worth," that is, the difference between simply having equal liberties and actually having equal means to make use of them (Rawls 1993). Formally speaking, citizens in most modern democracies are for the most part political equals, at least in the most fundamental way: everyone's vote is equal (taking into account the vagaries involved in the aggregation of votes within and across constituencies).[1] Substantively speaking, however, there are many reasons to expect a good degree of inequality, beginning with the fact that not everyone votes.

It is through this lens that an increasing number of scholars has begun to question the degree of homogeneity in opinion-policy relationships – essentially, the degree of equality in modern democracies. The reaction has been particularly strong in the United States. Indeed, concerns about rising inequality led to the American Political Science Association's 2003–5 Task Force on Inequality in American Democracy, and a resulting body of work chronicling the growing economic and political distance between the wealthy and the rest of the American citizenry (e.g., Jacobs and Skocpol 2005; Bartels 2008). Similar concerns have been evident in work by Robert Dahl. His seminal 1961 work, *On Democracy*, suggested a rather widespread, pluralistic distribution of power in 1950s New Haven, Connecticut; in 2006, *On Political Equality* revealed real concerns about increasing inequalities in American politics.

What do growing concerns about inequality suggest about the preceding exploration of opinion-policy relationships? In short, they suggest that we are missing part of the story. In preceding chapters, we have regarded public opinion as a simple summary of the opinions

---

[1] This is in a certain sense circular: most modern democracies exhibit procedural equality because procedural equality is one of the defining features of democracy. See, e.g., Dahl 1998.

of all citizens within the unit – country, state, or locality – of interest. We have ascribed roughly equal weight to each individual, essentially invoking formal equality.[2] In so doing, we have ignored three related possibilities: (1) certain characteristics, demographic or otherwise, may predispose citizens toward being at one or the other end of the range of preferences, (2) opinion-policy links may be stronger for some groups than for others, and (3) because of 1 and 2, policy may be more representative of the (different) preferences of certain groups.

The first possibility, that levels of policy support vary across certain characteristics, requires little argument. There is a huge volume of work demonstrating such differences – that wealthier citizens are less supportive of redistributive policies, for instance (see Erikson and Tedin 2004). People will have differing levels of support for policy in various domains for any number of reasons, well beyond what would seem to be obvious self interest. These differences, while important, in many cases have little consequence for our examination, however. That is, consistently differing levels of support across groups matter not at all to the longitudinal relationship between preferences and policy. As long as the preferences of different groups move in parallel over time, public responsiveness and policy representation will be indistinguishable for any number of groups. Just as one group's preferences are increasing (or decreasing), so too are the others. (Of course, differences in levels of support across groups may matter a good deal for levels of policy, but this is a different subject and one that we at least begin to consider in the concluding section of this chapter and also in the concluding chapter.)

The story is somewhat different if public support does not move in perfect synchronization across different groups – that is, if there are not parallel publics. In this case, the second and third possibilities become relevant: the magnitude of citizens' responsiveness to policy can vary across groups, as can policy representation. Indeed, the two are expected to be intertwined. We have already suggested that the opinion-policy relationship may be driven at least in part by differences

---

[2] Do recall that it is difficult to perfectly summarize most distributions of preferences, as even the mean or median of a distribution will produce substantial inequality in representation, i.e., the positions of those to the left and right will not be represented in policy.

in the responsiveness of different groups. Politicians, we have argued, are likely to pay more attention to the opinions of those who are paying attention to them. Inequality in representation is thus to be expected, at least to the extent that different groups' attentiveness differs.

Differences in citizen attentiveness need not be detrimental to democratic responsiveness. That is, highly attentive citizens can provide the incentive for policymakers to represent public preferences. They also can provide effective cues for less attentive citizens. (Recall the discussion in Chapter 2; also see the discussion in the next section.) Differences in information and attentiveness may lead to inequalities in representation, however, and produce a persistent power differential between groups – broadly speaking, a difference between those with knowledge and influence, and those without. This has been a central concern in the recent U.S. literature.

GROUP DIFFERENCES IN THE LITERATURE

The seminal work on heterogeneity in public opinion is a 1964 study by Converse arguing that while some people have well-developed preferences and are attentive to, and therefore informed about, politics, most people fall far short of this ideal. When making political judgments, most citizens rely instead on more primitive cues, such as party and social group identifications, or else short-term forces such as economic performance. Various other scholars have confirmed these large differences in political knowledge. (See Delli Carpini and Keeter's (1996) extensive study.) These differences also constitute the starting point for much of the work on deliberative democracy. (See, e.g., Fishkin 1991, 1995; Gastil 2000).

Recent work argues that voters can rely on cues or heuristics to over-come their limited information (Lupia 1994; Lupia and McCubbins 1998; Popkin 1991; Sniderman et al. 1991; Lau and Redlawsk 2006; Gabel and Scheve 2007). In this way, and without knowing much about policy activities, the argument goes, most voters can hold politicians accountable. The research on cue-taking clearly is encouraging, as there is evidence that it works, at least to some degree. There also is a body of evidence – from statistical simulations (Bartels 1996; Althaus 1998, 2003; Fournier 2005) and quasi-experimental studies (Luskin et al. 2002; Kuklinski et al. 2000) – suggesting that the benefits of cues are limited. This work shows that, although they help the less sophisticated mimic the more sophisticated, cues and heuristics do not fully bridge the gap in information. Other recent research (Lau and Redlawsk 2006) demonstrates more powerful effects. Regardless, most of this work does not address questions of policy, especially responsiveness to policy change. Can the less attentive citizens mimic the more attentive ones? Does cue-taking function equally well across all policy domains?

Research indicates that there may be more similarity than difference. Of particular note is Page and Shapiro's classic book, *The Rational Public* (1992), in which they document a striking pattern of opinion change over time. Page and Shapiro show that opinion change on a wide range of issues is effectively parallel across various subcategories of the American public. In effect, despite differences in the levels of preferences, people move together over time in the same liberal or conservative direction. (Also see Stimson 1989; Ferejohn and Kuklinski 1990; Sniderman, Brody, and Tetlock 1991; Lupia 1994; Soroka and Wlezien 2008; Enns and Kellstedt 2008; Ura and Ellis 2008.) These results suggest that people generally react to new information in the same way. But, do people respond similarly to all new information? In particular, are people equally responsive to policy, or are some, for example, the highly sophisticated, more responsive to policy than others?

A related question is whether highly sophisticated people are also better represented than less sophisticated people. Inequalities in representation are certainly of increasing salience at present, though most research is focused less on sophistication and more on another dimension across which preferences may vary: income. Bartels (2005, 2008) relates average scores on the National Election Study (NES) ideology question, as well as a number of policy-specific questions, by income tercile, to U.S. senators' roll-call votes. In doing so, he finds that senators' roll-call voting records are better accounted for by variation in the ideological and policy preferences of upper-income citizens (across states) than by the ideological or policy preferences of middle- or lower-income citizens. Gilens (2004, 2005) examines the association between levels of public support for policy change – imputed for different income categories – and (binary) policy change (or stasis) within the following four years. His results are similar to

Bartels's policy change is better explained by higher-income citizens' support for policy change than by support among lower-income citizens.

Jacobs and Page (2005) explore a different though related theme. They do not look specifically at the effects of public preferences across income categories, but examine the varying associations between U.S. foreign policy officials and those of business leaders, experts, labor leaders, or the general public. More so than others, however, they directly examine opinion change, and find that one-period change in policy support found amongst U.S. foreign policy officials most closely matches one-period change in the preferences of business leaders and experts. This provides further – albeit indirect – evidence of a representational bias toward upper-income citizens.

Each of these works provides evidence that policy in the United States is related principally to the preferences of the wealthiest citizens. Each suggests that U.S. politics is characterized by a high level of inequality. To what extent is this true? In particular, to what extent does it affect the dynamics of representation we have observed here? We explore the possibility of heterogeneity in policy representation in the following sections. Given our interest in the thermostatic model, and in particular our assertion that policy representation is limited or enhanced by public responsiveness, we begin by examining heterogeneity in public responsiveness to policy.

PARALLEL PUBLICS?

To what extent do preferences differ across groups at particular points in time? More importantly for our purposes, to what extent do the preferences of groups differ *over* time? We address these questions here using the same measure of net preferences used in previous chapters, but calculated separately for sub-aggregates of education, income, and party identification. For education, survey response categories vary across countries, but we nevertheless are able to classify all respondents using three comparable categories: (1) did not finish high school, (2) did finish high school, and (3) had some education beyond high school. This threefold scheme divides survey samples into three relatively equal groups, although the sizes of the groups do change over time in predictable ways; that is, in each country, the percentage of people not finishing high school declines as the percentage of people with some college experience increases.

For income, we begin with preferences aggregated by the income response categories in the individual-level survey files, and then collapse these into terciles based on the distribution in the survey file – the General Social Survey (GSS) in the United States or the Environics polls in Canada. (For the United Kingdom, we do not have a measure of income and so rely on a standard measure of social class, discussed later.) When survey response categories overlap the divide between two income terciles, respondents in this category are sorted into the terciles proportionally, based on where the tercile division lies in the response category. Note that using terciles from the GSS survey files has the advantage of keeping the three categories equal in size – that is, the number of respondents in each category is the same, and no one category is more (or less) susceptible to measurement error.[3] (The total sample size is just over 1,100, on average, but approximately 5 percent of respondents do not answer the income question, leaving an average N of about 1050, or 350 in each income category.) As noted, income data are not available in the United Kingdom, but Gallup surveys there do include measures of one standard British class variable, where respondents are separated into "manual" and "nonmanual" categories. We use these two categories – essentially blue collar and white collar – as coarse proxies for income in the United Kingdom. In fact, this variable may capture much more than differences in income.

For party identification (PID), in the United States we rely on the standard 7-point scale, and net support is calculated separately for Democrats, Republicans, and Independents, where Independents include both those identifying themselves as independent, and those who only "lean" toward one of the parties. PID questions are not regularly part of commercial omnibus surveys in either Canada or the United Kingdom, but vote intention questions are always included. We thus use these items to separate respondents into three partisan groups in each

[3] Given that the income distribution reported in GSS is always somewhat lower than what we see in Census data, we also calculated using terciles from the U.S. Bureau of the Census. This makes virtually no difference to any of the results – specifically, using the Census distribution slightly expands the range of differences.

of these countries: in the United Kingdom, Labour, Liberal Democrat, and Conservative; in Canada, the New Democrats (NDP), Liberals, and Conservatives, where Conservatives include Progressive Conservatives, as well as – from 1992 – Reform and then Canadian Alliance voters.[4]

The resulting data are illustrated in Figures 8.1 to 8.3. Each figure shows defense spending preferences, welfare preferences (for the United States and Canada), and combined health and education preferences. The latter domains are combined for expository purposes, as the patterns are very similar; we keep welfare separate because there are some important differences in this domain, as we shall see. Because there are quite different levels in preferences across domains, the y-axes necessarily cover different values – from –60 to +60 for U.S. defense, for instance, and from –20 to +100 for U.S. health. The range in every case is 120 points, however, so the apparent magnitude of difference (or similarity) is directly comparable across figures. Finally, note that the U.K. data shown in Figure 8.3 are rather spotty. The original U.K. opinion series are drawn from published reports. In order to break series into sub-aggregates, we need to use the individual-level files, only seven of which are publicly available (through the Roper archive). We include the resulting data in these figures, then, but exclude the United Kingdom from multivariate analyses – there are just too few cases.

Results across the three countries are quite similar. There are differences in levels of support across groups in some cases, but preferences often are indistinguishable. Even when there are differences in levels, there is a good degree of parallelism over time. Take the first panel of Figure 8.1, which displays U.S. defense spending preferences by level of education. The low-education group is consistently more supportive of defense spending than the high-education group, and the average difference between the two over the period is quite large (28 points). The relationship over time is very strong, as is clear in

---

[4] In Canada, Quebec voters are included in the sample but for the sake of parsimony in graphs and analyses we do not track Bloc Quebecois votes. Results for this party do not change the story presented here, however. Note also that partisan groups in the United States are roughly equal in size, but that the same is not true for the United Kingdom and Canada. In those countries, Liberal Democrat and NDP identifiers are always considerably smaller. There is as a consequence a greater margin of error in these data series, which we should take into account when interpreting results.

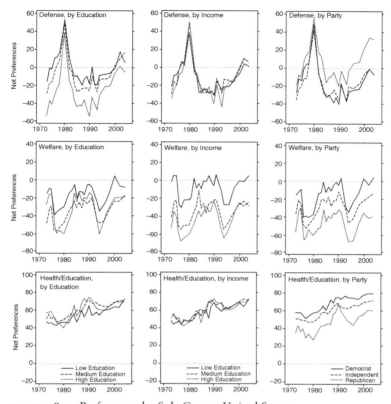

FIGURE 8.1. Preferences by Sub-Group, United States

the figure. We can also provide a more formal measure of over-time parallelism across the three series using Cronbach's alpha. Alpha summarizes bivariate correlations between more than two series; it ranges from 0 to 1, and it gives us a sense for how closely each set of three series moves together over time, that is, of the degree to which the differences or similarities across groups are reliable.[5] In this case, the alpha measure for all three education groups is a rather high .96. Clearly, these preferences move in parallel over time. The same is found to be true when looking at defense preferences by income and party identification in the second and third columns. Across income

---

[5] Note, however, that alphas can be taken to overstate the parallelism between series. For instance, an average bivariate correlation of .5 produces an alpha of .75.

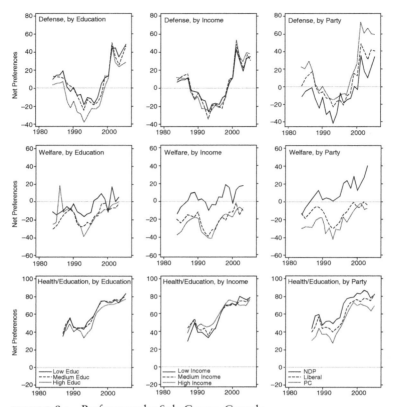

FIGURE 8.2. Preferences by Sub-Group, Canada

levels, there are very few differences in either levels or changes over time. For partisan groups there are greater differences in levels, that is, polarization, between Democrats and Republicans after the mid-1980s, and especially from 2002, but again there also is a good degree of parallelism.

Welfare preferences by income level (in the center panel of Figure 8.1) exhibit by far the greatest cross-sectional difference – and that income groups show a large difference is unique to this domain. Indeed, the difference in means for the nonwelfare domains (including those not pictured here) is less than four points on average and only three points when comparing people with high and low incomes. None of these differences is even close to statistically significant. In contrast, for welfare the means differ by more than 30 points, five times what we observed

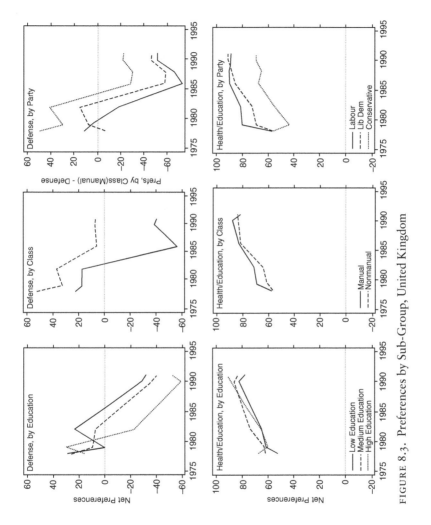

FIGURE 8.3. Preferences by Sub-Group, United Kingdom

155

for the other seven domains on average. Notice also that the differences in welfare preferences across income levels are not symmetrical: the mean preference for people with middling incomes is much more like the mean for people with upper incomes than that for people with lower incomes. This asymmetry may have important implications: to the extent that policymakers represent the median preference, policy will better represent the preferences of the rich than the poor. (We will return to this issue below.)

Trends in the Canadian data (Figure 8.2) largely mirror those in the United States. Income does not show especially great differences in levels in defense or health and education, but clearly shows a large difference for welfare. Again, middle- and high-income preferences for welfare are very close, indeed almost indistinguishable, and consistently more than 20 points away from low-income preferences. As in the United States, the high-education group consistently shows more over-time variance than the other education groups. The tendency seems to contrast with what we might expect based on Converse (1964) and Zaller (1992), who imply greater stability in attitudes for the more sophisticated. For relative preferences, however, we expect more change among the highly educated, reflecting a greater degree of updating, that is, of thermostatic responsiveness, among the former. But again, there is considerable parallelism even across education groups. Across the three domains and three sets of groups shown in Figure 8.2, the average alpha score is .96.

Data from the United Kingdom present a much choppier picture, although, to the extent that we can make comparisons, the results are not very different. That is, there is considerable parallelism. The notable difference in levels between manual and nonmanual workers on defense post-1985 reflects, we suspect, the fact that "class" captures more than simply income. Given the paucity of data in the United Kingdom, however, we cannot (and do not) make too much of this particular finding.

What do these data suggest regarding heterogeneity in responsiveness and representation? On the one hand, they suggest that heterogeneity in public responsiveness and policy representation is likely to be relatively limited. Differences in responsiveness and representation are dependent, after all, on differences in preferences, and Figures 8.1 to 8.3 suggest that these differences are in many cases rather small.

Across all domains and all three types of groups there is also considerable parallelism. This comports with Page and Shapiro's (1992) examination of various issues and sub-groupings. There is, as a consequence, little scope for difference in the dynamic relationship between policy and the preferences of one group or another.

Nevertheless, there is in some domains a degree of difference across groups that we do not wish to ignore. Given the recent U.S. literature, differences in welfare preferences across income levels are of particular interest. And where public responsiveness is concerned, that the highly educated consistently shows more over-time variance than others is intriguing, and is also in line with the expectation that this group may be especially attentive to policy change.

GROUPS AND PUBLIC RESPONSIVENESS

Having determined the extent to which the structure of preferences differs across groups, we now examine in more detail whether the opinion-policy relationship differs. We do so by first modeling relative preferences for three sub-aggregates (R^A, R^B and R^C) as follows:

$$R^A_t = P^{*A}_t + \pi_A P_t + \varepsilon_1$$
$$R^B_t = P^{*B}_t + \pi_B P_t + \varepsilon_2$$
$$R^C_t = P^{*C}_t + \pi_C P_t + \varepsilon_3, \qquad\qquad (8.1)$$

where the preferred levels of preferences (and residual variances) are allowed to vary across groups. Note that this is a simple extension of the model of public responsiveness set out in Chapter 2. In this case, we simply identify R for three separate sub-aggregates (low-, middle-, and high-education, for instance), and model each separately. We are most interested in the parameter of responsiveness to policy, π. If different groups respond in the same way, the parameter will be indistinguishable across the equations. (That is, $\pi_A = \pi_B = \pi_{C}$.) If groups respond differently, these parameters will differ. Preceding figures suggest, for instance, that a parameter for high education citizens might be larger than one for low- and middle-education citizens, reflecting a greater degree of responsiveness amongst the more sophisticated.

Results for these estimations are shown in Tables 8.1 and 8.2. We do not produce results for the United Kingdom because of a lack of data, as noted above. For both the United States and Canada, we show

TABLE 8.1. *Public Responsiveness, by Sub-Group, United States*

Education	Low	Middle	High
Defense	−.230**	−.250**	−.308**
Welfare	−.674**	−.562**	−.718**
Health & Education	−.105*	−.097**	−.201**
Income	*Low*	*Middle*	*High*
Defense	−.234**	−.270**	−.287**
Welfare	−.696**	−.707**	−.710**
Health & Education	−.143**	−.132**	−.154**
Party	*Dem*	*Ind*	*Rep*
Defense	−.289**	−.237**	−.277**
Welfare	−.599**	−.513**	−.915**
Health & Education	−.038*	−.094**	−.204**

Cells contain OLS coefficients, where * $p < .10$; ** $p < .05$. Full models are listed in Appendix Table 2.

results for defense, welfare, and health and education combined.[6] As in previous chapters, only the feedback coefficients are shown in these tables, with full models included in Appendix Table 3. Because we are interested in comparing across groups within domains, we do not need to use standardized coefficients – spending is the same across all models in each single domain.

Table 8.1 displays results for the different education, income and PID sub-groups in the United States. What is most noteworthy from this table is that every one of the spending coefficients is negative and significantly different from zero. The public responsiveness found earlier clearly does not merely reflect the behavior of peculiarly attentive issue publics; rather, it holds across education and income levels and party identification. This is an important finding, for it indicates that people with very different backgrounds and circumstances respond in much the same way to changes in policy, on average. Each group receives (and processes) basic information about the direction and magnitude of policy change.

[6] Results differ only slightly when the health and education domains are examined independently – see Wlezien and Soroka n.d.

Although there is considerable homogeneity in people's responses to policy, there are differences as well. Consider the first row of Table 8.1, which shows defense coefficients for the three education groups, from low education in column 1 to high education in column 3. Here we can see that the magnitude of responsiveness increases slightly as we move from low to middle to high. The pattern is similar in the social domains – again, the high-education group is most responsive to policy change. There are some differences in the dynamics of preferences across education groups, then; this said, all differences are rather slight and all but one – between low- and high-education groups for health and education – are not statistically different in magnitude. This should come as no surprise, given how closely the series track together.[7]

A similar pattern is evident across income levels in the United States. In each domain, the coefficient is (marginally) larger for the high-income group, with the greatest difference being in defense. The extent to which this pattern parallels that for education suggests a possibly common source, for example, that education actually drives the differences across income groups.[8] But in no case is the difference statistically significant. The over-time flow of preferences across both income and education sub-groups in the United States is thus much more similar than it is different. All groups respond fairly equally to policy change, and they seemingly react in like fashion to other events.

The pattern across partisan groups looks rather different. Democrats appear marginally more responsive to defense policy, although the difference here is not statistically significant. There is a significant difference for both welfare and combined health and education spending,

---

[7] Testing whether feedback coefficients are statistically different is a bit complicated, given that each coefficient is generated from a separate regression model (as in equation 8.1). It is possible to test directly whether coefficients are different by estimating a single time-series cross-sectional panel, where there is a separate panel for each of the three groups, and where interactions allow each coefficient to take on a different value within each panel. This single model produces the same coefficients as the separate models presented here, and facilitates testing the equality of feedback coefficients directly. Discussions of significant differences in this section rely on this procedure.

[8] If so, then there is little difference owing to income *per se*, though the difference still may be important, particularly if policymakers are more responsive to those with higher incomes. Of course, it may be that there is something about income above and beyond education levels, and this would imply more direct consequences for the representational connection.

TABLE 8.2. *Public Responsiveness, by Sub-Group, Canada*

Education	Low	Middle	High
Defense	−4.539**	−3.851	−4.863*
Welfare	−.799**	−1.337**	−1.197**
Health & Education	−.944**	−.920**	−.808**

Income	Low	Middle	High
Defense	−4.069*	−4.566	−4.583
Welfare	−.994**	−1.545**	−1.572**
Health & Education	−.976**	−.882**	−.780**

Party	NDP	Lib	Con
Defense	−4.108	−4.405	−5.731*
Welfare	−.815**	−1.105**	−1.468**
Health & Education	−.979**	−.849**	−.984**

Cells contain OLS coefficients, where * p < .10; ** p < .05. Full models are listed in Appendix Table 2.

however, and in these cases Republicans are most responsive. The results are somewhat counterintuitive, in that they suggest that partisans are most attentive to what politicians do for "other partisans," that is, assuming that defense spending is more salient to Republicans and social spending more salient to Democrats.

Canadian results in Table 8.2 reveal an only slightly different picture. As we saw in Chapter 5, there is relatively little public responsiveness to defense spending in Canada. This holds across the various sub-aggregates – although there is weak evidence of responsiveness for some groups, most are not significant and the coefficients are not very different, substantively or statistically. The one notable exception is for party affiliation: Conservatives appear to be (slightly) more responsive to defense policy change.

Where Canadian social policy is concerned, there is clearly greater responsiveness to welfare spending among the highly educated. There appears to be an opposite effect for combined health and education spending, where the low-educated seem more responsive, but it is not statistically significant. We detect a similar pattern across income levels: significantly greater responsiveness to welfare for the high-income group, and a hint of greater responsiveness from low-income respondents in the combined health and education domains. Where party is concerned there are few significant differences. Note that the greater responsiveness from Conservatives in the welfare domain is similar to our U.S. results, suggesting that partisan groups may be most responsive to what politicians do for "other partisans." It does not fit well with results for defense, however, where Conservatives are also most responsive.

Overall, the story in Tables 8.1 and 8.2 is predominantly one of similarity, with some small but interesting differences in some domains. Most important is the pervasive evidence of feedback in by-group results; which by and large reflects results found in previous chapters. In most cases, there are no significant differences from one group to another. Even where differences are apparent, they are rather small. The main finding, therefore, is parallelism across a wide range of socio-economic circumstances and political orientations. There is essentially a uniform swing of opinion in response to spending changes.

GROUPS AND POLICY REPRESENTATION

Is there heterogeneity in representation? The foregoing analysis suggests that there is not much difference in the representation of groups, as there is little difference over time in the preferences of to begin with. Even if policymakers represent one group more than another, the resulting pattern of policy change would be pretty much as we would predict using the preferences of other groups. Still, there are slight differences that might provide the basis for differential representation.

The following analyses come closest to mimicking work by Gilens (2004, 2005) and Bartels (2005) – they estimate directly the degree to which policy reflects the preferences of one group or another. The most direct way to assess the focus of representation is to include preferences of different groups in the basic representation equation from Chapter 7:

$$\Delta P_t = \rho + \gamma_{1A} R^A_{t-1} + \gamma_B R^B_{t-1} + \gamma_{1C} R^C_{t-1} + \gamma_2 G_{t-1} + \mu_t \qquad (8.2)$$

where R^A_{t-1}, R^B_{t-1}, and R^C_{t-1} are preferences for the different groups A, B, and C. Applying this approach here is complicated by very high multicolinearity resulting from the substantial parallelism in preferences that we have demonstrated across groups in all domains. (For instance, the mean bivariate correlation between welfare preferences for the three education

TABLE 8.3. *Policy Representation, by Sub-Group, United States*

Education	Low	Middle	High
Defense	.820**	.719**	.682**
Welfare	.364**	.303**	.185*
Health & Education	.960**	.818**	.646**
Income	*Low*	*Middle*	*High*
Defense	.824**	.749**	.662**
Welfare	.293**	.343**	.237*
Health & Education	.841**	.756**	.661**
Party	*Dem*	*Ind*	*Rep*
Defense	.685**	.742**	.746**
Welfare	.285**	.318**	.227*
Health & Education	.722**	.937**	.646**

Cells contain OLS coefficients, where * p < .10; ** p < .05. Full models are listed in Appendix Table 3.

groups is .887.) To assess differential responsiveness, therefore, we separately model the effect of each group's preferences, as follows:

$$\Delta P_t = \rho_A + \gamma_{1A} R^A_{t-1} + \gamma_{2A} G_{t-1} + \mu_{tA}$$
$$\Delta P_t = \rho_B + \gamma_{1B} R^B_{t-1} + \gamma_{2B} G_{t-1} + \mu_{tB}$$
$$\Delta P_t = \rho_C + \gamma_{1C} R^C_{t-1} + \gamma_{2C} G_{t-1} + \mu_{tC} \qquad (8.3)$$

where policy change is now modeled as a function of the relative preferences for the three different groups. Here we want to see whether the effect of preferences differs or is the same ($\gamma_{1A} = \gamma_{1B} = \gamma_{1C}$) – to put it more substantively, whether policy responds more to the preferences of some groups than others.

Results for the United States and Canada are summarized in Tables 8.3 and 8.4, respectively. As for the analysis of public responsiveness, we show only the representation coefficients, with full results in Appendix Table 3. The results generally are quite similar to what we observed for public responsiveness: every one of the opinion coefficients in Table 8.3 is positive and statistically significant. As suspected given the analysis of preferences, policy moves with the highly parallel flow of opinion across various groups. Budgetary policy change clearly

TABLE 8.4. *Policy Representation, by Sub-Group, Canada*

Education	Low	Middle	High
Defense	.014**	.010	.009*
Welfare	.096	.293**	.276**
Health & Education	.207**	.211**	.164**

Income	Low	Middle	High
Defense	.013*	.010*	.009
Welfare	.059	.255**	.232**
Health & Education	.139**	.172*	.223**

Party	NDP	Lib	Con
Defense	.010	.012*	.009*
Welfare	.090	.373**	.203**
Health & Education	.157*	.150*	.156**

Cells contain OLS coefficients, where * p < .10; ** p < .05. Full models are listed in Appendix Table 3.

does not only reflect the preferences of a particular group or set of groups.

Comparing the raw coefficients across groups is complicated by the fact that the variance in preferences is in some cases quite different from one group to another. Indeed, the variance in preferences is systematically (though usually not significantly) greater for the higher-education or higher-income groups – a consequence of their slightly greater responsiveness to spending, which we observed in Tables 8.1 and 8.2. This can be viewed in two ways: high-education and high-income groups are more responsive to a given change in spending, or each unit of preference has less monetary value for those groups.[9]

The different variances in the preferences series matter to our interpretation of the representation coefficients here. Take, for instance, the U.S. results for defense representation across education levels, in the first row of Table 8.3. The variance in defense preferences for the high-education group is roughly 21.4 points; for the low-education group,

[9] Note that the former provides an incentive for greater spending responsiveness to a unit of net support, whereas the latter provides an incentive for less.

roughly 16.9. If governments respond to the preferences of different groups proportionally – that is, taking into account the greater or lesser responsiveness of different groups – then we should expect the coefficient to be somewhat smaller for the higher-variance group. Looking across education groups, this is indeed evident for defense as well as the various social programs.

We can of course consider results taking into account the variance in preferences, by adopting the standardized measure of representation used in Chapter 7: a one-standard-deviation shift in preferences as a proportion of the average level of spending over the period.[10] Considering education groups, for instance, the standardized coefficients for defense are, from low to high, 4.5, 4.3, and 4.7. The apparent difference in raw coefficients, taking into account the variance in preferences, is not so great. That said, real differences in welfare and combined health and education remain: although the difference across groups is somewhat smaller using standardized measures, representation still appears somewhat greater for the low-education group.[11] In contrast, there are only very small differences across income levels, and – notably – no evidence of overrepresentation of high-income preferences.

Looking across partisan groups, the only notable difference is in welfare, where Democrats are better represented than Republicans but Independents have the greatest impact. This finding may be surprising, given that it was Republicans that seemed most responsive in this domain (see Table 8.1). The patterns of representation thus do not reinforce differences in public responsiveness across partisan groups; if anything, they are countervailing. Where responsiveness is strongest, representation is comparatively weak. As a result, net representation of partisan groups may be essentially the same (also see Wlezien and Soroka n.d.).

Canadian results suggest somewhat more difference. Again, there is rather weak representation in the defense domain, and no significant differences across groups. There are consistent differences in

---

[10] Taking into account the standard deviation makes a real difference here, but dividing by the average level of spending in this case matters little, as the denominator is the same for all models in each domain. We use the measure for the sake of consistency with Chapter 7 results.

[11] Standardized coefficients for welfare, from low to high education are 4.1, 3.6, and 3.0; for health and education, 5.9, 5.2, and 4.8.

welfare, however: namely, greater representation for middle- and high education and income groups. Using standardized measures (as in Chapter 7) actually augments the differences between the different categories of both income and education.[12] To be sure, there are in many cases only small differences in the magnitude of representation across groups. But where differences do exist – in welfare – both responsiveness and representation are lowest for the low-education and low-income groupings. Despite a high level of similarity in preferences over time, then, there are some differences, and these appear to matter for spending policy itself.

THE HOMOGENEITY OF OPINION-POLICY DYNAMICS

Our analyses reveal a striking amount of homogeneity in opinion-policy dynamics. Where previous chapters demonstrated clear and strong evidence of responsiveness in the aggregate, results in this chapter show that the relationship holds across various sub-aggregates. Indeed, in most domains people with less than a high school education, on average, respond as much as do those with a college education. The preceding aggregate results do not mask heightened responsiveness by one especially attentive group or set of groups.

The same is true for representation. Where preceding chapters found strong representation of public preferences in policy, we find it here as well, and to roughly the same degree across groups. In most cases, representation is neither markedly better nor markedly worse when we look solely at certain groups. Based on our analyses, the dynamics of democracy are not the preserve of the attentive few or of a well-heeled elite.

That said, there are a few significant differences in the representation of groups. Interestingly, it is the welfare domain in Canada that exhibits the dynamic closest to the one that has concerned U.S. scholars: greater representation of higher-income (and higher-education) groups. There is in contrast little evidence here that U.S. welfare spending follows high-income or education preferences to

---

[12] For instance, standardized coefficients for welfare, from low to high education levels, are 1.5, 4.3, and 4.8; for low to high income levels, 0.8, 4.3, and 4.0.

the disadvantage of low-income or education respondents.[13] Even in Canada the differences in welfare representation are between low-income preferences and the rest; that is, the representation of those with middle and high incomes is indistinguishable. This is of obvious importance, for it reveals that, even where representation differs across groups, the average person is effectively represented. It is about all we can expect even where there is perfect political equality and everyone is given equal weight – just because each person counts equally does not mean that each person's policy position wins (also see Wlezien and Soroka n.d.).

Differences in responsiveness thus matter most when preferences differ. And the preferences of groups do differ, as we have seen, especially for welfare spending. Recall the pattern across income levels in Canada in Figure 8.2. There we saw a sizable gap between low-income people on the one hand and middle- and high-income people on the other. (In Figure 8.1 we saw virtually the same pattern in the United States, though the preferences of middle- and high-income people are less similar.) These differences in preferences matter. In representing middle- or high-income preferences, for example, politicians would provide less welfare spending than we would get were low-income citizens driving policy.[14] This is important, though notice that this is exclusive to the welfare spending domain. In the other spending domains, as we saw in the figures, substituting the preferences of one income group for another makes virtually no

---

[13] Given the existing literature, one might well ask why do our data show such small differences in policy preferences across income terciles. There are several possibilities, including: (a) preferences tend to be more clearly different in policy domains where self-interest is paramount, (b) income terciles may actually be quite limited in their ability to reflect self-interest, (c) terciles may not be the relevant groupings, and stronger differences may emerge when we look at the top and bottom 10% of income earners, for instance. These and other differences are discussed in more detail in Soroka and Wlezien (2008).

[14] Simulating the effect of representing low- or middle- versus high-income preferences in the United States implies a considerably greater increase in spending over the long term. Indeed, assuming that policymakers represent high-income preferences and then substituting in middle-income preferences implies an 18% net increase in spending over the period examined here. (This is based on an approach which estimates how much spending is necessary to drive preferences down to the level we observe for high-income respondents. The estimate actually is a liberal one, as it presumes that the preference equilibrium would remain unchanged, i.e., not increase.)

difference.[15] There are other aspects of inequality as well. Education has been one focus here, and in this case we see much bigger gaps.[16] We might also consider inequality in representation across other sub-aggregates, including race, ethnicity, and gender. Griffin and Newman (2005) find that voters are better represented than nonvoters, and this may underpin any differential representation that we observe across groups. Partisanship may also matter. If representatives focus on co-partisans – those citizens most likely to re-elect them (see Fenno 1978; also Hill and Hurley 2003) – partisan groups should receive unequal representation, albeit varying over time with the party control of government. This time-varying inequality in representation may matter quite a lot given the large differences in preferences by party identification surveyed above.[17] All of this said, based on our analyses, there is no escaping the conclusion that public responsiveness and policy representation are strikingly similar across a set of politically important groups – income, education, and party. There simply is a limited basis in our set of spending domains for unequal representation over time.

[15] Even for welfare spending, where preferences do differ, there really is little escaping unequal representation. As we noted above, politicians have to pick some policy position and there is no reason to expect them to represent those with low income instead of the middle, who have electoral power, or the rich, who have money and are politically active.

[16] A more direct measure of political sophistication might produce even larger gaps, though we cannot tell given the limited data that are available over time.

[17] It would also help explain striking shifts in policy when the partisan control of government changes.

9

Degrees of Democracy

Preceding chapters have examined in some detail the nature and scope of public responsiveness and policy representation in the United States, the United Kingdom, and Canada. There is nonetheless much more to do. We do not attempt to cover all the remaining bases here, though we do want to highlight the critical findings and their implications, and point to some possibilities for future research. We begin by revisiting our analyses of public responsiveness and policy representation. We then consider the facilitating (or debilitating) effects of political institutions, what the results tell us about "system efficiency" and, finally, the broader implications of our findings for the study of representative democracy.

ON RESPONSIVENESS AND REPRESENTATION

Is thermostatic public responsiveness too good to be true? There is a considerable body of work detailing the extent of what individuals *do not* know about politics and policy. It may consequently be rather surprising for some that a considerable portion of American, British, and Canadian publics are able to adjust their preferences for policy change based on policy itself. Nevertheless, we have in Chapters 1 and 2 made the case that thermostatic responsiveness requires relatively little of the public, for at least the following reasons:

- The policy decisions citizens are required to make are typically much simplified. Indeed, the thermostatic model only requires that people can tell whether policy has gone "too far" in one direction or else "not far enough," given their preferences.

- Not *all* citizens need respond *all* the time. Attentiveness can and does vary across individuals, and all that is required for effective public responsiveness is that some (not insubstantial) segment of the public actually notices policy change.
- Thermostatic responsiveness need not be evident in *all* policy domains. We expect responsiveness only in domains of some public importance – that is, we do not (and should not) expect citizens to respond in domains about which they care relatively little.[1]

We thus see thermostatic public responsiveness as a quite reasonable expectation in some domains, and previous chapters have found strong evidence of this. When policy increases (decreases), preferences for more policy decrease (increase), other things being equal. And while allowing for the possibility of positive feedback, our analyses clearly indicate that negative feedback overwhelms positive feedback over the long term. This does not preclude the possibility that for certain periods more policy on one issue may actually lead to more, rather than less, demand. Indeed, this is precisely what we would expect from Baumgartner and Jones's (2002) recent work suggesting that, although negative-feedback-driven policymaking may dominate over the long run, it can be interrupted by rapid policy change and positive feedback over the short run (in the form of, e.g., "bandwagon effects" or "cascades"). Apart from these circumstances, however, negative feedback is expected to predominate, and this is what we observe.

More surprising than thermostatic responsiveness in general, perhaps, is the fact that it is evident among more than just a small, highly attentive group. Not all citizens respond equally, but we have seen (in Chapter 8) that there is a high degree of parallelism in preferences across a number of population subdivisions, including education levels. This is an important finding. We cannot tell how different people actually learn about policy change, but we can infer that the information necessary to update relative preferences is fairly minimal. Otherwise, it is difficult

---

[1] Indeed, responsiveness does not require that people notice policy change in specific domains. It may be, for instance, that they do follow what happens in particular salient domains and that responsiveness in less salient domains depends on more "global" policy trends across domains. See also the discussion in Chapter 6.

to imagine people with very different abilities and interests reacting so similarly over time. Borrowing from Lupia (1994), individuals are not "encyclopedias" and evidently need not be. Indeed, it appears that the extra information that highly informed citizens have about policy not only is not necessary for thermostatic responsiveness, it is not useful on average. High information may improve the complexity of preferences but it seemingly does not help people, on average, assess the direction and magnitude of policy change. This has important implications for representation: the relatively homogenous pattern of public responsiveness not only provides a strong incentive for policymakers to represent public opinion, it provides an incentive to represent people relatively equally. Whether politicians actually do so of course is another matter, as there are other reasons for politicians to be more attentive to certain groups than others. Still, as we saw in Chapter 8, representation is strikingly similar across a range of groups.

Public responsiveness is not equivalent across all domains, but this too is as we should expect. Citizens can and should not be equally attentive to all issues all the time. Attentiveness, and responsiveness, should be greatest in the policy domains that are most "important," and we have seen a strong connection between measures of issue salience and the strength of public responsiveness. This link between salience and responsiveness also tells us something about the micro-level story behind aggregate-level public responsiveness, and lends further support to the likelihood of thermostatic responsiveness. In short, issue salience is not equal across individuals. It may be that some individuals are highly responsive in some domains, and other individuals are highly responsive in others. We need not rely on the same citizens across all domains, then; issue publics (see, e.g., Neuman 1986; Krosnick 1990) may play a critical role in aggregate-level public responsiveness.[2] Even so, as we have noted, the parallelism in preferences suggests that issue publics are only part of the story. In highly salient domains, thermostatic responsiveness is pervasive. And even as the magnitude of responsiveness decreases in relatively low-salience domains, the extent to which responsiveness is evident is roughly

---

[2] We see hints of this in Chapter 8, where responsiveness varies slightly across partisan groups.

similar across groups. The similarities we observe across groups are much greater than the differences.

Just as public responsiveness varies across domains, so too does representation. This is not just because the incentive to represent – a monitoring public – varies, but because so too does the practical value of public preferences. As we have noted, expressed relative preferences are meaningful only if they reflect policy itself; otherwise, they tell us nothing about whether and to what extent the public really wants policy to change. Not surprisingly, we find a close connection between salience, public responsiveness, and representation. Where the public cares more and pays attention, there is a good deal of representation. In less salient domains, where public responsiveness is weak, the opinion-policy connection is itself quite weak. In low-salience domains where the public does not notice what policymakers do, there is no discernible representation connection. This is precisely what we should expect.

Even in those domains where we do find representation, the connection is not perfect. Politicians clearly are more responsive in some domains than others, and policy is driven by various other things. Political parties are of special importance, sometimes more important than the public itself. We saw in Chapter 7 the strong effects of party control of government, particularly in the United States (also see Alt 1985; Hibbs 1987).[3] Other factors matter as well. Indeed, representation may not reflect actual responsiveness to public opinion. It may be, as noted earlier on, that the public and politicians are "co-responsive" to something else, such as shifts in the need for more spending.[4] It may be, as Achen (1978) has suggested, that politicians produce policy that corresponds with public preferences because they are simply a representative sample of citizens. Dynamic representation may result as well, as politicians move alongside the larger public. It also may be that public opinion matters, but only indirectly – mediated by the

---

[3] It also may be that political parties are not equally responsive to public opinion (see, e.g., Norris and Lovenduski 2004; Adams et al. 2006; Nagel and Wlezien n.d.). We did not explicitly consider this possibility, mostly because the power of such tests are limited by the length of our time series, particularly in the United Kingdom and also Canada.

[4] However, note that if politicians are not following public opinion, they must themselves behave thermostatically when making policy. Otherwise we cannot explain representation of "thermostatic" public preferences.

behavior of other actors rather than actively represented by reelection-seeking politicians. For instance, as classic pluralist theorists (e.g., Truman 1951) suggest, interest groups may effectively mediate opinion representation over time (also see Hansen 1991; Burstein 2003). We do not directly assess this hypothesis here. What we can say for sure is that current public preferences are regularly connected with budgetary policy in the subsequent fiscal year; we thus can infer that, to the extent they play a decisive role in the political process in Canada, the United States and the United Kingdom, interest groups do not substantially distort the dynamic representation of public preferences in spending policy. This is of obvious relevance given the importance of interest groups in modern political life (Schaatschneider 1960).

One other caveat is in order. Our goal has not been to explain all policy change in all domains; rather, we want to assess the role of public opinion in those domains for which we can measure public opinion. In one sense, then, what we have shown overstates the level of democratic representation. That is, our results have been based on analyses of those policy domains where we actually have regular measures of opinion. These presumably are salient domains, at least more so than the domains about which survey organizations do not ask. There is a host of less salient domains where public preferences are unmeasured (see esp. Burstein 2006), and where representation is likely to be very weak or nonexistent. Representation may also be weak – or strong, we simply do not know – in areas that are not well captured by our budgetary measures. We look only at broad levels of spending, after all – we capture how much governments spend, but not how. Our results also say very little about policy representation where regulation is concerned. Indeed, the growing importance of regulation as a policy tool (in environmental policy, for instance) points to an increasingly wide range of policy to which the preceding results do not directly speak.

Also note that – just as negative feedback does not preclude intermittent positive feedback in public preferences – our results do not preclude the possibility of sometimes grossly unrepresentative policy decisions. Any policy scholar can recall specific legislative outcomes that seemed at odds with the state of public opinion at the time. And work that takes a policy-by-policy approach to the opinion-policy link regularly finds that a significant minority of policy shifts conflict with concurrent public preferences (see, e.g., Monroe 1979, 1998; Page and Shapiro 1983).

This is not surprising given our analyses, which demonstrate that other things matter for policy, particularly the party control of government. Substantial disjunctures with public preferences in the short term can exist even as policy reflects those preferences over the long term.

To the extent policymakers follow the public, how do they learn what people want? As with public responsiveness, we cannot be sure about the mechanisms behind policy representation. It is important to keep in mind that representation need not be driven by policymaker responsiveness to public opinion polls *per se*. Policymakers may learn about public preferences by other means– in discussions with constituents, through media content, or through interest groups, for example.[5] It also may be that policymakers do not just respond – they may anticipate trends in public opinion, such as public responsiveness to policy itself. Indeed, one can imagine politicians trying to assess exactly how far they should (or can) go with policy based on a shift in public preferences. Regardless, the result is essentially the same: policy and preferences move together over time. We have presented ample evidence of this in earlier chapters, and to some this is what matters most of all. Whether policymakers actually *respond* to preferences clearly does matter, however, normatively if not practically. But teasing out the specific mechanisms driving the opinion-policy relationship requires a quite different approach to the one taken here.

INSTITUTIONS AND REPRESENTATIVE DEMOCRACY

Institutions make a difference to the connections between public opinion and policy. Federalism confuses the signal citizens receive about policy change, impeding public responsiveness and, by implication, reducing the incentive to represent. The checks and balances in a Madisonian presidential system encourage policy representation in a way that is not evident in parliamentary systems. The opinion-policy link, we posit, should thus be strongest in a system that we have not investigated here – a unitary presidential system, where the policy signal is clear and both the executive and legislature represent

---

[5] Note that if media or interest groups matter, they do a very good job of reflecting public preferences, perhaps unwittingly, at least in those domains where we find strong representation.

opinion; it should by corollary be weakest in a federal parliamentary system, where the signal is confused and the legislature cannot effectively check the executive or correct its representational errors. (Recall Figure 3.3.)

We have paid a good deal of attention to these divisions of power, and for good reason. The United States, the United Kingdom, and Canada capture important variation in these institutional factors, and there is strong evidence that public responsiveness and policy representation co-vary as we would expect. To be more circumspect, we have presented rather strong evidence that federalism matters – we have seen differences both across countries, and within countries but across domains. Our evidence on presidentialism is somewhat weaker. We can compare only across countries, so we have but three cases and only one presidential system. The Madisonian system itself is, too, relatively rare, as the distribution of power in presidential systems typically is more highly skewed toward the executive. One might look to include other presidential systems, as well as parliamentary ones, with varying balances of executive–legislative power. But there seemingly are no other cases quite like the United States.

Non-Madisonian presidential systems might well behave in different ways. We have suggested that the greater presidential power is, the more the system will behave like a parliamentary one. Semi-presidential systems – in which there is both a president and a parliament and executive power is shared (Duverger 1980; Schleiter and Morgan-Jones n.d.)[6] – offer other interesting possibilities. The classic case is France, but it is not singular.[7] Here, we might expect the patterns of opinion representation to be in between that for presidential and parliamentary systems, though this may depend on whether control of the presidency and parliament is divided, that is, whether there is "cohabitation." Both non-Madisonian presidential and semi-presidential systems present worthy avenues of research, then, though neither can currently be pursued given the available data. For the time being, all we can do is speculate.

[6] Also see Shugart 2005.
[7] Finland also is semi-presidential, and the number of these systems has grown substantially in recent years as many of the new democracies in Eastern Europe and the former Soviet Union have adopted this design, including Romania, Russia, and the Ukraine.

The effects of federalism also deserve further study, though this actually can be taken up, if not by extending our sample of domains and countries, then by exploring the different and overlapping levels at which representation may exist in the federal countries examined here. The picture we have painted above is a relatively simple one in which public responsiveness and policy representation are measured nationally. The function of a federal system need not be to enhance national-level policymaking, however. These systems may well accomplish policy representation through multiple sources; we have already seen hints of this in the Canadian case, where consolidated spending often shows greater representation and responsiveness than either federal or provincial spending taken separately.

Federal systems can facilitate policy differences across subnational units. Indeed, the strength of a federal system may hinge in part on the degree to which it allows policies to covary with regional differences in policy preferences. The United States and Canada are two cases in point. In both, federalism allows for the representation of quite different interests across states or provinces, and at the local level. Our analyses have focused on the national level, but the latter clearly matter as well.

There already exists a literature focusing on differences in preferences and policy across U.S. states. Extending these cross-sectional analyses to other countries is important to understanding how federalism structures opinion-policy relationships. Extending the analysis of subnational units over time is important as well. Some state or provincial policies may better represent changing public opinion than others. This representation also might vary across states and provinces: a high-salience policy in one state may be a low-salience policy in the next; a domain central to one province may be peripheral to another. Both public responsiveness and policy representation may vary accordingly. Summing state and provincial preferences and spending thus may mask some quite strong, and some quite weak, opinion-policy interactions.

Issues of federalism may be particularly salient given worldwide trends in multi-level governance. Recent years have seen growing decentralization in both Canada and the United Kingdom, as well as in a host of other countries not considered here, including France, Italy, Belgium, Spain, and New Zealand, and across the developing world (see, e.g., Ansell and Gingrich 2003; Bahl and Wallace 2005). The European Union (EU) presents a particularly interesting venue in which to explore the potential advantages and disadvantages of federalism. The existing literature highlights the problems of executive dominance in a complicated federal and multinational system (see, e.g., Follesdal and Hix 2006). This literature may actually understate the problem, since the tangled federal structure also makes public responsiveness much more difficult. Note further that, where public responsiveness is concerned, difficulties with the EU relate not just to EU institutions: as a policy signal becomes a combination of policy made at both the EU and the national levels, the potential for public responsiveness at the national level may decrease as well. To make things even more difficult for the EU, it still mostly deals with comparatively low-salience issues.

Indeed, the EU might be close to a worst-case scenario where the opinion-policy link is concerned, were it not for its presidential elements.[8] Although data limitations there make it difficult to pursue the kind of investigation we have undertaken here, a good deal of research has accumulated showing that the EU functions exactly as we would predict: the usual characterization is of a "democratic deficit," in which public opinion is considered to play only a very weak role (e.g., Andersen and Burns 1996; Weiler et al. 1995). The results of recent EU constitutional referenda (in 2005 in France and the Netherlands, and 2008 in Ireland) only underscore the point.

The effect of horizontal and vertical divisions of power on the opinion-policy relationship should also be evident beyond the EU. We stated at the outset that the scope of our hypotheses would far outstrip our ability to test them, and have certainly accomplished that objective. But we hope that we have in the process illustrated a structure to opinion-policy relationships that can be further explored in other countries. We also hope that the institutional hypotheses investigated here stimulate considerations of how a much broader set of political institutions may affect the opinion-policy link.

Holding electoral systems constant has been rather useful for our purposes, but electoral systems clearly have a major impact on the composition of governments and play a critical role in providing

---

[8] In effect, it is a highly decentralized semi-presidential system.

the incentives for representation. We have suggested that, although proportional systems provide a stronger link between vote and seat distributions, majoritarian systems may actually enhance representation between elections, at least insofar as they produce single-party governments. We have not tested this here, however. Nor have we examined the effects of disproportionality and vote-seat elasticities. Rogowski and Kayser (2002) argue that majoritarian systems are more responsive to consumer (rather than producer) interests because marginal increases in vote share are more likely to matter (to the office-seeking politician) in majoritarian systems. The dynamic representation of public preferences may be similarly enhanced by this greater vote-seat elasticity.

Other institutions may have systematic effects on the opinion-policy relationship as well. We have given no consideration to corporatist versus pluralist processes, the organization and power of the legislature, the strength of party discipline, and so on. In short, political scientists still have much to learn about how a wide range of political institutions affect the principal function of representative democracy – producing a systematic link between public opinion and policy.

THE "EFFICIENCY" OF POLITICAL SYSTEMS

In Chapter 1 we outlined the similarities between the thermostatic model investigated here and the functionalist theories of David Easton and Karl Deutsch. Both of these authors describe an idealized political system as one that is self-maintaining, where inputs (preferences) are converted into outputs (policy) and outputs are monitored and feed back on inputs. This is a caricature of a representative democracy, of course – it certainly does not capture everything we want in this kind of political system. It does describe a dynamic central to representative democracy, however. Deutsch refers to the reciprocal process relating public inputs and outputs as the "efficiency" of a policy system – how quickly and fully the system facilitates both political representation and public responsiveness. We discussed efficiency in Chapter 3. Results in subsequent chapters allow us to provide assessments of efficiency in the three countries considered here. That is, we can assess the net effect of representation and feedback, and doing so provides a useful summary of the effects of government institutions.

What happens when preferences increase? Imagine a one-unit shock in the public's underlying preferred level of spending. How quickly does it take for the system to re-equilibrate? How long does it take for spending to adjust? The simplest and best way to capture and measure system efficiency is to simply multiply the raw feedback and representation coefficients in each country. System efficiency (ζ, zeta) for domain d in country c is thus:

$$\zeta_{cd} = \beta_{1cd} * \gamma_{1cd} \qquad\qquad (9.1)$$

where β_1 is the public responsiveness coefficient from equation 2.3, and γ_1 is the representation coefficient from equation 2.7. The product of these two coefficients, ζ, tells us how much of a given shock is corrected in each year.[9]

Following a hypothetical punctuation in preferences for policy, we might envision at least two quite different ways of reaching equilibrium. In the first case, the efficiency coefficient is less than zero but greater than minus one ($-1 < \zeta < 0$). In this instance, we should see a gradual return to equilibrium – policymakers respond in part and preferences adjust accordingly, policymakers respond in part again and preferences adjust accordingly, and so on. The resulting dynamic is illustrated in Figure 9.1, where efficiency equals –.3. In the second case, the efficiency coefficient is less than minus one but greater than minus two ($-2 < \zeta < -1$), a consequence of highly reactionary policymaking in which, when the public wants just a little more (or less) policy, policymakers provide much more (or less). Preferences respond accordingly, reversing signs, policymakers overcompensate again, and so on. The resulting dynamic is also illustrated in Figure 9.1, where efficiency equals -1.7. Note that in both conditions illustrated in Figure 9.1 preferences reach equilibrium at roughly the same time, though they follow quite different paths.[10]

---

[9] Note that the use of a lower-case zeta (ζ) for system efficiency is purposeful. In control theory, a branch of engineering concerned with dynamical systems like those discussed by Weiner, ζ is used to represent the damping ratio of a spring system – essentially, the rate at which a system returns to equilibrium.

[10] Figure 9.1 does not capture all the various possibilities where system efficiency is concerned. It may be that $\zeta > 0$, for instance, because of either (a) positive feedback and positive representation, or (b) negative feedback and negative representation, and then we have a system that will not return to equilibrium. Here, preferences and policy will drift off in one direction or another, in what time series econometrics

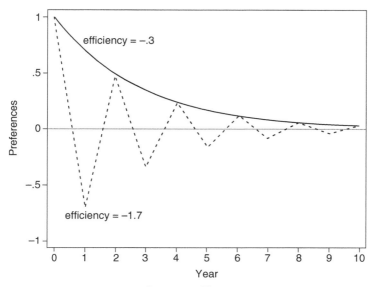

FIGURE 9.1. Two Forms of System Efficiency

   The paths illustrated in the figure correspond to two plausible real-world conditions. The possibility of hyper-responsiveness to preferences has been a concern for those interested in modes of representation (including Burke and Mill). Representatives who face very strong electoral pressures, or are prone to being highly reactive to public interests, may tend to regularly over-shoot equilibrium. By contrast, we might expect that representatives with a broader, more temperate, and longer-term view than their constituents will respond more incrementally. Indeed, it may not be just the raw behavior of representatives that matters: given that we are talking about policy, a system-level outcome, institutional design can limit the potential consequences of highly reactive representatives. We can see this line of thinking in theoretical work by Burke and Mill, and of course in the *Federalist Papers*, where the Senate is discussed as a check on the potential hyper-responsiveness of the House.

   refers to as an "explosive process." It also may be that $\zeta < -2$, the product of quite different dynamics certainly, though which also will not return to equilibrium. Here, preferences and policy would drift off in both directions, increasingly alternating negative and positive over time.

In short, working through the consequences of different magnitudes of feedback and representation for policymaking, and for "system efficiency," can be a useful way to think about institutional design. Attributing real values to ζ can be similarly valuable, as a kind of directly comparable summary measure of the way political systems – policymakers and publics combined – react over time. Actually doing so is relatively simple, drawing on results for public responsiveness (from Table 5.2) and policy representation (from Table 7.2).

Figure 9.2 plots simulated preferences based on ζ for the combined social domains in each country. Note first that the downward-sloping pattern in the figure suggests that when responding to a shock in public preferences, at least where social domains are concerned, politicians tend to be conservative. That is, they tend to undershoot what the public wants. It may be that politicians are wary of overshooting, and perhaps for good reason, but there might be other explanations. For instance, the traditional budgeting literature emphasizes incrementalism as a normative decision-making approach. Alternatively, it may be that certain actors attempt a more complete response but that

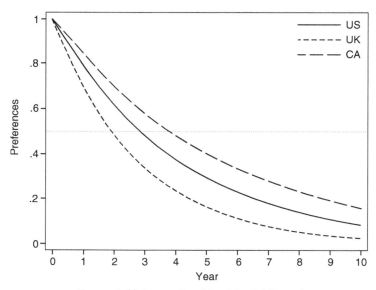

FIGURE 9.2. System Efficiency, Combined Social Domains

institutional friction prevents it (Jones et al., 2009). We cannot sort among these possibilities (or others). What we can say is that of the two paths illustrated in Figure 9.1, our data suggest an incremental return to equilibrium is more prevalent in the domains and countries investigated here.

Differences between the three countries appear to be rather modest, and they are not statistically significant, though they are illustrative. Consider that the half life of a hypothetical one-unit shock in U.K. preferences is roughly two years; in the United States it is three years; in Canada it is more than four years. What accounts for these differences in system efficiency? One source of inefficiency is to a certain degree endogenous to the system: weak public responsiveness begets weak policy representation. Or, at least, weak public responsiveness precludes strong policy representation. The importance of public responsiveness in this regard is underscored in Figure 9.2. Recall that the United States showed rather strong representation in comparison with the United Kingdom and Canada. Indeed, representation was by our standardized measure stronger in the United States in every major domain. Public responsiveness was less so – lower than the United Kingdom for defense and education, and lower than Canada for health. It is this somewhat muted responsiveness that limits the estimate of U.S. system efficiency here.[11]

Put differently, the figure implies that – through its effects on public responsiveness – the differences in federalism between the United Kingdom and the United States matter more than the differences in parliamentarism versus presidentialism. That is, the impact of the vertical division of powers on public responsiveness is somewhat greater than the (in this particular case, countervailing) impact of the horizontal division of powers on policy representation. The United States exhibits somewhat weaker system efficiency as a result. And things are even worse for Canada: while the United States benefits from presidentialism, and the United Kingdom benefits – at least was benefited – from a unitary system, Canada benefits from neither.

---

[11] Note, however, that U.K. results do not include welfare, a high-salience issue in the United States. Unless welfare is of relatively low salience in the United Kingdom, including it might enhance the difference between the United Kingdom and United States (and Canada).

Figure 9.2 thus illustrates the net effect of our institutional hypotheses. It also makes particularly clear that dynamic, representative policy-making depends in large part on reactive public preferences.

FINAL THOUGHTS

Democracy works. To be exact, representative democracy works. It is not perfect, to be sure, and it certainly works better under some conditions than others. Some of these conditions are exactly as we should expect. The public salience of issues clearly matters. Expecting representative democracy to represent preferences that do not exist, in domains about which people do not care, is unreasonable. The ways in which issues become more or less salient are thus of critical importance. Politicians may attempt to influence and manage issue salience; mass media, interest groups, and policy advocates surely matter as well. But the people ultimately decide. Some domains simply do not attract much attention – they are uninteresting or obscure or simply very small.[12] Those domains exhibit at best a representation of some "global" trend in preferences, but often little representation of any kind at all.

Representation also depends on institutional conditions – and, importantly, these are not usually within the control of the citizenry but in the hands of politicians themselves. That is, politicians can to some extent choose institutional arrangements in policy areas, such as their federal quality. Our examination here indicates that politicians may have real incentives to do so, for example, either to diffuse responsibility or else to make responsibility more clear.[13] This is an important possibility. Concerns about the capacity of citizens may be well founded, and the public surely plays a central role in producing "degrees" of democracy. But it also may be that democracy works only as well as politicians want it to. This is an empirical question, of course, and one for future research.

---

[12] On the implications that "concreteness" versus "abstractness" may have for opinion responsiveness, see Yagade and Dozier 1990, Soroka 2002. Note also that the salience of policy domains seems very closely related to program size, which is highly intuitive.

[13] This has also been the subject of some recent work on public policy, esp. Harrison 1996.

Appendix

This appendix includes information on data sources, descriptives for the preferences and spending data used through the book (Appendix Table 1), as well as detailed regression results for all preceding models of public responsiveness (Appendix Table 2) and policy representation (Appendix Table 3).

For Appendix Tables 2 and 3, regression results are shown in the order in which they appear in the text. In each case, regression models are also preceded by a reference to the table in the text in which the abbreviated results appear. The first models in Appendix Table 2 appear in Table 5.2 of the text, for instance; the first models in Appendix Table 3 appear in Table 7.2. In cases where only certain domains appear in the main text but models were estimated for other domains, they too are included under the relevant table heading.

DATA SOURCES

Public Preferences

Net preferences for policy are measured using questions about government spending, and both the question wording and the "net support" measure are described in detail in Chapter 4. The General Social Survey, from which we draw the U.S. data, is available from the National Opinion Research Archive (NORC) at the University of

Chicago. Aggregate results from U.K. Gallup are available in King and Wybrow (2001); for Chapter 8, where preferences are broken down by sub-group, we rely on the U.K. Gallup surveys available from the Roper Center for Public Opinion Research. Environics Focus Canada surveys are available at the Canadian Opinion Research Archive (CORA) at Queen's University, Kingston, Ontario.

Chapter 6 includes two other measures of preferences in the United States. The Roper data are available from the Roper Center for Public Opinion Research at the University of Connecticut. Monthly Trendex data were graciously provided by Robert Shapiro. (For his work using these data, see, e.g., Shapiro and Young 1986; Shapiro et al. 1987.)

Government Spending (Including Federalism)

The principal measures of spending are also discussed in detail in Chapter 4. U.S. data are drawn from the *Historical Tables* provided by the Office of Management and Budget (OMB); U.K. data are from Soroka, Wlezien, and MacLean (2006), supplemented by data for 1978 and 1979 recalculated by HM Treasury for Public Expenditure Statistical Analysis (PESA). Canadian data from FY1988 onward are from Statistics Canada, CANSIM matrix 385–0001, and data for previous years are from the terminated CANSIM matrix 2780. The functions used for each of the domains examined above are as follows.

- United States (both outlays and appropriations): for cities, "Community and Regional Development" excluding "Disaster Relief and Insurance"; for crime, "Administration of Justice"; for education, "Education," excluding "Training and Employment"; for environment, "Environment"; for foreign aid, two subfunctions from "International Affairs" – "International Development and Humanitarian Assistance" and "International Security Assistance"; for health, "Health"; for welfare, "Income Security" excluding "General Retirement and Disability Insurance," "Federal Employee Retirement and Disability," and "Unemployment Compensation." For more information, see the *Historical Tables, Budget of the United States Government*, available from OMB.
- United Kingdom: The domains used here are drawn from functions of the same name – "Defense," "Education," "Health," and

"Transport." For more information, see Soroka, Wlezien, and MacLean (2006).

• Canada: for defense, "National Defense"; for education, "Education"; for environment, "Environment"; for health, "Health"; for transportation, "Transportation and Communication" excluding federal expenditures on "Telecommunications" (provincial expenditures on "Telecommunications" are unavailable); for welfare, "Social Assistance." Complete descriptions of functions and subfunctions are available from Statistics Canada, *Financial Management System* (FMS) 2002. For data before FY1988, the functions in CANSIM matrix 2780 (with which current functions are interpolated; see Chapter 4) are: for defense, "Foreign Affairs and International Assistance"; for education, "Education"; for environment, "Environment"; for health, "Health"; for transportation, "Transportation and Communications"; for welfare, "Social Services."

Additional spending data are used for our measure of federalism in Chapters 5 and 7, and to examine the difference between federal, provincial, and consolidated spending in Chapter 6. For Canada, data on provincial and local government spending is included in the same Statistics Canada matrix as the consolidated and federal spending figures. In the United States, the OMB's *Historical Tables* do not include state spending. Our federalism measure there relies on federal data from the *Historical Tables* and state-level spending data drawn from *Annual State and Local Government Finance Data*, published by the Public Policy Institute of California. Data are available for 29 years between 1972 to 2004. We approximate the functional spending domains from the OMB as follows: welfare includes "Social Services," excluding "Veterans' Benefits"; education includes both "K-12 Education" and "Higher Education"; health includes "Health"; environment includes "Environment and Housing" excluding "Housing," "Sewerage," and "Solid Waste."

Nongovernment Spending

Data for unemployment rates, issue salience, crime rates, healthcare, and measures of government partisanship were obtained from the sources noted below.

- Unemployment rate: For the Canadian models including the unemployment rate, we generated fiscal-year unemployment rates from the monthly unemployment data from the Statistics Canada CANSIM database. Similar data were generated for the United States and United Kingdom using month unemployment data from the U.S. Department of Labor, Bureau of Labor Statistics, and from National Statistics.
- Issue salience: The measure of issue salience used first in Chapter 5 is based on all available polls with the "most important problem" question, from 1982 to 2001, from Gallup in the United States and United Kingdom, and IPSOS-Reid (formerly Angus Reid) in Canada. U.S. Gallup data were made available by Gallup online; U.K. Gallup data are from King and Wybrow (2001); Angus Reid data were drawn from *Reid Reports* archived at the University of British Columbia. All data are collected in Stuart Soroka, *Comparative MIP Data, 1939–2001*, where response categories, which vary over time, are recoded using the Policy Agendas coding scheme from Baumgartner and Jones (2002).
- Crime rates: Annual data on violent and nonviolent crime rates, used in Chapter 6, are available from the U.S. Bureau of Justice Statistics at the National Archive of Criminal Justice.
- Healthcare: Data on the number of acute care hospital beds per 1,000 people was drawn from OECD Health Data 2008. Where necessary, missing data were filled in using linear interpolation.
- Government partisanship: All measures of government partisanship, including the measures of marginality used in Chapter 7, were collected by the authors using electoral results readily available online.

APPENDIX TABLE 1. *Descriptive Statistics for Preferences and Spending Measures*

Cells contain descriptives for Preferences and Spending variables, based on all available cases (raw, rather than interpolated data for preferences) during the periods of study for each country: U.S., 1973–2004; U.K., 1978–1999; Canada (CA), 1984–2004.

		Preferences					Spending				
		Obs	Mean	SD	Min	Max	Obs	Mean	SD	Min	Max
US	Cities	29	34.175	9.345	17.000	48.420	32	10.129	3.585	6.897	19.854
	Crime	30	62.229	5.956	49.000	70.853	32	15.886	9.366	7.006	41.744
	Defense	30	−9.291	18.870	−33.281	47.956	32	308.099	55.911	227.575	417.519
	Education	30	55.333	10.219	39.415	70.031	32	41.673	10.721	28.696	73.339
	Environment	29	50.540	10.771	31.000	71.135	32	22.337	3.163	15.388	28.234
	Foreign Aid	29	−64.976	7.247	−75.527	−50.000	32	14.794	3.130	8.046	21.708
	Health	30	59.519	7.080	49.112	73.661	32	88.937	56.070	30.151	219.943
	Space	29	−32.907	10.372	−55.431	−17.000	32	11.305	2.414	8.040	15.370
	Welfare	26	−30.093	12.431	−49.827	−16.124	32	100.979	41.095	36.819	176.555
UK	Defense	15	−25.000	21.720	−48.000	20.000	22	27.958	3.053	22.596	32.495
	Education	15	69.467	10.378	44.000	82.000	22	35.792	4.000	31.053	41.895
	Health	15	76.600	9.723	59.000	87.000	22	38.252	7.886	27.539	52.974
	Transport	15	44.767	11.431	23.000	57.000	22	10.917	1.591	8.679	14.143
CA	Defense	17	−1.373	20.211	−28.000	46.000	21	12.773	1.045	10.745	14.265
	Education	14	54.786	11.157	39.000	72.000	21	57.350	6.843	45.604	68.322
	Environment	17	44.320	13.489	27.000	70.000	21	8.375	1.628	5.485	11.850
	Health	16	49.029	18.911	24.000	77.000	21	58.771	12.658	40.572	85.878
	Transport	15	13.241	14.623	−3.000	45.000	17	19.048	1.343	17.400	21.220
	Welfare	18	−13.765	9.538	−33.000	0.000	17	86.728	8.074	67.268	94.766

APPENDIX TABLE 2. *Public Responsiveness*

Cells contain OLS coefficients with standard errors in parentheses. DW is the Durbin-Watson test for correlated standard errors. DhF is an F-test, and Dhp the p-value, from a Durbin's h test, used to test for correlated standard errors when a lagged depending variable is included in the model.

* p < .10; ** p < .05; *** p <.01.

Full Results for Table 5.2

	Spend$_t$	Prefs$_{t-1}$	Counter	Counter^2	US–Russia
US Social	−.169**	.624**		.066**	
	(.043)	(.105)		(.016)	
US Defense	−.258**		1.175**		.360**
	(.051)		(.524)		(.112)
US Welfare	−.627**	.550**	1.542**	.044**	
	(.185)	(.123)	(.680)	(.019)	
US Health	−.284**	.542**	−.693*	.082**	
	(.115)	(.145)	(.386)	(.029)	
US Education	−.288*		1.219**		
	(.145)		(.160)		
US Environment	−2.265**		.786**		
	(.567)		(.200)		
US Cities	−2.195**		−.248*		
	(.400)		(.146)		
US Crime	−.838**		.433**		
	(.197)		(.191)		
US Foreign Aid	−.193		.548**		
	(.298)		(.095)		
US Space	−1.225*	.751**	.286		
	(.622)	(.097)	(.174)		
UK Social	−1.355**		3.909**		
	(.190)		(.343)		
UK Defense	−9.542**				.326**
	(.963)				(.059)
UK Health	−2.323**		4.132**		
	(.298)		(.343)		
UK Education	−3.497**		3.756**		
	(.709)		(.473)		
UK Transport	−2.641**	.692**			
	(.902)	(.126)			

Post-911	Unemp	Constant	N	Rsq	Adj Rsq	DW	DhF	Dhp
		−21.560** (5.136)	32	.837	.819		.412	.527
31.684** (9.246)		−32.508** (11.975)	31	.594	.532	1.024		
		−38.349** (11.353)	32	.725	.685		3.935	.058
		−15.797** (6.206)	32	.685	.639		4.507	.043
		−19.497** (2.729)	33	.774	.758	1.243		
		−12.575** (3.507)	33	.386	.346	1.034		
		3.973 (2.568)	33	.542	.511	1.678		
		−6.927** (3.153)	33	.517	.484	1.528		
		−8.766** (1.774)	33	.525	.493	2.598		
		−4.429 (2.844)	32	.769	.745		.066	.799
		−33.227** (2.960)	18	.953	.946	1.836		
		−15.018** (3.363)	18	.870	.852	1.830		
		−35.126** (2.957)	18	.954	.948	1.766		
		−31.923** (4.108)	18	.888	.873	1.734		
		.000 (1.306)	18	.792	.764		.011	.916

(*continued*)

APPENDIX TABLE 2. *(continued)*

Full Results for Table 5.2

	Spend$_t$	Prefs$_{t-1}$	Counter	Counter²	US–Russia
CA Social	−.361**	.420**		.151**	
	(.092)	(.159)		(.035)	
CA Defense	−4.424*	.880**			
	(2.513)	(.131)			
CA Welfare	−2.226**	.468**	2.247**		
	(.578)	(.126)	(.544)		
CA Health	−2.143**	.619**		.334**	
	(.616)	(.146)		(.091)	
CA Education	−.716*	.466**	1.632**		
	(.365)	(.207)	(.553)		
CA Environment	−7.869**	.825**		.101**	
	(2.651)	(.114)		(.031)	
CA Transport	−2.040**	1.023**			
	(.950)	(.081)			

Full Results for Table 6.1

	Spend$_t$	Prefs$_{t-1}$	Counter	Counter²	US–Russia
Defense (Out)	−.246**				.156**
	(.049)				(.069)
Defense (App)	−.233**				.263**
	(.048)				(.072)
Welfare (Out)	−.629**	.478**	2.656**	.020	
	(.179)	(.120)	(.716)	(.023)	
Welfare (App)	−.460**	.365**	−.618	.082**	
	(.105)	(.121)	(.634)	(.030)	
Health (Out)	−.241*	.526**	.085	.063*	
	(.129)	(.158)	(.429)	(.036)	
Health (App)	−.140	.557**	.184	.038	
	(.107)	(.167)	(.437)	(.032)	
Education (Out)	−.266		1.173**		
	(.157)		(.195)		
Education (App)	−.164		1.084**		
	(.137)		(.189)		
Environment (Out)	−2.291**		.805**		
	(.674)		(.223)		

Post-911	Unemp	Constant	N	Rsq	Adj Rsq	DW	DhF	Dhp
		−11.678** (2.850)	16	.944	.929		.320	.583
		−.000 (2.610)	20	.745	.715		1.652	.217
	5.486** (2.477)	−65.024** (25.606)	16	.938	.915		4.687	.056
		−33.074** (9.129)	18	.931	.916		.084	.776
		−13.872** (4.780)	18	.895	.873		2.893	.113
		−10.044** (3.315)	18	.831	.795		.203	.659
		.000 (1.373)	18	.918	.907		.363	.556

Post-911	Unemp	Constant	N	Rsq	Adj Rsq	DW	DhF	Dhp
39.845** (8.754)		−9.219** (3.536)	29	.602	.554	1.134		
46.116** (9.517)		−13.355** (3.734)	29	.585	.535	1.247		
		−42.526** (10.388)	29	.782	.746		13.172	.001
		−13.195** (3.369)	29	.816	.785		.493	.490
		−17.987** (7.350)	29	.695	.645		5.483	.028
		−12.815* (6.427)	29	.675	.620		3.721	.066
		−16.415** (2.928)	29	.686	.662	1.216		
		−15.172** (2.854)	29	.670	.644	1.121		
		−11.269** (3.514)	29	.388	.341	1.025		

(*continued*)

APPENDIX TABLE 2. *(continued)*

Full Results for Table 6.1

	Spend$_t$	Prefs$_{t-1}$	Counter	Counter^2	US-Russia
Environment (App)	−.984*		.697**		
	(.555)		(.266)		
Cities (Out)	−1.945**		−.097		
	(.471)		(.208)		
Cities (App)	−.719*		.264		
	(.419)		(.238)		
Crime (Out)	−.847**		.440*		
	(.232)		(.257)		
Crime (App)	−.924**		.599**		
	(.245)		(.289)		
Foreign Aid (Out)	−.136		.592**		
	(.323)		(.119)		
Foreign Aid (App)	.028		.599**		
	(.203)		(.120)		
Space (Out)	−1.172*	.660**	.230		
	(.634)	(.116)	(.180)		
Space (App)	−.671	.663**	.114		
	(.665)	(.122)	(.184)		

Full Results for Table 6.3

	Spend$_t$	Prefs$_{t-1}$	Counter	Counter^2	US-Russia
Defense (Roper-GSS)	.003	.789**			.009
	(.036)	(.120)			(.058)
Defense (GSS-Roper)	−.175**	.412**			.097
	(.047)	(.168)			(.075)
Social (Roper-GSS)	.043	.701**		.000	
	(.027)	(.079)		(.013)	
Social (GSS-Roper)	−.274**	.515*		.124**	
	(.059)	(.251)		(.030)	

Full Results for Table 6.4

	Spend$_t$	Prefs$_{t-1}$	Counter	Counter^2	Crime
Crime, VI	−1.215**		.674**		
	(.313)		(.270)		

Post-911	Unemp	Constant	N	Rsq	Adj Rsq	DW	DhF	Dhp
		−9.751**	29	.211	.150	.923		
		(4.157)						
		1.359	29	.569	.536	1.667		
		(3.127)						
		−3.699	29	.359	.309	1.209		
		(3.605)						
		−6.162	29	.540	.504	1.541		
		(3.698)						
		−8.392*	29	.550	.516	1.494		
		(4.126)						
		−8.289**	29	.494	.455	2.688		
		(1.945)						
		−8.393**	29	.491	.452	2.647		
		(1.959)						
		−3.219	29	.600	.552		.387	.540
		(2.689)						
		−1.597	29	.563	.510		.132	.719
		(2.753)						

Post-911	Unemp	Constant	N	Rsq	Adj Rsq	DW	DhF	Dhp
		−.338	27	.777	.748	1.810		
		(2.754)						
		−3.677	27	.654	.609	1.124		
		(3.646)						
		−.003	17	.966	.959	2.173		
		(1.282)						
		−11.715**	17	.870	.840	1.206		
		(2.968)						

Post-911	Unemp	Constant	N	Rsq	Adj Rsq	DW	DhF	Dhp
		−8.768**	27	.478	.434	1.625		
		(3.610)						

(*continued*)

APPENDIX TABLE 2. *(continued)*

Full Results for Table 6.4

	Spend$_t$	Prefs$_{t-1}$	Counter	Counter^2	Crime
Crime, v2	−.948**		.570*		.003
	(.458)		(.302)		(.004)
Crime, v3			.020		.008**
			(.152)		(.003)

Full Results for Table 6.5

	Spend$_t$	Prefs$_{t-1}$	Counter	Counter^2	Acute Care
US Health, v1	−.284**	.542**	−.693*	.082**	
	(.115)	(.145)	(.386)	(.029)	
US Health, v2	−.284**	.542**	−.693	.082**	.000
	(.118)	(.149)	(.419)	(.033)	(8.192)
US Health, v3		.527**	−.273	.011	−2.921
		(.161)	(.413)	(.016)	(8.788)
US Health, v4		.543**			−4.113**
		(.156)			(1.883)
UK Health, v1	−2.317**		4.106**		
	(.292)		(.354)		
UK Health, v2	−1.847**		3.595**		−3.404
	(.508)		(.574)		(3.024)
UK Health, v3			1.548**		−12.452*
			(.157)		(2.398)
CA Health, v1	−2.143**	.619**		.334**	
	(.616)	(.146)		(.091)	
CA Health, v2	−2.533**	.483**		.407**	−2.690
	(.887)	(.215)		(.109)	(14.949)
CA Health, v3		.895**		.141*	25.962*
		(.199)		(.072)	(13.790)

Full Results for Table 6.6

	Spend$_t$	Prefs$_{t-1}$	Counter	Counter^2	US-Russia
Welfare (Cons)	−2.226**	.468**	2.247**		
	(.578)	(.126)	(.544)		
Welfare (Fed)	−.891**	.520**	.302		
	(.205)	(.125)	(.206)		
Health (Cons)	−2.143**	.619**		.334**	
	(.616)	(.146)		(.091)	

Post-911	Unemp	Constant	N	Rsq	Adj Rsq	DW	DhF	Dhp
		-10.412** (4.173)	27	.492	.426	1.700		
		-8.868* (4.378)	27	.397	.347	1.630		

Post-911	Unemp	Constant	N	Rsq	Adj Rsq	DW	DhF	Dhp
		-15.797** (6.206)	32	.685	.639		4.507	.043
-.000 (8.192)		-15.797 (16.085)	32	.685	.625		4.334	.048
-2.921 (8.788)		3.406 (15.142)	32	.615	.558		.166	.687
-4.113** (1.883)		3.908* (1.983)	32	.605	.578		.221	.642
		-30.795** (2.709)	16	.946	.937	1.227		
-3.404 (3.024)		-15.686 (13.689)	16	.951	.939	1.304		
-12.452** (2.398)		29.637** (7.904)	16	.897	.881	.919		
		-29.655** (8.253)	18	.931	.916		.084	.776
-2.690 (14.949)		-33.858** (12.431)	17	.935	.913		1.076	.322
25.962* (13.790)		-30.921* (15.422)	17	.890	.865		.294	.598

Post-911	Unemp	Constant	N	Rsq	Adj Rsq	DW	DhF	Dhp
	5.486** (2.477)	-27.173** (8.616)	16	.938	.915		4.687	.056
		-2.263 (1.763)	16	.892	.865		1.972	.188
		-33.074** (9.129)	18	.931	.916		.084	.776

(*continued*)

APPENDIX TABLE 2. *(continued)*

Full Results for Table 6.6

	Spend$_t$	Prefs$_{t-1}$	Counter	Counter^2	US-Russia
Health (Fed)	−.918**	.444**		.104**	
	(.343)	(.200)		(.041)	
Education (Cons)	−.716*	.466**	1.632**		
	(.365)	(.207)	(.553)		
Education (Fed)	−1.690*	.523**	.630		
	(.940)	(.210)	(.420)		
Environment (Cons)	−7.869**	.825**		.101**	
	(2.651)	(.114)		(.031)	
Environment (Fed)	−26.243**	.483**		.086**	
	(9.440)	(.180)		(.028)	
Transport (Cons)	−2.040**	1.023**			
	(.950)	(.081)			
Transport (Fed)	−2.852**	.899**			
	(1.187)	(.096)			

Full Results for Table 8.1

	Spend$_t$	Prefs$_{t-1}$	Counter	Counter^2	US-Russia
Defense (1st Income)	−.234**		.553		.248**
	(.042)		(.426)		(.092)
Defense (2nd Income)	−.270**		1.194**		.369**
	(.049)		(.501)		(.108)
Defense (3rd Income)	−.287**		1.662**		.501**
	(.055)		(.556)		(.119)
Welfare (1st Income)	−.696**	.463**	1.524*	.056**	
	(.219)	(.139)	(.779)	(.026)	
Welfare (2nd Income)	−.707**	.491**	1.656**	.051*	
	(.212)	(.134)	(.801)	(.025)	
Welfare (3rd Income)	−.710**	.543**	1.693**	.058**	
	(.212)	(.125)	(.753)	(.023)	
Social (1st Income)	−.143**			.058**	
	(.064)			(.015)	
Social (2nd Income)	−.132**	.709**		.037**	
	(.052)	(.119)		(.013)	
Social (3rd Income)	−.154**	.720**		.042**	
	(.066)	(.121)		(.016)	

Post-911	Unemp	Constant	N	Rsq	Adj Rsq	DW	DhF	Dhp
		−10.297** (4.309)	18	.914	.896		1.672	.219
		−13.872** (4.780)	18	.895	.873	2.304		
		−5.354 (3.679)	18	.891	.868	2.336		
		−10.044** (3.315)	18	.831	.795		.203	.659
		−8.560** (3.068)	18	.823	.785		.786	.391
		.000 (1.373)	18	.918	.907		.363	.556
		.000 (1.334)	18	.923	.912		.642	.436

Post-911	Unemp	Constant	N	Rsq	Adj Rsq	DW	DhF	Dhp
31.742** (7.527)		−19.268** (9.364)	31	.654	.601	.958		
32.137** (8.851)		−33.169** (11.012)	31	.632	.575	.813		
34.088** (9.817)		−45.073** (12.214)	31	.639	.584	.952		
		−40.046** (12.603)	31	.617	.558		.505	.484
		−40.383** (12.452)	31	.602	.540		3.308	.081
		−43.043** (12.745)	31	.788	.755		13.932	.001
		−17.698** (4.580)	31	.768	.751	1.029		
		−11.401** (4.071)	31	.876	.863		.012	.912
		−12.667** (4.901)	31	.812	.791		.711	.407

(*continued*)

APPENDIX TABLE 2. *(continued)*

Full Results for Table 8.1

	Spend$_t$	Prefs$_{t-1}$	Counter	Counter^2	US-Russia
Defense (1st Educ)	−.230** (.044)		.599 (.445)		.302** (.095)
Defense (2nd Educ)	−.250** (.051)		1.228** (.520)		.347** (.112)
Defense (3rd Educ)	−.308** (.055)		2.288** (.558)		.495** (.120)
Welfare (1st Educ)	−.674** (.186)	.455** (.131)	1.760** (.663)	.049** (.022)	
Welfare (2nd Educ)	−.562** (.189)	.533** (.136)	1.372* (.732)	.045** (.021)	
Welfare (3rd Educ)	−.718** (.260)	.607** (.123)	1.960** (.921)	.048 (.030)	
Social (1st Educ)	−.105* (.053)			.050** (.012)	
Social (2nd Educ)	−.097** (.042)	.790** (.107)		.027** (.010)	
Social (3rd Educ)	−.201** (.066)	.725** (.104)		.052** (.016)	
Defense (PID:Dem)	−.289** (.051)		.648 (.514)		.336** (.110)
Defense (PID:Ind)	−.237** (.052)		1.131** (.531)		.354** (.114)
Defense (PID:Rep)	−.277** (.045)		1.965** (.457)		.466** (.098)
Welfare (PID:Dem)	−.599** (.231)	.556** (.136)	1.813** (.847)	.040 (.026)	
Welfare (PID:Ind)	−.513** (.192)	.581** (.133)	1.268* (.725)	.040* (.022)	
Welfare (PID:Rep)	−.915** (.213)	.372** (.130)	1.801** (.776)	.075** (.024)	
Social (PID:Dem)	−.038* (.019)	.596** (.135)	.644** (.203)		
Social (PID:Ind)	−.094** (.033)	.762** (.100)		.028** (.009)	
Social (PID:Rep)	−.204** (.070)	.758** (.109)		.053** (.017)	

Post-911	Unemp	Constant	N	Rsq	Adj Rsq	DW	DhF	Dhp
30.348** (7.850)		−21.487** (9.766)	31	.649	.595	.826		
34.033** (9.181)		−33.161** (11.423)	31	.595	.532	.848		
28.846** (9.854)		−54.154** (12.259)	31	.639	.583	.903		
		41.321** (10.949)	31	.710	.665		3.228	.084
		34.195** (11.540)	31	.704	.659		3.099	.091
		−43.927** (15.152)	31	.726	.684		6.136	.020
		−15.103** (3.788)	31	.827	.814	1.506		
		−8.107** (3.180)	31	.901	.890		1.482	.234
		15.938** (4.935)	31	.833	.814		.014	.907
34.856** (9.073)		−23.832** (11.288)	31	.671	.620	.956		
28.484** (9.372)		−31.379** (11.660)	31	.552	.483	.796		
34.576** (8.067)		−48.761** (10.036)	31	.713	.669	.958		
		−39.268** (13.914)	31	.726	.684		2.273	.144
		−31.186** (11.531)	31	.693	.646		2.502	.126
		−49.974** (12.428)	31	.651	.597		1.296	.266
		−9.665** (3.080)	31	.936	.929		1.185	.286
		−8.440** (2.734)	31	.944	.938		.125	.726
		−16.263** (5.146)	31	.841	.823		1.900	.180

(*continued*)

APPENDIX TABLE 2. *(continued)*

Full Results for Table 8.2

	Spend$_t$	Prefs$_{t-1}$	Counter	Counter^2	US-Russia
Defense (1st Income)	−4.069* (2.250)	.882** (.135)			
Defense (2nd Income)	−4.566 (2.924)	.851** (.147)			
Defense (3rd Income)	−4.583 (2.802)	.873** (.135)			
Welfare (1st Income)	−.994** (.314)		1.207** (.361)		
Welfare (2nd Income)	−1.545** (.260)		1.633** (.299)		
Welfare (3rd Income)	−1.572** (.222)		1.882** (.255)		
Social (1st Income)	−.976** (.260)	.426** (.166)	1.909** (.881)	.163** (.062)	
Social (2nd Income)	−.882** (.261)	.384* (.179)	1.315 (.803)	.175** (.067)	
Social (3rd Income)	−.780** (.166)	.468** (.130)	1.709** (.634)	.104** (.036)	
Defense (1st Educ)	−4.539** (2.064)	.934** (.118)			
Defense (2nd Educ)	−3.851 (2.571)	.870** (.141)			
Defense (3rd Educ)	−4.863* (2.750)	.844** (.129)			
Welfare (1st Educ)	−.799** (.365)		1.443** (.420)		
Welfare (2nd Educ)	−1.337** (.213)		1.488** (.245)		
Welfare (3rd Educ)	−1.197** (.161)	.448** (.083)	1.213** (.168)		
Social (1st Educ)	−.944** (.188)	.281* (.141)	1.914** (.684)	.163** (.041)	
Social (2nd Educ)	−.920** (.192)	.395** (.139)	1.572** (.637)	.161** (.045)	

Post-911	Unemp	Constant	N	Rsq	Adj Rsq	DW	DhF	Dhp
		.000 (2.339)	20	.733	.701		1.275	.276
		−.000 (3.039)	20	.684	.647		1.229	.284
		.000 (2.904)	20	.732	.701		2.494	.134
		−9.055** (3.137)	16	.557	.489	1.962		
		−12.250** (2.602)	16	.794	.762	1.901		
		−14.116** (2.219)	16	.861	.840	1.430		
		−32.383** (7.832)	18	.945	.928		3.522	.085
		−28.515** (7.178)	18	.929	.907		3.882	.072
		−24.807** (5.187	18	.957	.944		1.441	.253
		(−.000) (2.146)	20	.800	.776		1.121	.305
		−.000 (2.673)	20	.703	.668		1.743	.205
		−.000 (2.833)	20	.747	.717		.837	.374
		−10.820** (3.653)	16	.505	.429	2.533		
		−11.161** (2.126)	16	.819	.791	1.919		
		−9.095** (1.409)	16	.960	.950		.530	.482
		−32.410** (6.049)	18	.962	.950		2.240	.160
		−29.288** (5.778)	18	.959	.947		.741	.406

(continued)

APPENDIX TABLE 2. *(continued)*

Full Results for Table 8.2

	Spend$_t$	Prefs$_{t-1}$	Counter	Counter^2	US-Russia
Social (3rd Educ)	−.808**	.517**	1.692**	.126**	
	(.219)	(.153)	(.700)	(.055)	
Defense	−4.108	.648**			
(PID:NDP)	(3.267)	(.194)			
Defense	−4.405	.889**			
(PID:Lib)	(2.626)	(.139)			
Defense	−5.731*	.923**			
(PID:Con)	(2.753)	(.108)			
Welfare	−.815**		2.184**		
(PID:NDP)	(.313)		(.360)		
Welfare	−1.105**	.389**	1.014**		
(PID:Lib)	(.175)	(.101)	(.183)		
Welfare	−1.468**		2.116**		
(PID:Con)	(.250)		(.287)		
Social	−.979**	.336*	2.534**	.121*	
(PID:NDP)	(.276)	(.182)	(.970)	(.060)	
Social	−.849**	.489**	1.430	.150**	
(PID:Lib)					
	(.268)	(.171)	(.883)	(.065)	
Welfare	−.984**	.518**	2.710**	.094	
(PID:Con)	(.261)	(.147)	(.922)	(.057)	

Post-911	Unemp	Constant	N	Rsq	Adj Rsq	DW	DhF	Dhp
		−26.915** (6.321)	18	.954	.939		5.359	.039
		.000 (3.249)	20	.494	.435		2.575	.128
		−.000 (2.728)	20	.725	.693		3.571	.077
		.000 (2.843)	20	.830	.810		.861	.367
		−16.378** (3.128)	16	.743	.703	2.000		
		−7.604** (1.530)	16	.940	.925		.357	.562
		−15.871** (2.498)	16	.842	.817	2.334		
		−33.529** (8.530)	18	.921	.896		.205	.659
		27.060** (7.506)	18	.927	.904		5.249	.041
		−32.329** (7.781)	18	.940	.922		12.591	.004

Cells contain OLS coefficients with standard errors in parentheses. DW is the Durbin-Watson test for correlated standard errors. DhF is an F-test, and Dhp the p-value, from a Durbin's h test, used to test for correlated standard errors when a lagged depending variable is included in the model.
* p < .10; ** p < .05; *** p <.01.

Full Results for Table 7.2

	Prefs$_{t-1}$	Govt1	Govt2	Unemp	Spend$_{t-1}$
US Social	1.287**	−5.511	−.740**		
	(.249)	(3.950)	(.354)		
US Defense	.705**	14.577**	1.088**		
	(.125)	(4.878)	(.402)		
US Welfare	.326**	−3.915	−.401*		
	(.136)	(3.106)	(.224)		
US Health	.563**	−.939	.081		
	(.107)	(1.566)	(.134)		
US Education	.207*	.693	−.160		
	(.105)	(1.955)	(.198)		
US Environment	.052*	−.377	−.065		
	(.027)	(.557)	(.042)		
US Cities	.070**	.139	−.011		
	(.015)	(.279)	(.025)		
US Crime	−.029	−.077	.077		
	(.068)	(.789)	(.073)		
US Foreign Aid	−.035	.394	.085		
	(.092)	(1.065)	(.112)		
US Space	.043**	.306	−.033		
	(.010)	(.218)	(.020)		
UK Social	.224**	−6.769**		.543**	
	(.056)	(1.883)		(.210)	
UK Defense	.048**	−.909			.364**
	(.017)	(.815)			(.147)
UK Health	.112**	−3.441**		.286*	
	(.037)	(1.259)		(.160)	
UK Education	.075**	−2.365*		.217*	
	(.032)	(1.113)		(.117)	
UK Transport	.033	−.672			
	(.025)	(.882)			
CA Social	.464**	9.737**	1.140		
	(.149)	(2.212)	(1.214)		

1977	1978	Constant	N	Rsq	Adj Rsq	DW
		37.155** (17.114)	33	.493	.441	2.044
		−58.748** (18.896)	33	.596	.555	1.767
		20.720* (11.143)	33	.183	.099	2.215
		−3.069 (6.403)	33	.546	.499	1.250
		6.859 (9.278)	33	.127	.037	2.698
		3.189 (1.987)	33	.168	.082	1.530
3.321** (.795)	5.833** (.830)	.122 (1.197)	33	.752	.706	2.369
		−3.433 (3.407)	33	.064	−.032	2.567
		−4.122 (5.087)	33	.027	−.074	1.821
		1.323 (.934)	33	.401	.339	1.777
		3.852** (1.299)	18	.545	.447	1.807
		−9.755** (4.309)	18	.505	.399	
		1.919** (.791)	18	.418	.293	1.704
		1.237 (.853)	18	.335	.192	1.659
		.597 (.825)	18	.108	−.011	1.893
		−5.143** (2.319)	16	.701	.626	2.201

(continued)

APPENDIX TABLE 3. *(continued)*

Full Results for Table 7.2

	Prefs$_{t-1}$	Govt1	Govt2	Unemp	Spend$_{t-1}$
CA Defense	.011*	.256			
	(.006)	(.236)			
CA Welfare	.322**	3.210**		1.541**	
	(.090)	(1.288)		(.653)	
CA Health	.092**	1.872**			
	(.019)	(.767)			
CA Education	.110**	2.560**			
	(.036)	(.744)			
CA Environment	.025**	−.302			
	(.009)	(.235)			
CA Transport	.035**	−.060			
	(.016)	(.619)			

Full Results for Table 7.3

	Prefs$_{t-1}$	Govt1	Govt2	Unemp	Spend$_{t-1}$
Defense (Out)	.670**	15.700**	1.011**		
	(.138)	(5.279)	(.445)		
Defense (App)	.854**	9.293	1.051*		
	(.163)	(6.212)	(.523)		
Welfare (Out)	.345**	−4.141	−.452*		
	(.156)	(3.490)	(.258)		
Welfare (App)	.860**	−11.328*	−.513		
	(.253)	(5.654)	(.384)		
Health (Out)	.562**	−.645	.073		
	(.117)	(1.740)	(.149)		
Health (App)	.572**	−.394	−.002		
	(.203)	(3.009)	(.257)		
Education (Out)	.234*	.380	−.182		
	(.137)	(2.234)	(.220)		
Education (App)	.006	3.843	.298		
	(.172)	(2.806)	(.277)		
Environment (Out)	.062**	−.921*	−.022		
	(.025)	(.533)	(.041)		
Environment (App)	.078**	.351	.179**		
	(.034)	(.728)	(.060)		
Cities (Out)	.061**	.010	.013		
	(.016)	(.281)	(.026)		

1977	1978	Constant	N	Rsq	Adj Rsq	DW
		−.115 (.158)	20	.200	.106	1.851
		−3.841** (1.052)	16	.786	.732	2.090
		−.588 (.348)	17	.622	.568	2.262
		−.885** (.348)	17	.495	.423	2.471
		.086 (.109)	17	.367	.276	2.154
		.085 (.321)	17	.271	.167	1.806

1977	1978	Constant	N	Rsq	Adj Rsq	DW
		−48.344** (20.882)	29	.572	.520	1.815
		−53.740** (24.572)	29	.561	.509	2.075
		27.656** (12.852)	29	.181	.083	2.194
33.567** (11.858)		29.062 (19.107)	29	.388	.286	2.149
		3.335 (7.087)	29	.540	.485	1.227
		.336 (12.251)	29	.277	.190	1.542
		9.840 (10.480)	29	.119	.013	2.715
		−15.931 (13.167)	29	.129	.025	2.397
3.235** (1.339)		1.598 (1.946)	29	.339	.229	1.997
9.121** (1.829)	10.898** (1.855)	−9.136** (2.866)	29	.704	.640	2.443
3.618** (.778)	5.986** (.802)	−1.116 (1.243)	29	.787	.741	2.459

(continued)

APPENDIX TABLE 3. *(continued)*

Full Results for Table 7.3

	Prefs$_{t-1}$	Govt1	Govt2	Unemp	Spend$_{t-1}$
Cities (App)	.064	.784	.127		
	(.061)	(1.052)	(.096)		
Crime (Out)	−.026	−.116	.083		
	(.074)	(.881)	(.082)		
Crime (App)	.034	−.187	.092		
	(.064)	(.759)	(.071)		
Foreign Aid (Out)	.000	.540	.039		
	(.100)	(1.119)	(.121)		
Foreign Aid (App)	−.124	.158	.137		
	(.179)	(2.003)	(.216)		
Space (Out)	.047**	.262	−.028		
	(.019)	(.257)	(.022)		
Space (App)	.008	.435	.003		
	(.033)	(.464)	(.039)		

Full Results for Table 7.4

	Prefs$_{t-1}$	Govt1	Govt2	Unemp
US Social	1.764**	−2.723	−1.172**	
	(.384)	(4.195)	(.508)	
UK Social	.051	−4.927*		.552**
	(.169)	(2.588)		(.226)
CA Social	.501	9.324**		1.194
	(.631)	(2.685)		(1.318)

Full Results for Table 7.5

	Ch Spend$_t$	Ch Spend$_{t-1}$
US Defense	.173	−.322**
	(.134)	(.132)
US Social	.072	−.149**
	(.067)	(.066)
UK Defense	1.474	−8.714**
	(2.930)	(2.767)
UK Social	−.528	−1.100**
	(.403)	(.407)

1977	1978	Constant	N	Rsq	Adj Rsq	DW
19.175** (2.977)		-6.969 (4.463)	29	.652	.594	2.495
		-2.808 (3.851)	29	.064	-.048	2.570
		-4.114 (3.318)	29	.066	-.046	1.847
		-1.798 (5.524)	29	.017	-.101	1.790
		-6.371 (9.892)	29	.024	-.094	1.957
		1.302 (1.037)	29	.324	.243	1.809
		-.406 (1.868)	29	.053	-.060	2.935

Vote Margin	Prefs* VMargin	Constant	N	Rsq	Adj Rsq	DW
-1.951 (1.210)	-.158* (.089)	60.616** (26.750)	32	.562	.478	2.468
.001 (.113)	.018 (.016)	1.885 (2.313)	18	.586	.414	2.180
.189 (.594)	.005 (.061)	-6.261 (7.434)	16	.709	.563	2.284

Constant	N	Rsq	Adj Rsq	DW
.000 (2.077)	32	.171	.114	1.872
-.000 (.790)	32	.150	.091	2.312
.000 (2.753)	17	.438	.358	2.313
-.000 (.697)	17	.435	.355	2.109

(*continued*)

APPENDIX TABLE 3. *(continued)*

Full Results for Table 7.5

	Ch Spend$_t$	Ch Spend$_{t-1}$
CA Defense	−.183	2.663
	(5.658)	(5.635)
CA Social	.061	−.503**
	(.230)	(.229)

Full Results for Table 8.3

	Prefs$_{t-1}$	Govt1	Govt2	Unemp
Defense (1st Income)	.824**	15.636**	1.485**	
	(.147)	(4.810)	(.398)	
Defense (2nd Income)	.749**	17.166**	1.269**	
	(.119)	(4.573)	(.371)	
Defense (3rd Income)	.662**	15.164**	1.036**	
	(.104)	(4.474)	(.368)	
Welfare (1st Income)	.293**	−3.440	−.297	
	(.140)	(3.303)	(.212)	
Welfare (2nd Income)	.343**	−4.090	−.364*	
	(.136)	(3.155)	(.212)	
Welfare (3rd Income)	.237*	−2.503	−.427*	
	(.119)	(3.077)	(.246)	
Social (1st Income)	.841**	2.573	−.459	
	(.207)	(2.624)	(.299)	
Social (2nd Income)	.756**	.950	−.284	
	(.164)	(2.534)	(.252)	
Social (3rd Income)	.661**	.061	−.107	
	(.154)	(2.650)	(.241)	
Defense (1st Educ)	.820**	15.021**	1.526**	
	(.133)	(4.537)	(.379)	
Defense (2nd Educ)	.719**	16.356**	1.139**	
	(.127)	(4.827)	(.392)	
Defense (3rd Educ)	.682**	18.336**	.600	
	(.110)	(4.674)	(.384)	
Welfare (1st Educ)	.364**	−2.941	−.495**	
	(.134)	(2.768)	(.230)	
Welfare (2nd Educ)	.303**	−2.970	−.435*	
	(.144)	(3.141)	(.242)	

Constant	N	Rsq	Adj Rsq	DW
−.000 (2.997)	19	.014	−.109	2.118
.000 (1.020)	15	.358	.251	1.973

Constant	N	Rsq	Adj Rsq	DW
−77.426** (18.830)	32	.607	.565	1.806
−68.536** (17.489)	32	.653	.615	1.874
−56.677** (17.314)	32	.656	.619	1.901
15.682 (10.512)	32	.159	.069	2.300
19.152* (10.531)	32	.208	.123	2.094
21.019* (12.175)	32	.148	.057	2.233
19.293 (13.882)	32	.419	.357	1.494
12.324 (11.903)	32	.474	.417	1.590
4.831 (11.471)	32	.444	.385	1.494
−78.908** (17.898)	32	.646	.608	1.605
−62.085** (18.468)	32	.610	.568	1.793
−38.776** (17.841)	32	.646	.608	1.793
24.383** (11.305)	32	.230	.147	2.286
21.667* (12.059)	32	.160	.070	2.279

(*continued*)

APPENDIX TABLE 3. *(continued)*

Full Results for Table 8.3

	Prefs$_{t-1}$	Govt1	Govt2	Unemp
Welfare (3rd Educ)	.185* (.106)	−2.589 (3.321)	−.322 (.228)	
Social (1st Educ)	.960** (.192)	2.454 (2.405)	−.485* (.263)	
Social (2nd Educ)	.818** (.181)	1.055 (2.549)	−.281 (.255)	
Social (3rd Educ)	.646** (.158)	−1.756 (2.854)	−.081 (.245)	
Defense (PID:Dem)	.685** (.118)	16.026** (4.743)	1.620** (.396)	
Defense (PID:Ind)	.742** (.130)	15.865** (4.780)	1.223** (.391)	
Defense (PID:Rep)	.746** (.112)	16.110** (4.365)	.657* (.364)	
Welfare (PID:Dem)	.285** (.128)	−3.609 (3.241)	−.512* (.257)	
Welfare (PID:Ind)	.318** (.152)	−3.455 (3.303)	−.434* (.242)	
Welfare (PID:Rep)	.227* (.120)	−1.885 (2.956)	−.212 (.205)	
Social (PID:Dem)	.722** (.170)	2.578 (2.583)	−.326 (.271)	
Social (PID:Ind)	.937** (.187)	1.484 (2.420)	−.473* (.262)	
Social (PID:Rep)	.646** (.122)	−1.412 (2.478)	−.165 (.220)	

Full Results for Table 8.4

	Prefs$_{t-1}$	Govt1	Govt2	Unemp
Defense (1st Income)	.013* (.007)	.247 (.232)		
Defense (2nd Income)	.010* (.006)	.239 (.236)		
Defense (3rd Income)	.009 (.006)	.273 (.239)		
Welfare (1st Income)	.059 (.111)	5.265** (1.745)		−.129 (.769)

Constant	N	Rsq	Adj Rsq	DW
16.280	32	.123	.029	2.140
(11.338)				
20.536	32	.513	.461	1.528
(12.255)				
12.155	32	.466	.409	1.476
(12.006)				
4.766	32	.422	.360	1.521
(11.770)				
−83.781**	32	.620	.579	1.797
(18.742)				
−65.597**	32	.614	.572	1.710
(18.408)				
−39.972**	32	.677	.642	1.935
(17.000)				
25.582*	32	.174	.086	2.274
(12.880)				
21.917*	32	.160	.070	2.395
(12.154)				
10.824	32	.137	.045	2.170
(9.861)				
13.216	32	.437	.377	1.455
(12.621)				
20.620	32	.513	.461	1.448
(12.266)				
8.379	32	.538	.489	1.581
(10.526)				

Constant	N	Rsq	Adj Rsq	DW
−.111	20	.222	.131	1.856
(.156)				
−.108	20	.192	.097	1.838
(.159)				
−.123	20	.183	.087	1.851
(.160)				
−1.407	16	.567	.459	1.674
(1.276)				

(*continued*)

APPENDIX TABLE 3. *(continued)*

Full Results for Table 8.4

	Prefs$_{t-1}$	Govt1	Govt2	Unemp
Welfare (2nd Income)	.255** (.055)	3.495** (1.042)		1.214** (.461)
Welfare (3rd Income)	.232** (.070)	4.127** (1.219)		1.161* (.600)
Social (1st Income)	.139** (.063)	4.624** (1.466)		-.401 (.671)
Social (2nd Income)	.172* (.080)	3.986** (1.422)		-.199 (.760)
Social (3rd Income)	.223** (.089)	5.147** (1.465)		-.300 (.642)
Defense (1st Educ)	.014** (.006)	.272 (.226)		
Defense (2nd Educ)	.010 (.006)	.234 (.239)		
Defense (3rd Educ)	.009* (.005)	.284 (.239)		
Welfare (1st Educ)	.096 (.079)	5.667** (1.467)		-.041 (.570)
Welfare (2nd Educ)	.293** (.122)	3.798** (1.503)		1.431 (.878)
Welfare (3rd Educ)	.276** (.067)	2.380* (1.292)		1.627** (.598)
Social (1st Educ)	.207** (.092)	5.232** (1.558)		-.220 (.726)
Social (2nd Educ)	.211** (.089)	4.733** (1.443)		-.010 (.770)
Social (3rd Educ)	.164** (.065)	4.375** (1.372)		-.327 (.634)
Defense (PID: NDP)	.010 (.007)	.307 (.252)		
Defense (PID:Lib)	.012* (.006)	.284 (.232)		
Defense (PID:Con)	.009* (.004)	.318 (.237)		
Welfare (PID: NDP)	.090 (.080)	5.980** (1.501)		.031 (.632)

Constant	N	Rsq	Adj Rsq	DW
−3.327** (.771)	16	.843	.803	2.290
−3.427** (1.021)	16	.770	.712	2.015
−.826 (1.259)	16	.590	.488	2.310
−.957 (1.329)	16	.583	.479	2.276
−1.172 (1.253)	16	.623	.529	2.421
−.122 (.151)	20	.270	.184	1.853
−.105 (.160)	20	.174	.077	1.829
−.128 (.159)	20	.192	.097	1.837
−1.696 (1.096)	16	.607	.508	1.800
−3.823** (1.432)	16	.702	.627	2.264
−3.740** (.925)	16	.815	.769	1.929
−1.205 (1.372)	16	.594	.492	2.467
−1.466 (1.406)	16	.607	.509	2.425
−.828 (1.154)	16	.624	.529	2.389
−.138 (.166)	20	.134	.032	1.802
−.128 (.155)	20	.233	.142	1.954
−.143 (.157)	20	.218	.126	1.804
−1.925 (1.262)	16	.599	.499	1.656

(continued)

APPENDIX TABLE 3. *(continued)*

Full Results for Table 8.4

	Prefs$_{t-1}$	Govt1	Govt2	Unemp
Welfare	.373**	1.839		2.073**
(PID:Lib)	(.081)	(1.252)		(.619)
Welfare	.203**	4.714**		.957
(PID:Con)	(.065)	(1.196)		(.577)
Social	.157*	4.858**		−.399
(PID:NDP)	(.082)	(1.577)		(.740)
Social	.150*	4.199**		−.356
(PID:Lib)	(.070)	(1.435)		(.701)
Welfare	.156**	4.912**		−.340
(PID:Con)	(.058)	(1.391)		(.602)

Constant	N	Rsq	Adj Rsq	DW
−4.392**	16	.841	.801	2.587
(.943)				
−3.235**	16	.757	.696	2.330
(1.022)				
−1.014	16	.560	.449	2.137
(1.454)				
−.785	16	.583	.479	2.420
(1.270)				
−1.120	16	.640	.551	2.551
(1.183)				

Bibliography

Abramowitz, A.I. 1994. "Issue Evolution Reconsidered: Racial Attitudes and Partisanship in the U.S. Electorate." *American Journal of Political Science* 38:1–24.

Abramson, Jeffrey B., F. Christopher Arterton and Gary R. Orren. 1988. The *Electronic Commonwealth: The Impact of New Media Technologies on Democratic Politics.* New York: Basic Books.

Achen, Christopher H. 1978. "Measuring Representation." *American Journal of Political Science* 22:475–510.

Adams, James, Michael Clark, Lawrence Ezrow, and Garrett Glasgow. 2006. "Are Niche Parties Fundamentally Different from Mainstream Parties? The Causes and the Electoral Consequences of Western European Parties' Policy Shifts 1996–1998." *American Journal of Political Science* 50:513–529.

Almond, Gabriel. 1950. *The American People and Foreign Policy.* 2nd ed. New York: Harcourt, Brace, Jovanovich.

Alt, James E. 1985. "Political Parties, World Demand, and Unemployment: Domestic and International Sources of Economic Activity." *American Political Science Review* 79:1016–1040.

Althaus, Scott L. 2003. *Collective Preferences in Democratic Politics: Opinion Surveys and the Will of the People.* Cambridge: Cambridge University Press.

——— 1998. "Information Effects in Collective Preferences." *American Political Science Review* 92: 545–558.

Andersen, S.S., and Burns, T. 1996. "The European Union and the Erosion of Parliamentary Democracy: A Study of Post-Parliamentary Governance." In Andersen, S.S. and Eliassen, K.A., eds. *The European Union: How Democratic Is It?* London: Sage.

Andersen, Robert, James Tilley and Anthony F. Heath. 2005. "Political Knowledge and Enlightened Preferences: Party Choice Through the Electoral Cycle." *British Journal of Political Science* 35: 285–302.

Anderson, Cameron. 2006. "Economic Voting and Multilevel Governance: A Comparative Individual-level Analysis," *American Journal of Political Science* 50(2):446–460.

Ansell, Christopher, and Jane Gingrich. 2003. "Trends in Decentralization." In Bruce E. Cain, Russell J. Dalton and Susan E. Scarrow, eds. *Democracy Transformed? Expanding Opportunities in Advanced Industrial Democracies*, pp. 140–163. Oxford: Oxford University Press.

Arceneaux, Kevin. 2005. "Do Campaigns Help Voters Learn? A Cross-National Analysis." *British Journal of Political Science* 36:159–173.

Arrow, Kenneth J. 1951. *Social Choice and Individual Values*. New York: Wiley.

Bagehot, Walter. 1867. *The English Constitution*. London: Fontana.

Bahl, Roy, and Sally Wallace. 2005. "Public Financing in Developing and Transition Countries." *Public Budgeting & Finance* 25(4s):83–98.

Barker, Ernest. "Burke and his Bristol Constituency," in *Essays on Government*. Oxford: The Clarendon Press.

Barnes, Samuel H. 1977. *Representation in Italy: Institutionalized Tradition and Electoral Choice*. Chicago: University of Chicago Press.

Bartels, Larry M. 2008. *Unequal Democracy: The Political Economy of the New Gilded Age*. Princeton: Princeton University Press.

  2005. "Economic Inequality and Political Representation." Paper presented at the Annual Meeting of the American Political Science Association, Boston, September 2002. Revised August 2005.

  1993. "Messages Received: The Political Impact of Media Exposure." *American Political Science Review* 87(2):267–285.

  1991. "Constituency Opinion and Congressional Policy Making: The Reagan Defense Build Up." *American Political Science Review* 85(2):457–474.

Baumgartner, Frank R., and Bryan D. Jones. 2002. "Positive and Negative Feedback in Politics," In Frank R. Baumgartner and Bryan D. Jones, eds. *Policy Dynamics*. Chicago: University of Chicago Press.

  1993. *Agendas and Instability in American Politics*. Chicago: University of Chicago Press.

Beitz, Charles. 1990. *Political Equality: An Essay in Democratic Theory*. Princeton: Princeton University Press.

Bentham, Jeremy. 1989. *First Principles Preparatory to the Constitutional Code*, Philip Schofield, ed. Oxford: Clarendon.

Berelson, Bernard R., Paul F. Lazarsfeld and William N. McPhee. 1954. *Voting: A Study of Opinion Formation in a Presidential Campaign*. Chicago: University of Chicago Press.

Berinsky, Adam J. 2004. *Silent Voices: Public Opinion and Political Participation in America*. Princeton: Princeton University Press.

Bianco, William T. 1994. *Trust: Representatives and Constituents*. Ann Arbor: University of Michigan Press.

Birch, Anthony H. 2001. *Concepts and Theories of Modern Democracy*, 2nd ed. London: Routledge.

1971. *Representation*. New York: Praeger.

Blais, André, Donald Blake and Stephane Dion. 1996. "Do Parties Make a Difference? A Reappraisal." *American Journal of Political Science* 40:514–520.

Blais, André, and Marc André Bodet. 2006. "Does Proportional Representation Foster Closer Congruence Between Citizens and Policy Makers?" *Comparative Political Studies* 39:1243–1262.

Blekesaune, Morten. 2007. "Economic Conditions and Public Attitudes to Welfare Policies." *European Sociological Review* 23:393–403.

Brady, Henry E., and Richard Johnston. 1987. "What's the Primary Message: Horse Race or Issue Journalism?" In Gary R. Orren and Nelson W. Polsby, eds. *Media and Momentum*. Chatham, NJ: Chatham House.

Brand, Jack. 1992. *British Parliamentary Parties: Policy and Power*. Oxford: Oxford University Press.

Bratton, Kathleen A. and Kerry L. Haynie. 1999. "Agenda Setting and Legislative Success in State Legislatures: The Effects of Gender and Race." *Journal of Politics* 61:658–679.

Bratton, Kathleen A. and Leonard P. Ray. 2002. "Descriptive Representation, Policy Outcomes, and Municipal Day-Care Coverage in Norway." *American Journal of Political Science* 46(2):428–437.

Brehm, John. 1993. *The Phantom Respondents: Opinion Surveys and Political Representation*. Ann Arbor: University of Michigan Press.

Brody, Richard. 1991. *Assessing the President: The Media, Elite Opinion, and Public Support*. Stanford: Stanford University Press.

Brooks, Clem. 2006. "Voters, Satisficing and Public Policymaking: Recent Directions in the Study of Electoral Politics." *Annual Review of Sociology* 32:191–211.

Brooks, Clem, and Jeff Manza. 2007. *Why Welfare States Persist: Public Opinion and the Future of Social Provision*. Chicago: University of Chicago Press.

2006. "Social Political Responsiveness in Developed Democracies." *American Sociological Review* 71:474–494.

Brooks, Joel E. 1990. "The Opinion-Policy Nexus in Germany." *Public Opinion Quarterly* 54:508–529.

1987. "The Opinion-Policy Nexus in France – Do Institutions and Ideology Make a Difference?" *Journal of Politics* 49:465–480.

1985. "Democratic Frustration in the Anglo-American Polities: A Quantification of Inconsistency between Mass Public Opinion, and Public Policy." *Western Political Quarterly* 38:250–261.

Budge, I., Robertson, D., and Hearl, D. eds. 1987. *Ideology, Strategy and Party Change: Spatial Analyses of Post-War Election Programmes in 19 Democracies*. Cambridge: Cambridge University Press.

Burstein, Paul. 2006. "Why Estimates of the Impact of Public Opinion on Public Policy Are Too High," *Social Forces* 84:2273–2290.

    2003. "The Impact of Public Opinion on Public Policy: A Review and an Agenda." *Political Research Quarterly* 56:29–40.

    1979. "Some 'Necessary Conditions' for Popular Control of Public Policy: A Critique." *Polity* 12:23–37.

Cain, Bruce E., John A. Ferejohn and Morris P. Fiorina. 1987. *The Personal Vote: Constituency Service and Electoral Independence.* Cambridge, MA: Harvard University Press.

    1979. "The House Is Not a Home: British MPs in Their Constituencies." *Legislative Studies Quarterly* 4(4):501–523.

Campbell, Angus, Philip E. Converse, Warren E. Miller and Donald E. Stokes. 1964. *The American Voter.* Chicago: University of Chicago Press.

Clarke, Harold D., David Sanders, Marianne C. Stewart and Paul Whiteley. 2004. *Political Choice in Britain.* Oxford: Oxford University Press.

Clausen, Aage R. 1973. *How Congressmen Decide: A Policy Focus.* New York: St. Martin's.

Chong, Dennis, and James N. Druckman. 2007. "Framing Theory." *Annual Review of Political Science* 10: 103–126.

Cohen, Jeffrey E. 1999. *Presidential Responsiveness and Public Policy-Making.* Ann Arbor: University of Michigan Press.

Converse, Philip E. 1990. "Popular Representation and the Distribution of Information." In John A. Ferejohn and James H. Kuklinski, eds. *Information and Democratic Processes*, pp. 369–388. Urbana and Chicago: University of Illinois Press.

    1964. "The Nature of Belief Systems in Mass Publics." In D. E. Apter, ed. *Ideology and Discontent*, pp. 206–261. New York: The Free Press.

Converse, Philip E. and Roy Pierce. 1986. *Political Representation in France.* Cambridge, MA: Harvard University Press.

Cowley, Philip. 2002. *Revolts & Rebellions – Parliamentary Voting Under Blair.* London: Politico.

Cox, Gary W. 1997. *Making Votes Count: Strategic Coordination in the World's Electoral Systems.* Cambridge: Cambridge University Press.

Cox, Gary W. 1987. *The Efficient Secret: The Cabinet and the Development of Political Parties in Victorian England.* Cambridge: Cambridge University Press.

Cox, Gary W., and Scott Morgenstern. 2001. "Latin America's Reactive Assemblies and Proactive Presidents." *Comparative Politics* 33(2): 171–189.

Cutler, Fred. 1999. "Jeremy Bentham and the Public Opinion Tribunal." *Public Opinion Quarterly* 63(3):321–346.

Dahl, Robert A. 2000. *On Democracy.* New Haven: Yale University Press.

    1971. *Polyarchy.* New Haven: Yale University Press.

1970. *Frontiers of Democratic Theory*. New York: Harper and Row.

1967. *Pluralist Democracy in the United States*. Chicago: Rand McNally.

1956. *A Preface to Democratic Theory*. Chicago: University of Chicago Press.

Delli Carpini, Michael X, and Scott Keeter. 1996. *What Americans Know About Politics and Why It Matters*. New Haven: Yale University Press.

Devine, Donald J. 1970. *The Attentive Public: Polyarchical Democracy*. Chicago: Rand McNally.

Deutsch, Karl W. 1963. *Nerves of Government*. New York: The Free Press.

Downs, Willam W. 1999. "Accountability Payoffs in Federal Systems? Competing Logics and Evidence from Europe's Newest Federation." *Publius* 29: 87–110.

Downs, Anthony. 1956. *An Economic Theory of Democracy*. New York: Harper.

Druckman, James, and Lawrence Jacobs. 2006. "Lumpers and Splitters: The Public Opinion Information That Politicians Collect and Use." *Public Opinion Quarterly* 70(4):453–476.

Durr, Robert H. 1993. "What Moves Policy Sentiment?" *American Political Science Review* 87(1):158–170.

Duverger, Maurice. 1980. "A New Political System Model: Semi-Presidential Government. *European Journal of Political Research* 8:165–187.

Easton, David. 1965. *A Framework for Political Analysis*. Englewood Cliffs, NJ: Prentice-Hall.

1985. "Political Language and Political Reality." *PS: Political Science and Politics* 18:10–19.

Eichenberg, Richard, and Richard Stoll. 2003. "Representing Defense: Democratic Control of the Defense Budget in the United States and Western Europe." *Journal of Conflict Resolution* 47: 399–423.

Eisinger, Robert M. 2003. *The Evolution of Presidential Polling*. New York: Cambridge University Press.

Enns, Peter K. and Paul M. Kellstedt. 2008. "Policy Mood and Political Sophistication: Why Everyone Moves Mood." *British Journal of Political Science* 38:433–454.

Erikson, Robert S. 1990. "Roll Calls, Reputations, and Representation in the U.S. Senate." *Legislative Studies Quarterly* 15(4):623–642.

1978. "Constituency Opinion and Congressional Behavior: A Reexamination of the Miller-Stokes Representation Data." *American Journal of Political Science* 22:511–535.

Erikson, Robert S., Michael B. MacKuen, and James A. Stimson. 2002. *The Macro Polity*. Cambridge: Cambridge University Press.

Erikson, Robert S., John P. McIver and Gerald C. Wright. 1987. "Political Parties, Public Opinion, and State Policy in the United States." *American Political Science Review* 83:728–50.

Erikson, Robert S., Gerald C. Wright, and John P. McIver. 1993. *Statehouse Democracy; Public Opinion and Policy in the American States.* Cambridge: Cambridge University Press.

Erikson, Robert S. and Kent L. Tedin. 2004. *American Public Opinion.* New York: Longman.

Erickson, Lynda. 1997. "Might More Women Make a Difference? Gender, Party and Ideology among Canada's Parliamentary Candidates." *Canadian Journal of Political Science* 30(4):663–688.

Eulau, Heinz. 1967. "Changing Views of Representation." In Ithiel de Sola Pol, ed. *Contemporary Political Science: Toward Empirical Theory*, pp. 53–85. New York: McGraw-Hill.

Eulau, Heinz and Paul D. Karps. 1977. "The Puzzle of Representation: Specifying Components of Responsiveness." *Legislative Studies Quarterly* 2(3):233–254.

Eulau, Heinz, and Kenneth Prewitt. 1973. *Labyrinths of Democracy: Adaptations, Linkages, Representation, and Policies in Urban Politics.* Indianapolis, IN: Bobbs-Merrill.

Fairlie, John A. 1940. "The Nature of Political Representation." *American Political Science Review* 34(2):236–248.

Fenno, Richard. 1978. *Home Style: House Members in Their Districts.* New York: Little, Brown.

Ferejohn, J.A. 1990. "Information and the Electoral Process," In John Ferejohn, and James Kuklinski, eds. *Information and Democratic Processes.* Chicago: University of Illinois Press.

Ferejohn, J.A., and Kuklinski, J.H. eds. 1990. *Information and Democratic Processes.* Urbana: University of Illinois Press.

Fiorina, Morris P. 1997. "Professionalism, Realignment, and Representation." *American Political Science Review* 91:156–162.

    1981. *Retrospective Voting in American National Elections.* New Haven: Yale University Press.

    1974. *Representatives, Roll Calls, and Constituencies.* Lexington, MA: Lexington Books.

    1973. "Electoral Margins, Constituency Influence, and Policy Moderation: a Critical Assessment." *American Politics Research* 1:479–498.

Fishkin, James S. 1995. *The Voice of the People: Public Opinion and Democracy.* New Haven: Yale University Press.

    1991. *Democracy and Deliberation: New Directions For Democratic Reform.* New Haven: Yale University Press.

Follesdal, Andreas, and Simon Hix. 2006. "Why There is a Democratic Deficit in the EU: A Response to Majone and Moravcsik." *Journal of Common Market Studies* 44(3):533–562.

Fournier, Patrick. 2005. "Ambivalence and Attitude Change in Vote Choice: Do Campaign Switchers Experience Internal Conflict?" In Stephen C.

Craig and Michael D. Martinez, eds. *Ambivalence, Politics, and Public Policy*. New York: Palgrave Macmillan.

Franklin, Mark N. 2004. *Voter Turnout and the Dynamics of Electoral Competition in Established Democracies Since 1945*. Cambridge: Cambridge University Press.

Franklin, Mark N. and Wlezien, C. 1997. "The Responsive Public: Issue Salience, Policy Change, and Preferences for European Unification." *Journal of Theoretical Politics* 9:347–363.

Franklin, Mark N., Wouter van der Brug, and Cees van der Eijk. 2007. *The Economy and the Vote: Electoral Responses to Economic Conditions in 15 Countries*. New York: Cambridge University Press.

Froman, Lewis A. 1963. *Congressmen and Their Constituencies*. Chicago: Rand McNally.

Gabel, Matthew, and Kenneth Scheve. 2007. "Estimating the Effect of Elite Communications on Public Opinion Using Instrumental Variables." *American Journal of Political Science* 51:1013–1028.

Gastil, John. 2000. "Is Face-to-Face Citizen Deliberation a Luxury or a Necessity?" *Political Communication* 17:357–361.

Gay, Claudine. 2002. "Spirals of Trust? The Effect of Descriptive Representation on the Relationship between Citizens and Their Government." *American Journal of Political Science* 46(4):717–732.

Geer, John G. 2006. *In Defense of Negativity: Attack Ads in Presidential Campaigns*. Chicago: University of Chicago Press.

1996. *From Tea Leaves to Opinion Polls: A Theory of Democratic Leadership*. New York: Columbia University Press.

Gelman, Andrew, and Gary King. 1993. "Why Are American Presidential Election Campaign Polls So Variable When Votes Are So Predictable?" *British Journal of Political Science* 23:409–451.

Gilens, Martin. 2005. "Inequality and Democratic Responsiveness." *Public Opinion Quarterly* 65:778–796.

2004. "Public Opinion and Democratic Responsiveness: Who Gets What They Want from Government?" Social Inequality Working Paper, Russell Sage Foundation.

Goggin, M., and Wlezien, C. 1993. "Abortion Opinion and Policy in the American States." In M. Goggin, ed., *Understanding the New Politics of Abortion*, pp. 190–202. Newbury Park, CA: Sage.

Golder, Matt. 2005. "Democratic Electoral Systems Around the World 1946–2000." *Electoral Studies* 24: 103–121.

Gotell, Lise, and Janine Brodie. 1996. "Women and Parties in the 1990s: Less than Even an Issue of Numbers." In Hugh G. Thorbrun, ed. *Party Politics in Canada*, 7th ed. Scarborough, ON: Prentice Hall.

Graber, D. 1989. *Mass Media and American Politics*, 3rd ed. Washington, DC: CQ Press.

Griffin, J. D., and Newman, B. 2005. "Are Voters Better Represented?" *Journal of Politics*.

Groseclose, Tim. 2001. "A Model of Candidate Location When One Candidate Has a Valence Advantage." *American Journal of Political Science* 45:862–886.

Gulati, Girish J. 2004. "Revisiting the Link Between Electoral Competition and Policy Extremism in the U.S. Congress." *American Politics Research* 32:495–520.

Habermas, Jürgen. 1962. *The Structural Transformation of the Public Sphere: An Inquiry into a Category of Bourgeois Society. Trans. Thomas Burger.* Cambridge, MA: MIT Press.

Hansen, John Mark. 1991. *Gaining Access: Congress and the Farm Lobby, 1919–1981.* Chicago: University of Chicago Press.

Harrison, Kathryn. 1996. *Passing the Buck: Federalism and Canadian Environmental Policy.* Vancouver: UBC Press.

Hartley, Thomas, and Bruce Russett. 1992. "Public Opinion and the Common Defence: Who Governs Military Spending in the United States?" *American Political Science Review* 86:905–915.

Heise, D. R. 1969. "Separating Reliability and Stability in Test-Retest Correlations." *American Sociological Review* 34:93–101.

Heitshusen, Valerie, Garry Young and David M. Wood. 2005. "Electoral Context and MP Constituency Focus in Australia, Canada, Ireland, New Zealand, and the United Kingdom." *American Journal of Political Science* 49(1):32–45.

Herman, Edward S., and Noam Chomsky. 1988. *Manufacturing Consent: The Political Economy of the Mass Media.* New York: Pantheon Books.

Hero, Rodney E., and Caroline J. Tolbert. 1995. "Latinos and Substantive Representation in the U.S. House of Representatives: Direct, Indirect, or Nonexistent?" *American Journal of Political Science* 39(3):640–652.

Herrera, Cheryl Lyn, Richard Herrera, and Eric R.A.N. Smith. 1992. "Public Opinion and Congressional Representation." *Public Opinion Quarterly* 56(2):185–205.

Hibbs, Douglas A. 1987. *The American Political Economy.* Cambridge, MA: Harvard University Press.

Hill, Kim Q. and Angela Hinton-Anderson. 1995. "Pathways of Representation: A Causal Analysis of Public Opinion-Policy Linkages." *American Journal of Political Science* 39(4):924–935.

Hill, Kim Q., and Patricia. A. Hurley. 2003. "Beyond the Demand-Input Model: A Theory of Representational Linkages." *Journal of Politics* 65(2):304–26.

Hill, Kim Q., and Patricia A. Hurley. 1999. "Dyadic Representation Reappraised." *American Journal of Political Science* 43:109–137.

Hobolt, Sara B., and Robert Klemmensen. 2008. "Government Responsiveness and Political Competition in Comparative Perspective." *Comparative Political Studies* 41:309–337.

    2005. "Responsive Government? Public Opinion and Policy Preferences in Britain and Denmark." *Political Studies* 53:379–402.

Holsti, Ole R. 1996. *Public Opinion and American Foreign Policy*. Ann Arbor: University of Michigan Press.

Huber, John D. 1996. *Rationalizing Parliament: Legislative Institutions and Party Politics in France*. Cambridge: Cambridge University Press.

Hurley, Patricia A. 1982. "Collective Representation Reappraised." *Legislative Studies Quarterly* 7(1):119–136.

Hutchings, Vincent L. 2003. *Public Opinion and Democratic Accountability: How Citizens Learn About Politics*. Princeton: Princeton University Press.

Inglehart, Ronald and Paul Abramson. 1994. "Economic Security and Value Change." *American Political Science Review* 88:336–354.

Iyengar, Shanto, Helmut Norpoth and Kyu S. Hahn. 2004. "Consumer Demand for Election News: The Horserace Sells." *Journal of Politics* 66:157–175.

Jackman, Simon, and Paul Sniderman. 2002. "The Institutional Organization of Choice Spaces: A Political Conception of Political Psychology." pp. 209–223 In Kristen Monroe, ed., *Political Psychology*. Mahway, NJ: Lawrence Erlbaum.

Jacobs, Lawrence R. 1995. "The Rise of Presidential Polling: The Nixon White House in Historical Perspective." *Public Opinion Quarterly* 59:163–195.

    1993. *The Health of Nations: Public Opinion and the Making of Health Policy in the U.S. and Britain*. Ithaca, NY: Cornell University Press.

Jacobs, Lawrence R. and Benjamin I. Page. 2005. "Who Influences U.S. Foreign Policy?" *American Political Science Review* 99:107–123.

Jacobs, Lawrence R. and Robert Y. Shapiro. 2000. *Politicians Don't Pander: Political Manipulation and the Loss of Democratic Responsiveness*. Chicago: University of Chicago Press.

    1995. "The Rise of Presidential Polling: The Nixon White House in Historical Perspective." *Public Opinion Quarterly* 59:163–195.

Jacobs, Lawrence R. and Theda Skocpol, eds. 2005. *Inequality and American Democracy: What We Know and What We Need to Learn*. New York: Russell Sage Foundation.

Jennings, I. 1959. *Cabinet Government*, 3rd ed. Cambridge: Cambridge University Press.

Jennings, Will. 2009. "The Public Thermostat, Political Responsiveness and Error-Correction: Border Control and Asylum in Britain 1994–2007." *British Journal of Poltical Science*, 39(4):847–870.

Jennings, Will, and Peter John. 2009. "The Dynamics of Political Attention: Public Opinion and the Queen's Speech in the United Kingdom 1960–2001." *American Journal of Political Science* 53(4):838–854.

Johnston, Richard. 2008. "Polarized Pluralism in the Canadian Party System: Presidential Address to the Canadian Political Science Association." *Canadian Journal of Political Science* 41:815–834.

Johnston, Richard, Andre Blais, Elisabeth Gidengil, and Neil Nevitte. 1996. *The Challenge of Direct Democracy: The 1992 Canadian Referendum.* Montreal: McGill-Queen's University Press.

Johnston, Richard, Henry E. Brady and Jean Crete. 1992. *Letting the People Decide: Dynamics of a Canadian Election.* Montreal: McGill-Queen's University Press.

Johnson, Martin, Paul Brace, and Kevin Arceneaux. 2005. "Public Opinion and Dynamic Representation in the American States: The Case of Environmental Attitudes." *Social Science Quarterly* 86(1):87–108.

Jones, Bryan D. 1994. *Reconceiving Decision-Making in Democratic Politics: Attention, Choice, and Public Policy.* Chicago: University of Chicago Press.

Jones, Bryan D., Frank R. Baumgartner and James L. True. 1998. "Policy Punctuations: U.S. Budget Authority 1947–1995." *Journal of Politics* 60: 1–33.

Jones, Bryan D., Frank R. Baumgartner, Christian Breunig, Christopher Wlezien, Stuart Soroka, Martial Foucault, Abel François, Christoffer Green-Pedersen, Chris Koske, Peter John, Peter B. Mortensen, Frédéric Varone, Stefaan Walgrave. 2009. "A General Empirical Law of Public Budgets: An Empirical Analysis." *American Journal of Political Science* 53(4):855–873.

Joumard, Isabelle, and Per Mathis Kongsrud. 2003. "Fiscal Relations Across Government Levels." *OECD Economic Studies* 36:155–229.

Karol, David. 2007. "Has Polling Enhanced Representation? Unearthing Evidence from the Literary Digest Issue Polls." *Studies in American Political Development* 21:16–29.

Katz, Richard S. 1997. *Democracy and Elections.* New York: Oxford University Press.

Kelly, Nathan J. 2009. *The Politics of Income Inequality in the United States.* New York: Cambridge University Press.

Kelly, R.M., M.A. Saint-Germain and J.D. Horn. 1991. "Female Public Officials: A Different Voice?," *Annals of the American Academy of Political and Social Science* 515:77–87.

Kerr, Brinck, and Will Miller. 1997. "Latino Representation, It's Direct and Indirect." *American Journal of Political Science* 41(3):1066–1071.

Key, V.O., Jr. 1966. *The Responsible Electorate: Rationality in Presidential Voting 1936–1960.* New York: Vintage Books.

King, Anthony and Robert J. Wybrow. 2001. *British Political Opinion: 1937–2000, The Gallup Polls.* London: Politico.

Kingdon, John W. 1995. *Agendas, Alternatives and Public Policies*, 2nd ed. New York: Harper Collins.

　1981. *Congressmen's Voting Decisions*, 2nd ed. New York: Harper & Row.

　1973. *Congressmen's Voting Decisions*. New York: Harper & Row.

Klingemann, Hans-Dieter, Andrea Volkens, Judith Bara, Ian Budge, and Michael McDonald. 2006. *Mapping Policy Preferences: Estimates for Parties, Electors, and Governments in Eastern Europe, European Union and OECD 1990–2003*. Oxford: Oxford University Press.

Krosnick, Jon. 1990. "Government Policy and Citizen Passion: A Study of Issue Publics in Contemporary America." *Political Behavior* 12(1):59–92.

　1989. "Question Wording and Reports of Survey Results: The Case of Louis Harris and Associates and Aetna Life and Casualty." *Public Opinion Quarterly* 53:107–113.

Kuklinski, James H. 1977. "District Competitiveness and Legislative Roll Call Behavior: A Reassessment of the Marginality Hypothesis." *American Journal of Political Science* 20:627–638.

　1978. "Representation and Elections: A Policy Analysis." *American Political Science Review* 72:165–177.

Kuklinski, James, Paul Quirk, Jennifer Jerit, David Schwieder and Robert Rich. 2000. "Misinformation and the Currency of Democratic Citizenship." *Journal of Politics* 62:790–816.

Kymlicka, Will. 1995. *Multicultural Citizenship*. Oxford: Oxford University Press.

　1993. "Group Representation in Canadian Politics." In *Equity and Community: The Charter, Interest Advocacy, and Representation*. F. L. Seidle, ed. Montreal: Institute for Research on Public Policy.

Lau, Richard R., and David P. Redlawsk. 2006. *How Voters Decide: Information Processing During Election Campaigns*. Cambridge: Cambridge University Press.

Laver, Michael, and Kenneth A. Shepsle. 1996. *Making and Breaking Governments: Cabinets and Legislatures in Parliamentary Democracies*. Cambridge: Cambridge University Press.

　1997. "Events, Equilibria, and Survival." *American Journal of Political Science* 42:28–54.

Lazarsfeld, Paul F., Bernard Berelson, and Hazel Gaudet. 1968. *The People's Choice: How the Voter Makes up his Mind in a Presidential Campaign*. New York: Columbia University Press.

Lijphart, Arend. 1999. *Patterns of Democracy*. New Haven: Yale University Press.

　1994. *Electoral Systems and Party Systems: A Study of Twenty-Seven Democracies 1945–1990*. Oxford: Oxford University Press.

　1984. *Democracies: Patterns of Majoritarian and Consensus Government in Twenty-One Countries*. New Haven: Yale University Press.

　1977. *Democracy in Plural Societies*. New Haven: Yale University Press.

Linz, Juan J. 1994. "Presidential or Parliamentary Democracy: Does It Make a Difference?" In Juan Linz and Arturo Valenzuela, eds. *Failure of Presidential Democracy*. Baltimore: Johns Hopkins University Press.

Lippmann, Walter. 1925. *The Phantom Public*. New York: Harcourt, Brace and Company.

Lupia, Arthur. 1994. "The Effect of Information on Voting Behavior and Electoral Outcomes: An Experimental Study of Direct Legislation." *Public Choice* 78:65–86.

Lupia, Arthur and Mathew D. McCubbins. 1998. *The Democratic Dilemma: Can Citizens Learn What They Need to Know?* Cambridge: Cambridge University Press.

Lupia, Arthur and Kaare Strom. 1995. "Coalition Termination and the Strategic Timing of Parliamentary Elections." *American Political Science Review* 89:648–665.

Luskin, Robert C., James S. Fishkin, and Roger Jowell. 2002. "Considered Opinions: Deliberative Polling in Britain." *British Journal of Political Science* 32:455–487.

MacRae, Duncan, Jr. 1952. "The Relation Between Roll Call Votes and Constituencies in the Massachusetts House of Representatives." *American Political Science Review* 46(4):1046–1055.

Maestas, Cherie. 2000. "Professional Legislatures and Ambitious Politicians: Policy Responsiveness of Individuals and Institutions." *Legislative Studies Quarterly* 25(4):663–690.

   2003 "The Incentive to Listen: Progressive Ambition, Resources, and Opinion Monitoring among State Legislators." *Journal of Politics* 65:439–456.

Manin, Bernard. 1997. *The Principles of Representative Government*. Cambridge: University of Cambridge.

Manin, Bernard, Adam Przeworski, and Susan Stokes. 1999. "Elections and Representation." In Adam Przeworski, Susan Stokes, and Bernard Manin, eds. *Democracy, Accountability, and Representation*. Cambridge: Cambridge University Press.

Mansbridge, Jane. 1999. "Should Blacks Represent Blacks and Women Represent Women? A Contingent 'Yes.'" *Journal of Politics* 61(3):628–657.

   1986. *Why We Lost the ERA*. Chicago: University of Chicago Press.

Manza, Jeff and Fay Lomax Cook. 2002. "Policy Responsiveness to Public Opinion: The State of the Debate." In Jeff Manza, Fay Lomax Cook, and Benjamin I. Page, eds. *Navigating Public Opinion: Polls, Policy, and the Future of American Democracy*. Oxford: Oxford University Press.

Matland, Richard E. and Donley T. Studlar. 1996. "The Contagion of Women Candidates in Single-Member District and Proportional Representation Electoral Systems: Canada and Norway." *Journal of Politics* 58(3):707–733.

Matthews, D.R., and Valen, H. 1999. *Parliamentary Representation: The Case of the Norwegian Storting.* Columbus: Ohio State Press.

Mayhew, David R. 1974. *Congress: The Electoral Connection.* New Haven: Yale University Press.

   1966. *Party Loyalty among Congressmen: The Difference Between Democrats and Republicans 1947–1962.* Cambridge, MA: Harvard University Press.

McCrone, Donald J. and James H. Kuklinski. 1979. "The Delegate Theory of Representation." *American Journal of Political Science* 23:278–300.

McDonald, Michael D., and Ian Budge. 2005. *Elections, Parties, Democracy: Conferring the Median Mandate.* Oxford: Oxford University Press.

McGann, Anthony, 2006. *The Logic of Democracy.* Ann Arbor: University of Michigan Press.

Mill, J.S. 1991 [1861]. *Considerations on Representative Government in John Stuart Mill On Liberty and Other Essays.* Oxford: Oxford University Press.

Miller, A.H., Miller, W.E., Raine, A.S., and Browne, T.A. 1976. "A Majority Party in Disarray: Policy Polarization in the 1972 Election." *American Political Science Review* 70:753–778.

Miller, Warren E. 1967. "Voting and Foreign Policy." *Domestic Sources of Foreign Policy.* James N. Rosenau, ed. New York: Free Press. pp. 213–230.

Miller, Warren E., Roy Pierce, Jacques Thomassen, Richard Herrera, Soren Holmberg, Peter Esaiasson, and Bernhard Wessels. 1999. *Policy Representation in Western Democracies.* Oxford: Oxford University Press.

Miller, Warren E. and Donald E. Stokes. 1963. "Constituency Influence in Congress." *American Political Science Review* 57(1):45–56.

Monroe, Alan. 1998. "Public Opinion and Public Policy 1980–1993." *Public Opinion Quarterly* 62:6–28.

   1979. "Consistency between Constituency Preferences and National Policy Decisions." *American Politics Quarterly* 12:3–19.

Morone, James A. and Theodore R. Marmor. 1981. "Representing Consumer Interests: The Case of American Health Planning." *Ethics* 91(3: Special Issue: Symposium on the Theory and Practice of Representation):431–450.

Murray, Shoon Kathleen. 2006. "Private Polls and Presidential Policymaking: Reagan as a Facilitator of Change." *Public Opinion Quarterly.* 70(4): 477–499.

Murray, Shoon Kathleen, and Peter Howard. 2002. "Variation in White House Polling Operations: Carter to Clinton." *Public Opinion Quarterly* 66:527–558.

Nagel, Jack and Christpher Wlezien. n..d. "Center-Party Strength and Major-Party Polarization in Britain." *British Journal of Political Science*, forthcoming.

Neuman, W. Russell. 1986. *The Paradox of Mass Politics*. Cambridge, MA: Harvard University Press.

Norrander, Barbara and Clyde Wilcox. 1999. "Public Opinion, and Policymaking in the States: The Case of Post-Roe Abortion Policy." *Policy Studies Journal* 27:707–722.

Norris, Pippa. 2000. *A Virtuous Circle? Political Communications in Post-Industrial Democracies*. Cambridge: Cambridge University Press.

   1985. "Women's Legislative Representation in Western Europe." *West European Politics* 8:90–101.

Norris, Pippa, and Joni Lovenduski. 2004. "Why Parties Fail to Learn: Electoral Defeat, Selective Perception and British Party Politics." *Party Politics* 10(1): 85–104.

Neumann, Russell W. 1986. *The Paradox of Mass Politics*. Cambridge, MA: Harvard University Press.

Newhouse, Joseph P. 1977. "Medical-Care Expenditure: A Cross-National Survey." *The Journal of Human Resources* 12(1):115–125.

Oldendick, Robert W. and Barbara Ann Bardes. 1982. "Mass and Elite Foreign Policy Opinions." *Public Opinion Quarterly* 46(3):368–382.

Page, Benjamin I. 2002. "The Semi-Sovereign Public." In J. Manza, F. L. Cook, & B. I. Page, eds. *Navigating Public Opinion: Polls, Policy, and the Future of American Democracy*. New York: Oxford University Press.

Page, Benjamin I. and Robert Y. Shapiro. 1992. *The Rational Public: Fifty Years of Trends in Americans' Policy Preferences*. Chicago: University of Chicago Press.

   1983. "Effects of Public Opinion on Policy." *American Political Science Review* 77:175–190.

Persson, T., Roland, G., and Tabellini, G. 1997. "Separation of Powers and Political Accountability." *Quarterly Journal of Economics* 112(4): 1163–202.

Petry, Francois. 1999. "The Opinion-Policy Relationship in Canada." *Journal of Politics* 61:540–550.

Petry, Francois and Matthew Mendelsohn. 2004. "Public Opinion and Policy Making in Canada, 1995–2001." *Canadian Journal of Political Science* 27:505–529.

Phillips, Anne. 1995. *The Politics of Presence*. Oxford: Oxford University Press.

Pitkin, H. F. 1967. *The Concept of Representation*. Berkeley: University of California Press.

Poole, Keith T. and Howard Rosenthal. 2007. *Ideology and Congress*. New Brunswick: Transaction.

Popkin, Samuel L. 1991. *The Reasoning Voter: Communication and Persuasion in Presidential Campaigns*. Chicago: University of Chicago Press.

1994. *The Reasoning Voter: Communication and Persuasion in Presidential Campaigns*, 2d ed. Chicago: University of Chicago Press.

Powell, G. Bingham, Jr. 2000. *Elections as Instruments of Democracy: Majoritarian and Proportional Views*. New Haven: Yale University Press.

Powell, G. Bingham, Jr., and Guy D. Whitten. 1993. "A Cross-National Analysis of Economic Voting: Taking Account of the Political Context." *American Journal of Political Science* 37:391–414.

Prior, Markus. 2007. *Post-Broadcast Democracy: How Media Choice Increases Inequality in Political Involvement and Polarizes Elections*. Cambridge: Cambridge University Press.

Przeworski, Adam, Susan Carol Stokes, and Bernard Manin. 1999. *Democracy, Accountability, and Representation*. Cambridge: Cambridge University Press.

Ranney, Austin. 1954. *The Doctrine of Responsible Party Government: Its Origins and Present State*. Urbana: The University of Illinois Press.

Rae, Douglas. 1981. "Two Contradictory Ideas of (Political) Equality." *Ethics* 91(3, Special Issue: Symposium on the Theory and Practice of Representation):451–456.

Rasinski, Kenneth A. 1989. "The Effect of Question Wording on Public Support for Government Spending." *Public Opinion Quarterly* 53: 388–394.

Rawls, John. 1993. *Political Liberalism*. New York: Columbia University Press.

Riker, William. 1982. "The Two-Party System and Duverger's Law: An Essay on the History of Political Science." *American Political Science Review* 76(4):753–766.

Rodden, Jonathan. 2004. "Comparative Federalism and Decentralization: Meaning and Measurement." *Comparative Politics* 36:481–500.

2003. "Reviving Leviathan: Fiscal Federalism and the Growth of Government." *International Organization* 57:695–729.

Rogowski, Ronald. 1981. "Representation in Political Theory and in Law." *Ethics* 91(3, Special Issue):395–430.

Rogowski, Ronald, and Mark Andreas Kayser. 2002. "Majoritarian Electoral Systems and Consumer Power: Price-Level Evidence from the OECD Countries." *American Journal of Political Science* 46(3):526–539.

Rosen, Harvey S. and Ted Gayer. 2008. *Public Finance*, 8th edition. New York: McGraw-Hill.

Rottinghaus, Brandon. 2006. "Rethinking Presidential Responsiveness: The Public Presidency and Rhetorical Congruency 1953–2001." *Journal of Politics* 68(3):720–732.

Rousseau, Jean-Jacques. 1762. *The Social Contract, or Principles of Political Right*.

Said, Edward W. 1997. *Covering Islam: How the Media Experts Determine How We See the Rest of the World*. Revised ed. New York: Vintage Books.

Sapiro, Virginia. 1981. "When Are Interests Interesting?" *American Political Science Review* 75(3):701–16.

Sartori, Giovanni. 1997. *Comparative Constitutional Engineering: An Inquiry into Structures, Incentives and Outcomes*, 2nd ed. New York: New York University Press.

Schattschneider E. E. 1975 (1960). *The Semi-Sovereign People*. Hinsdale, IL: Dryden Press.

   1942. *Party Government*. New York: Holt, Rinehart and Winston.

Schleiter, Petra, and Edward Morgan-Jones. N.d. "Citizens, Presidents, and Assemblies: The Study of Semi-Presidentialism beyond Duverger and Linz." *British Journal of Political Science*, forthcoming.

Schmidt, Manfred G. 1996. "When Parties Matter: A Review of the Possibilities and Limits of Partisan Influence on Public Policy," *European Journal of Political Research* 30(2):155–183.

Schumpeter, Joseph. 1942. *Capitalism, Socialism and Democracy*. New York: Harper & Row.

   1950. *Capitalism, Socialism and Democracy*, 3rd ed. New York: Harper & Row.

Shapiro, Catherine R., David W. Brady, Richard A. Brody, and John A. Ferejohn. 1990. "Linking Constituency Opinion and Senate Voting Scores: A Hybrid Explanation." *Legislative Studies Quarterly* 15(4):599–621.

Shapiro, Robert Y. and John T. Young. 1986. "The Polls: Medical Care in the United States." *The Public Opinion Quarterly* 50:418–428.

Shapiro, Robert Y., Kelly D. Patterson, Judith Russell and John T. Young. 1987. "A Report: Employment and Social Welfare." *Public Opinion Quarterly* 51:268–281.

Shugart, Matthew Soberg. 2005. "Semi-Presidential Systems: Dual Executive and Mixed Authority Patterns." *French Politics* 3:323–351.

Smith, Thomas. 1987. "That Which We Call Welfare by Any Other Name Would Smell Sweeter: An Analysis of the Impact of Question Wording on Response Patterns." *Public Opinion Quarterly* 51:75–83.

Sniderman, Paul M., Richard A. Brody and Philip Tetlock. 1991. *Reasoning and Choice: Explorations in Political Psychology*. Cambridge: Cambridge University Press.

Sniderman, Paul M., Joseph F. Fletcher, Peter H. Russell, Philip E. Tetlock and Brian J. Gaines. 1991. "The Fallacy of Democratic Elitism: Elite Competition and Commitment to Civil Liberties." *British Journal of Political Science* 21(3):349–370.

Sniderman, Paul M. and S. M. Theriault. 2004. "The Structure of Political Argument and the Logic of Issue Framing." In Paul M. Sniderman and W. E. Saris, eds. *Studies in Public Opinion*, pp. 133–165. Princeton: Princeton University Press.

Soroka, Stuart. 2002. *Agenda-Setting Dynamics in Canada*. Vancouver: UBC Press.

Soroka, Stuart, and Christopher Wlezien. 2008. "On the Limits to Inequality in Representation." *P.S.: Political Science & Politics* 41:319–327.

———. 2005. "Opinion-Policy Dynamics: Public Preferences and Public Expenditure in the United Kingdom." *British Journal of Political Science* 35:665–89.

———. 2004. "Opinion Representation and Policy Feedback: Canada in Comparative Perspective." *Canadian Journal of Political Science* 37(3):531–60.

Soroka, Stuart, Christopher Wlezien, and Iain McLean. 2006. "Public Expenditure in the U.K.: How Measures Matter." *Journal of the Royal Statistical Society, Series A* (**169**):255–71.

Stevenson, Randolph T. 2001. "The Economy and Policy Mood: A Fundamental Dynamic of Democratic Politics?" *American Journal of Political Science* 45:620–633.

Still, Jonathan W. 1981. "Political Equality and Election Systems." *Ethics* 91(3, Special Issue: Symposium on the Theory and Practice of Representation):375–394.

Stimson, James A. 1991. *Public Opinion in America: Moods, Cycles, and Swings*. Boulder, CO: Westview Press.

———. 1989. "The Paradox of Ignorant Voters, But Competent Electorate." In *Perspectives on American and Texas Politics*, Donald Lutz and Kent Tedin, eds. Dubuque, Iowa: Kendall/Hunt.

Stimson, James A., Michael B. MacKuen and Robert S. Erikson. 1995. "Dynamic Representation." *American Political Science Review* 89:543–565.

Stone, Walter J. 1979. "Measuring Constituency-Representative Linkages: Problems and Prospects." *Legislative Studies Quarterly* 4(4):623–639.

Strøm, Kaare. 2003. "Parliamentary Democracy and Delegation." In *Delegation and Accountability in Parliamentary Democracies*, eds. Kaare Strom, Wolfgang Muller, and Torbjorn Bergman, 55–106. Oxford: Oxford University Press.

Taagepera, Rein, and Matthew Soberg Shugart. 1989. *Seats and Votes: The Effects and Determinants of Electoral Systems*. New Haven: Yale University Press.

Teixeira, Ruy A. 1992. *The Disappearing American Voter*. Washington, DC: Brookings Institute.

Trudeau, Pierre E. 1968. *Federalism and French Canadians*. Toronto: MacMillan.

Truman, David. 1951. *The Governmental Process*. New York: Knopf

Tsebelis, George. 2002. *Veto Players: How Political Institutions Work*. New York: Russell Sage Foundation.

Ura, Joseph, and Christopher Ellis. 2008. "Income, Preferences and the Dynamics of Policy Responsiveness." *PS: Political Science and Politics* 41:785–794.

Uslaner, Eric M. and Ronald E. Weber. 1979. "U.S. State Legislators' Opinions and Perceptions of Constituency Attitudes." *Legislative Studies Quarterly* 4:563–585.

van der Eijk, C., and Franklin, Mark N. 1996. *Choosing Europe? The European Electorate and National Politics in the Face of Union.* Ann Arbor: University of Michigan Press.

Verba, Sidney and Norman H. Nie. 1972. *Participation in America: Political Democracy and Social Equality.* New York: Harper & Row.

Wahlke, John C. 1971. "Policy Demands and System Support: The Role of the Represented." *British Journal of Political Science* 1(3):271–290.

Watts, Ronald L. 1999. *Comparing Federal Systems.* 2nd ed. Montreal: McGill-Queen's University Press.

Weakliem, David. 2003. "Public Opinion Research and Political Sociology." *Research in Political Sociology* 12:49–80.

Weber, Ronald E. 1999. "The Quality of State Legislative Representation: A Critical Assessment," *The Journal of Politics* 61:609–627.

Weiler, J. H. H., Haltern, U. R. and Mayer, F. 1995. "European Democracy and its Critique." *West European Politics* 18(3):4–39.

Weissberg, Robert. 1978. "Collective vs. Dyadic Representation in Congress." *American Political Science Review* 72:535–47.

   1976. *Public Opinion and Popular Government.* Englewood Cliffs, NJ: Prentice-Hall.

Welch, Susan and John Hibbing. 1984. "Hispanics in Congress." *Social Science Quarterly* 65:328–335.

Wiener, Norbert. 1961. *Cybernetics, or Control and Communication in the Animal World.* New York: Wiley.

Wlezien, Christopher. 2005. "On the Salience of Political Issues: The Problem with 'Most Important Problem.'" *Electoral Studies* 24:555–79.

   2004. Patterns of Representation: Dynamics of Public Preferences and Policy." *Journal of Politics* 66:1–24.

   1996a. "Dynamics of Representation: The Case of U.S. Spending on Defense." *British Journal of Political Science* 26:81–103.

   1996b. "The President, Congress, and Appropriations 1951–1985." *American Politics Research* 24: 43–67.

   1995. "The Public as Thermostat: Dynamics of Preferences for Spending." *American Journal of Political Science* 39:981–1000.

   1993. "The Political Economy of Supplemental Appropriations." *Legislative Studies Quarterly* 18: 51–76.

Wlezien, Christopher, and Stuart Soroka. n.d. "Inequality in Policy Responsiveness?" In Peter Enns and Christopher Wlezien, eds, *Who Gets Represented?* New York: Russell Sage Foundation, forthcoming.

2007. "Relationships Between Public Opinion and Policy." In Russell Dalton and Hans-Deiter Klingemann, eds. *Oxford Handbook of Political Behavior*, pp. 799–817. Oxford: Oxford University Press.

2003. "Measures and Models of Budgetary Policy." *Policy Studies Journal* 31:273–286.

Wright, Gerald C. 1989. "Policy Voting in the U.S. Senate: Who Is Represented?" *Legislative Studies Quarterly* 14:465–486.

Yagade, A. and D. M. Dozier. 1990. "The Media Agenda-Setting Effect of Concrete versus Abstract Issues." *Journalism Quarterly* 67:3–10.

Zaller, John. 1998. "Monica Lewinsky's Contribution to Political Science." *PS: Political Science and Politics* 31:182–9.

1992. *The Nature and Origins of Mass Opinion.* Cambridge University Press.

Index

For EU product safety concerns, contact us at Calle de José Abascal, 56–1°,
28003 Madrid, Spain or eugpsr@cambridge.org.

www.ingramcontent.com/pod-product-compliance
Ingram Content Group UK Ltd.
Pitfield, Milton Keynes, MK11 3LW, UK
UKHW010040140625
459647UK00012BA/1507